Eurasian States

Policies and Practices

Eurasian States

Policies and Practices

Edited by
Arun Mohanty

KNOWLEDGE WORLD

KW Publishers Pvt Ltd
New Delhi

ISBN 978-93-86288-81-3 Hardback
eISBN 978-93-86288-82-0 ebook

Published in India by Kalpana Shukla

KNOWLEDGE WORLD

KW Publishers Pvt Ltd
4676/21, First Floor, Ansari Road
Daryaganj, New Delhi 110002
Phone: +91 11 23263498/43528107
Marketing: kw@kwpub.com
Editorial: jose@kwpub.com
Website: www.kwpub.com

Printed and Bound in India

Contents

Preface vii

1. The Indo-Russian Strategic Partnership: The Bullwark of a Multipolar World 1
   Sergei Lavrov

2. Pages from the History of the Establishment of Diplomatic Relations between India and Russia 6
   Arun Mohanty

3. Some Aspects of Regional Security in Central Asia: A Perspective from Kazakhstan 18
   Yerbulat Seilekhanov

4. Russia and India: Maintaining the Long-Range Vision 25
   Leonid Ivashov

5. CICA and the Contemporary World 31
   Jandos Asanov

6. Greater East Asia and Russia's Task 38
   Sergey Lounev and *Arun Mohanty*

7. Geopolitics at Work: The Georgia–Russia Conflict 60
   Peter W. Schulze

8. International System: Descending to Chaos or Looking up to New Opportunities? 75
   Kortunov S.V.

9. The Battle for Water in Central Asia and Regional Potential for Cooperation 97
   Stanislav Chernyavsky

10. Contemporary Japan–Central Asia Relations 114
    Elaheh Koolaee and *Mandana Tishehyar*

11. The Silk Route and Kazakhstan: A Historical Perspective 133
Sattar F. Mazhitov

12. Kazakhstan: A Land of Peace and Prosperity 145
Kairat Umarov

13. Socio-Economic Development of Uzbekistan and Indo-Uzbek Relations 161
Saidkamal Saydaminov

14. Economic Policy of the State Concerning Small Business: Experience of St. Petersburg 179
Vyachislav Shavshukov

15. External Energy Policy of Russia 209
V. N. Kharlamova and *N. A.Philimonova*

16. Energy Factor in Geopolitics 226
Valery Egozaryan

17. The New Silk Route and Chinese interests in Central Asia 234
Ramakrushna Pradhan

18. Diaspora: The Experience of Indian Diaspora for Russia 252
Felix Yurlov

19. Generation "Lost" and Generation "Next": The Two Generations of Russian Youth 273
Natalia Borozdina

20. Can Eurasian Countries Catch Up with the West? 281
Sergey Lounev

21. Institutional Developments and Political Practices in Kyrgyzstan 291
Sumant Kumar Swain

22. The Basic Directions of International Activity of the Russian Orthodox Church 308
Olga Tserpitskaya

Index 325

Preface

The current volume is a collection of articles written by eminent scholars and senior diplomats about developments in Eurasian states and their relations with India. The volume begins with the article written by Russian Foreign Minister Sergey Lovrov, who focuses on Russia–India strategic partnership and its contribution to the improvement of situations in international affairs. Lovrov argues that the Declaration on Strategic Partnership between the two countries was built on the basis of a common understanding that there is no alternative to the emergence of a multipolar world. It presumes the responsibility of Russia and India for the future of a modern civilisation, and a sound and adjusted approach to the realisation of the national interests of both the countries.

The second article, contributed by Professor Arun Mohanty, provides a detailed account of behind-the-scene developments that finally led to establishment of diplomatic relations between India and Russia on 13th April, 1947, despite British opposition. The establishment of diplomatic ties opened a new chapter in the history of bilateral relations though there was mutual suspicion in the immediate aftermath of mutual diplomatic recognition.

The next article written by Yerbulat deals with the security situation in Central Asia and emphasises the cooperation of the states of the continent in the framework of the Conference on Interaction and Confidence Building Measures in Asia (CICA), initiated by the Kazakh President N. Nazarbayev in 1992. However, given that the CICA is only at the initial stage of its development and faces certain difficulties, which hinder its potential to become a sort of European analogous structure (the OSCE), it is doubtful that it can be used at the present stage for the resolution of existing security issues.

The next contribution is made by a celebrated geopolitical thinker, General Leonid Ivashov, and draws attention to a loss of strategic vision as soon as our approach is reduced to mere commercial calculation, towards the sales of specific products and technologies. in other words, what we should consider is a large-scale complex programme of Russia–India cooperation embracing a broad range of issues. Importantly, the programme should aim at more than just particular financial results. it should be equally adequate for Russia's interests and those of "our strategic partners".

Jandos Asanov in his paper on "CICA and the Contemporary World" throws light on Asia's traditional military flashpoints, as well as on a number of non-traditional security challenges, now commonly known as New Threats and Challenges. While globalisation has brought unprecedented benefits in the form of rapid economic, technological and social changes, these changes have also spawned the much-more sinister byproduct of non-traditional security challenges. Some of the major non-traditional challenges being faced by Asia today are terrorism, transnational crime, and environmental degradation, the spread of infectious diseases and trafficking in human beings, illicit drugs and arms.

Globalisation has also been blamed for increasing the economic and social inequalities and consequent tensions in certain parts of Asia. He asserts that while poverty itself cannot be identified as a security challenge, it has certainly contributed to the rise of some of the new threats and challenges.

The next article written jointly by Sergey Lounev and Arun Mohanty discusses the perspectives for formation of a Greater East Asia and Russia's role in it. The possibility of the formation of a political integrated entity in the near future is at a minimum. Apart from that, there is a tendency to halt the traditional process in East Asia of development of relations in the security sphere and first of all, on a bilateral basis. The perspective for creating multifaceted cooperation in the sphere of security has emerged. However, that will be created on a wider basis than Greater East Asia. The US would remain as main actor in the macro-region in the political and military–political spheres.

Throwing light on history of the Russia–Georgia conflict, Peter Shulze in his article "Geopolitics at Work: the Georgia-Russia Conflict" argues that while the regional dimension of the war as lost its menacing character, this conflict acquired an international dimension from the beginning. The Russian counterattack which led to the temporary occupation of the core territories of Georgia alarmed the international community. The General Secretaries of the UN, the EU and the USA condemned the disproportional use of power, and demanded together an immediate ceasefire and the withdrawal of the Russian forces to the positions held before the war.

He further argues that the Kremlin did not need, nor did ask for, a military conflict with Georgia. But Moscow welcomed the opportunity to portray its willingness to punish the Georgian President for his anti-Russian politics. By doing so, the Kremlin aimed at drawing a clear line for the US-led influence in the CIS countries. The message was clear and meant containment to limit the Western influence in the territorial area which stretches from the Baltic Sea to the region between the Black and Caspian Sea—an area called "Zwischeneuropa".

Sergey Kortunov in his article analysing the state of the present world order says that the bipolar world that emerged after World War II presented a world of limited sovereignty (with the exception of thetwo superpowers) and in this capacity essentially contradicted the Westphalian system. The unipolar world that emerged after the

Soviet disintegration stood a greater contradiction to the Westphalian system, because there was only one country—USA—that enjoyed full sovereignty. Of course, this world did not reflect a Pax Americana (a long-time dream of the American rightist conservatives) and even a world hegemony of the USA. Rather, it was an attempt to assume world leadership with the help of "soft power".

The author firmly believes that the conflict potential in the world as a whole is rising, and a huge significance of power is being imposed upon the international community. The practice of unilateral and negative action, from the point of view of international law by some countries, as well as the attempt towards an unceremonial imposition of one's own position while ignoring the legitimate interests of the other partners, inflicts a serious damage to stability.

Stanislav Chernyavsky in his paper discusses the conflict around water distribution among the upstream and downstream countries of Central Asia and the potential for regional cooperation. He is of the opinion that the specifics of the water-energy balance of Central Asia have caused a serious debate about the use of market mechanisms of management of regional interaction in this direction. Nevertheless, that has not led to a significant closing of interests of the agrarian and energy sectors of the regional economy. All questions concerning the water–energy balance—the accumulation of hydro-resources for their further use during the irrigation period, the use of reserves of water for hydroelectric stations and potential projects for the expansion of water use in each of the Central Asian countries – are used as levers of pressure on the neighbours.

The obstacle for forming a constantly functioning and effective structure in the framework of the Eurasian Economic Community is the absence of political will on the part of the Central Asian leaders to overcome the differences. Nevertheless, a transborder character of water resources and a close interlinking between the water and energy supply in the region dictates the necessity for working out of a coordinated regional policy in the sphere of energy and water use.

The next article jointly contributed by Elaheh Koolaee and Mandana Tishehyar dwelling on Japan–Central Asia relations analyses the process of development of Japan's relations with the Central Asian countries and the existing challenges and opportunities. They are of the opinion that the feasibility of Central Asia as an alternative to Russia and the Middle East in meeting Japan's energy security needs appeared to be overestimated by the Japanese and exaggerated by the oil and gas-rich Central Asian states. In addition, talks with Russia over the disputed territories yielded no result. This led to a domestic criticism that Japan lacked a clearly defined strategy in engaging Central Asia. Despite the policy setback, it became increasingly clear that Central Asia is a region of growing geopolitical significance and that Japan's participation adds to the region's stability.

Sattar Mazhitov in his paper "The Silk Route and Kazakhstan: A Historical Perspective", talks about the possibility of Indo-Kazakh cooperation in building the Silk Route. According to him, the political scientists of Kazakhstan believe that a level of relations between Kazakhstan and India, despite their high potential, is not very high. Particularly, there is no legal foundation of mutual relations of a strategic character. Meanwhile, this moment is the determining factor for the promotion of cooperation between the two countries on the revived Silk Route.

He argues that this situation provides an impulse for the mutual participation of Kazakhstan and India in resolving the problem of revival of the Silk Route. Both states have a common understanding of the problem. The revived Silk Route would be a guarantor of world stability and the resolution of global issues.

The next article contributed by Kairat Umarov deals With political reforms and democratic transformation that have been instrumental in achieving domestic stability and consolidation of the society in Kazakhstan. The country does not stop at that: the Kazakhstan 2030 Programme sets an objective of establishing a common national identity to further unleash the creative power of the Kazakh people in building a unified and prosperous nation.

The article written by Saidkamal Saydaminov deals with Uzbekistan's socio-economic development and prospects for development of relations with India. He stresses that trade and economic relations between Uzbekistan and India over the years have largely been very successful. For the past decade, "our mutual trade turnover has grown by more than 12 times and in 2004 reached almost US$ 150 million". The close friendly relationship between India and Uzbekistan, which is characterised by a mutually beneficial all-round cooperation, is based not on their shared historical and cultural ties only; in the more recent times, the two countries have come to share common values such as secularism, tolerance and strong opposition to the forces of fundamentalism and terrorism. "We have a common vision of stability in our region, and peace and prosperity of our people, and we are determined to work together to achieve these aims", the author emphasises.

The paper written by Vyachislav Swastukov examines the issues of development of small business and its dependency on state policy, in the example of St. Petersburg. Its core task is the creation of favourable legal and administrative conditions for the development of national capital for the major sectors of the national economy. The strategic priorities for the development of St. Petersburg as a multipurpose megacity, the sphere of services, construction, transport, housing and communal services, and tourism demand a fuller use of the capital of all types of ownership in industrial production, innovations and cultures. The author concludes that the potential of the small businesses in their development is immense. However, the potentialities have not been harnessed.

V.N. Kharlamova and N.A Philimonova in their joint paper analysing the external energy policy of Russia emphasise that export–import relations between energy producers and consumers go beyond an exclusive economic arena. Energy resources, first of all, turn into some kind of indicator of the level of political–economic integration between states and as a serious foreign policy instrument. There is a direct dependency between the pricing policy of the main energy resources and the current state of international relations and global stability.

The next article written by Valery Egozaryan deals with the energy factor in geopolitics . For a long time, it has been clear that this topic is directly linked to the political issues of security. However, it is increasingly difficult to determine what is primary and what is secondary—the politics or economics—in each case.

The author argues that in a situation when the competition in the energy market gets aggravated, taking the demands of the US economy and the growing economic systems of India and China into account, the need for a political and economic partnership between India and Russia gets pre-determined. The strengthening of the geopolitical axis between Moscow and New Delhi will "permit us to resolve the issues of energy, security, etc." More effectively, the Shanghai Cooperation Organization, which is outwardly ignored by the West, can serve as a mutually beneficial, effective instrument of interaction.

Ramakrushna Pradhan in his paper discusses the Chinese interest in Central Asia and the challenges that Beijing may face there in pursuing its policies . China is also interested in maintaining close cooperation and boosting trade relations with the newly emerged Central Asian Republics. Therefore, the opening up of Central Asia and its emergence as a major source of energy resources beyond the western border of China has stimulated it to engage in a dialogue with the region and maintain close and cooperative relations with these countries for the achievement of its strategic interests and creating opportunities for trade, energy and security.

The next paper contributed by Felix Yurlov dwells on the Indian diaspora abroad and the lessons it holds for Russia. The contribution of the Indians living abroad to the fast-growing economy of India would form a significant part of all investments, because the people of Indian origin have deep links with this country, know its culture and the specific nature of its economy and the financial system pretty well. The Indian Diaspora will remain one of the instruments for strengthening the Indian influence abroad, particularly in the US, Britain, Canada and South Africa.

Natalia Borozdina in her article "Generation "Lost" and Generation Next: The Two Generations of Russian Youth", looks into the issues that the young generation faces. It believes that though it is argued that in most post-communist societies there exists a huge gap between legitimised social norms and moral values and those standards that guide our everyday behaviour, the generation "next" in Russia is more consistent in formulating its moral values and life priorities along with corresponding behavioral patterns. It is especially important to study the identity and world perception of the Russian youth today due to the fact that in transition societies it is the values of youth that in 10–15 years become dominant among the whole population of a country, as it was argued by Ronald Inglehart in his article "Changing Values, Economic Development and Political Change."

The next paper written by Sergey Lunev deals with the question of the Eurasian states can catch up with the West. Lounev stresses that the objective socio-economic situation of the Eurasian countries, stand in their way of building a new society. The presence of a huge unqualified population does not permit them to adopt many models of developed countries. There is no sense for applying a new resource-preserving technology because of the low cost of manual labour and the necessity to provide jobs to the huge population. It is not accidental that the majority of technological achievements are export-oriented. An annual exodus of tens of thousands of highly qualified specialists is also observed here, which may lead to a significant weakening of the positions of these states in the high-tech sphere, and a rapid deterioration of cultural dynamics in the future.

The article written by Sumant Swain on "Institutional Developments and Political Practices" emphasises that after the Cold War period, political development, especially in the communist bloc countries, provided a new imperative for political knowledge regarding the transitional political developments from the communist ideology to a democratic and liberal political system. The political culture, attitude, political behaviour and social acceptance of the general community as well as the political nomenclature of the communist society also changed according to the new political scenario.

Olga Tserpitskaya in her article "The Basic Directions of International Activity of the Russian Orthodox Church " discusses how unsettled relations between the Orthodox Churches can also affect relations with the other Christian and non-Christian religions, and become a reason of numerous reproaches from more "liberally adjusted" religious currents. Nevertheless, the Russian Orthodox Church has a very strong point which is difficult to challenge: the Russian Church at the given historical stage is the only major Church which has not admitted and allowed a dogmatic change or changes of traditional notion of divine service and the church life. Perhaps today, the Russian Orthodoxy remains one of the few that can freely carry on dialogue with the representatives of the other faiths or the secular organisations.

Unfortunately, few articles in the volume were written quite some time back and have not been updated. However, that does not diminish the relevance of issues raised in those papers. I owe sincere gratitude to many people for the successful completion of this volume. This is a Eurasian Foundation publication. First and foremost, my thanks go to my students, particularly Nivedita and Rekha, for their assistance in the preparation of the current volume. I am indebted to my wife, Namita, for taking care of my health that helped me in completing this volume. I am extremely grateful to KW Publishers for agreeing to publish the volume.

Arun Mohanty

1

The Indo-Russian Strategic Partnership: The Bullwark of a Multipolar World

Sergei Lavrov

Russia has been displaying a genuine interest towards India for a long time. Every Russian from his school days is acquainted with the name of Afanasi Nikitin, who during 1466–1472, long before the arrival of other European travellers, had visited India. After several years, and "travel beyond three seas", he left behind interesting descriptions of the traditions and rituals of its inhabitants. The Indo-Russian trade has been developing since the seventeenth century with Astrakhan being its centre. The Indian merchants established permanent settlements in large cities on the banks of the Volga. The Russian merchants on their part received the permission for doing trade with India in 1696. At the end of the eighteenth century, Russian scientists, researchers and representatives of creative professions started travelling to India.

The mutual interaction between the two countries found its official confirmation in the opening of the Russian consulate in the year 1900 at Bombay and ten years later at Kolkata.

The current year is the 70th anniversary of India's independence, which had been declared on August 15, 1947. Our country declared its decision to officially recognise India and to establish diplomatic ties even before it attained independence.

It is absolutely typical of international practice that our relations with India were neither affected by any serious differences nor based on contradictions. Rather, these relations were distinct in the understanding of commonality between the two countries and their people, which reflects the coincidence of long -term national interests and the similarity of positions on key international issues.

The Russian assistance in building a self-reliant economy and in strengthening the defence potential of India is the visible confirmation of friendly relations between the two countries. Several agreements were signed between them in order to develop the industrial foundation of the economy of independent India towards the end of the 1950s. The steel plants of Bhilai, Bokaro and Visakhapatnam, the aluminium plant at Korba, the heavy electrical machinery factory at Haridwar, the heavy machinery plant at Ranchi, the mining machinery factory at Durgapur, the oil refinery at Barauni, Koiyal and Mathura, and a whole range of hydro and thermal power stations and many other enterprises were built with Russian participation.

The Indo-Russian space cooperation found its beginning in the 1970s. The first Indian satellite *Aryabhatta* was sent to the Space Orbit from the Kapustin Yar Cosmodrom in 1975. The first Indian Cosmonaut Rakesh Sharma made his flight to space in the Soyuz T-11 spacecraft in 1984.

The end of the Cold War, the disintegration of the Soviet Union and dramatic changes in the international arena in the 1990s turned out to be a kind of testing of firmness of the Russia–India relations. Today, we can say with confidence that these relations not only stood the test but also convincingly showed that they remain as one of the most important aspects of international politics. The successful implementation of the Treaty of Friendship and Cooperation of the year 1993 and the Declaration on Strategic Partnership of the year 2000 bear testimony to that relationship.

The Declaration on Strategic Partnership between the two countries was built on the basis of a common understanding because there is no alternative to the emergence of a multipolar world. It presumes the responsibility of Russia and India for the future of a modern civilisation, and a sound and adjusted approach to the realisation of the national interests of both the countries.

The characteristic traits of the Russia-India partnership are regular and based on intensive political contacts. In the course of annual summits, relevant issues of international, regional and bilateral agenda are discussed in a trustworthy and constructive manner and priorities of further joint works are also determined.

The joint declaration speaks of common approaches of both countries on relevant international issues. Several inter-governmental and inter-departmental documents were signed as a result of the official visit of President Vladimir Putin to India on January 25 and 26, 2007, and also a joint declaration on cooperation in the sphere of peaceful use of nuclear energy was also signed.

Russia-India-China trilateral meetings are taking place on a regular basis. The first trilateral summit took place in July, 2006 on the sidelines of the G-8 summit held at St. Petersburg.

We attach great significance to the dialogue and joint action with India under the framework of the UN and regional forums. Russia also welcomed the inclusion of India in the Shanghai Cooperation Organization as an observer in 2005.

The development of trade and economic ties is among the joint priorities between the two countries. The bilateral trade turnover in the year went up by 25% and reached US$ 4 billion out of which US$ 3 billion constitutes Russia's exports to India. A target has been set to take the bilateral trade turnover to US$ 10 billion by 2010. The Russia–India Intergovernmental Commission on Trade and Economic, Scientific-Technical and Cultural Cooperation has to play an important role in achieving this target. The relationship between the business circles of both countries are successfully developing with the active participation of the Trade and Industry Chamber of Russia, the RSPP and the OPORA.

There are around 140 joint projects of applied and fundamental nature under implementation in the framework of a complex long-term programme for scientific cooperation. Several joint research centres have also been set up. The developments of new centres on non-ferrous metals, biomedical technology, catalysts and laser, and on transfer of technology are under formation. A number of agreements have been signed for Indi's participation in the Russian space navigation system, the GLONASS.

Healthy traditions formed in course of long years in the humanitarian sphere are continuing between the two countries. A programme for cultural exchanges is to be carried out in the period from 2007 to 2008. More than 4.5 thousand Indian students are studying in Russia and also cultural exchange programmes have been established in order to bring harmony in the academic sphere.

Important events in Russia-India relations would be holding the year of Russia in India in 2008 and year of India in Russia in 2009.

Russia highly values the centuries-old history of friendly ties with India. Our countries entered the twenty-first century as strategic partners. The sixty years experience of diplomatic relations gives the confidence that a mutually beneficial Russia–India cooperation would witness a new growth for the good of our states and people in the interests of peace and stability in the whole world.

(Courtesy: *Kommersant*)

2

Pages from the History of the Establishment of Diplomatic Relations Between India and Russia

Arun Mohanty

There were some kinds of diplomatic relations between Czarist Russia and British India ever since the beginning of the twentieth century. However, these relations were limited in nature as India was not independent, and Moscow had to deal exclusively with London in matters concerning India.

The campaign for establishing diplomatic ties with Moscow gathered momentum as India reached the final phase of its freedom struggle following the Second World War. Modern India's chief architect, Jawaharlal Nehru, had visualised a significant place for the former Soviet Union in India's foreign policy long before it attained independence.

The former Soviet Union, emerging victorious from the Second World War at a huge cost, had occupied a special place in Nehru's vision of the Indian foreign policy. It was evident from many facts.

Nehru, after being released from jail on June 15, 1945, met mediapersons the next day, at Delhi. The press conference was organised by the Indian Journalists' Union at the Imperial Hotel. Nehru, immediately after greeting the journalists, asked if there was any Soviet correspondent present in the press conference. When Oleg Arestov, the then *TASS* correspondent at Delhi, was introduced to him, Nehru asked him to sit next to him on the same sofa.

"I am glad that Soviet a journalist is present in India during these historic days," said Nehru, signalling a message for the Soviet government to which Nehru attached a lot of importance. Nehru's demonstrative gesture was designed to convey the significance he was attaching to the former USSR in his foreign policy thinking. He obviously hoped that the *TASS* correspondent would convey the message to the Soviet government. Nehru was clear that the establishment of diplomatic relations with the former Soviet Union that emerged as a great victorious power from the ruins of the war, would send a signal to the members of the international community to recognise India's independence.

The formation of the interim government of India by the nationalist–patriotic forces, its bid to pursue an independent foreign policy, and fruitful political cooperation of its delegation with the Soviet representatives at the UN set the important task for the establishment of diplomatic relations between New Delhi and Moscow as soon as possible. One of the first steps that Nehru took after joining the interim government was to search for ways to establish diplomatic relations with Russia, recalls the veteran diplomat, K.P.S. Menon.[1]

Jawaharlal Nehru had been pronouncing India's independent foreign policy from different platforms earlier. However, it was in his capacity as the Vice President of the Viceroy's Executive Council and Member of External Affairs that he made the first official declaration of India's independent foreign policy on September 7, 1946, in which he emphasised that India would participate in international conferences as a free nation "with our own policy and not merely as a satellite of other nations". Speaking warmly about the former Soviet Union, Nehru, in this historic speech, said: "to that other great nation of the modern world, the Soviet Union, which carries a vast responsibility for shaping world events, we send our greetings. They are our neighbours in Asia and inevitably we shall have to undertake many common tasks and have much to do with each other".[2]

The interim government of India soon approached various countries with the objective of establishing diplomatic relations with them. In Europe, V.K. Krishna Menon, secretary of the India League in London and a close friend of Nehru, was assigned with this job. In a press conference held in New Delhi on September 26, 1946, Nehru said that India so far had had no direct diplomatic contact with the former USSR, as it had with the US, and he proposed to explore the possibilities of establishing such contacts.

Subsequently, Nehru sent his trusted lieutenant V.K. Krishna Menon to Paris in order to meet the head of the Soviet delegation participating in the Paris Peace Conference without informing about it to the British Viceroy, who was the formal head of the interim government. Krishna Menon met the Soviet Foreign

Minister, Vyachislav Molotov, on September 28, 1946, at Paris where the latter was participating in the Paris Peace Conference following the Second World War. The *Reuters* correspondent at Paris in his dispatch about the meeting said that "the purpose of Mr. Menon's interview was to gain Soviet support to India's new Central Government to offset, particularly in foreign relations, the predominant British influence". Later, Krishna Menon himself after returning to London, while explaining the purpose of his meeting with Molotov, said:

> I went to Paris to see V. Molotov ... because the Government of India cabled me to consider what assistance the Soviet people could give in the present food crisis. Secondly, I visited M. Molotov because the policy of the Indian Government – announced both when Pandit Nehru assumed office afterwards – is that the new government will open up relations with all the countries as soon as practicable. The Government of India, having sent that message to Molotov, I was asked to see him and follow it up.[3]

According to Sarvepalli Gopal, the celebrated author of *Jawaharlal Nehru: A Biography*, Krishna Menon, exceeding Nehru's instructions, had also raised with the Soviet Foreign Minister Molotov, the possibility of some Soviet military experts visiting India. This anguished not only the British government but also several of Nehru's colleagues in the Congress party. It is interesting to note that Nehru did not oppose Krishna Menon's move, although he cautioned him to keep those people in India in mind who might be critical of such overtures to Moscow.[4]

Krishna Menon handed over a letter from Nehru to Molotov that contained the desire to establish diplomatic relations between India and the Soviet Union. The letter said, "We sincerely desire to develop friendly relations with the Soviet Union and exchange diplomatic and other representatives with your country. We hope that cooperation between India and Russia will be mutually beneficial and serve the interests of peace and progress in the whole world".[5] Regarding the matter of food assistance, Krishna Menon said that Molotov had given him the impression that the former Soviet Union was quite anxious "to assist, but her own scarcity in this area might prevent her from doing so".

Both sides expressed a complete readiness in establishing diplomatic relations between the two countries and decided to have further talks in this regard. Krishna Menon on behalf of Nehru and the interim government distanced himself from the anti-Soviet statements appearing in some Indian media from time to time, and gave the impression that these statements reflected the official position of the interim government of India.

The then Soviet government sent a reply to Nehru at the beginning of October 1946, expressing readiness to promote friendly relations with India. The letter expressed an understanding of the special difficulties that the new government had to overcome at the beginning, and wished success to Jawaharlal Nehru in fulfilling the tasks of the new Indian government in the interests of the Indian people.

In October, 1946, K.P.S. Menon, who was part of the Indian delegation to the UN General Assembly at New York at that point of time, was instructed to hold talks with Molotov for an exchange of diplomatic missions between the two countries.[6]

In November 1946, Jawaharlal Nehru declared in the Constituent Assembly that Molotov had confirmed his desire to exchange a diplomatic mission with India, and clarified that this desire of the former USSR had been conveyed by Molotov to Krishna Menon during their meeting.

The Department of External Affairs of the interim government of India, on November, 28, 1946, sent a telegram to London with the information that the Government of India had appointed K.P. S. Menon as its special representative to visit Moscow after the end of the UN General Assembly session in order to hold the official talks, started by Krishna Menon, for the exchange of diplomatic representatives between India and the former Soviet Union. The letter contained the request to issue instructions to the British ambassador in Moscow for extending all assistance to K.P. S. Menon.

The British government, scared of the establishment of diplomatic relations between the Indian interim government and the former USSR, did everything possible to prevent this from happening or at least, to delay the process. According to available documents, the movements of Krishna Menon and

K.P.S. Menon from the very beginning were placed under the strict watch of British intelligence. Even their correspondences with Pandit Nehru were intercepted.

While putting foreign affairs under the jurisdiction of the interim government, the British authorities did not refrain from making attempts to control Indian activities in the international arena and to exert influence on it. The legal foundation for the British control over the Indian foreign policy was provided by the then existing constitution that said that the "responsibility for Indian steps in international arena lies with the British government". India's independent stand on the issue of world affairs was construed as violation of the constitution by the British authorities, which time and again, reminded Nehru about it.

In connection with the proposed visit of K.P. Menon to Moscow, the British Foreign Ministry sent instructions to its ambassador at Moscow for taking steps to create hurdles in the establishment of diplomatic relations between India and the former USSR. The secret message sent by the British foreign office to its ambassador in Moscow said, "The government of India shows signs that it wants to establish diplomatic relations with the USSR, and we are interested in delaying the process as much as possible till the situation in India gets clearer".[7]

Events paving the Way for the Establishment of Diplomatic Ties

There were numbers of events that facilitated close contacts and productive cooperation leading to the establishment of diplomatic ties between India and the former USSR in April 1946. One such platform of fruitful cooperation was the UN that brought both the countries closer. India and the former Soviet Union came closer to each other's view point at the first session of the UN General Assembly. Both countries held identical views in the forum on issues such as the treatment of Indians in South Africa, the future of South West Africa, the trusteeship agreements, and the principle of unanimity of the Great Powers in the Security Council. The Indian delegation to the UN, consisting of Vijayalakshmi Pandit, V. K. Krishna Menon and

M.C. Chagla had been appointed by the interim government of India and its composition was apparently Nehru's choice.

The Indian and Soviet delegations not only shared common views on the above issues but also the Soviet delegation used the debate for granting quick independence to India. Molotov, stressing India's sovereignty in his general speech to the Assembly on October 29, 1946, said that, "although India is a member of the United Nations, and consequently, in accordance with the Charter, her relationship with Great Britain should be based on sovereign equality, have you not heard here in the General Assembly India's appeal for support and assistance? It is time that the just demands of India were recognized".[8]

It was thanks to the Indian and Soviet efforts that the UN General Assembly approved a resolution condemning racial discrimination of Indians in South Africa. The Soviet delegation very forcefully linked the issue of racial discrimination of the Indians in South Africa with broader issues of the recognition of India's independence.

Vijayalakshmi Pandit, leader of the Indian delegation to the UN, highly assessing the significance of the Soviet Foreign Minister's speech at the UNGA said, "We welcome Vyachislav Molotov's declaration on India. This is a sign of understanding and friendship between our countries. It was a very brave speech".[9]

Though Indian position on the issue was strongly supported by many countries, especially from Asia, Middle East and Latin America, the Soviet support to the Indian stand was the most eloquent.

In the meantime, the preparations for establishing diplomatic relations between the two countries went ahead in full spirit, notwithstanding the obstacles created by the British government. Following the Menon–Molotov meeting at Paris in late September and Nehru's announcement in the Constituent Assembly on November 12, 1946, the Indian interim government in early December, 1946 directed KP.S. Menon, its Agent- General in China, to proceed to Moscow for this purpose. Nehru's eagerness for the quick establishment of diplomatic ties with the former Soviet Union was reflected in his speech in January when he spoke at a reception organised in honour of the visiting Soviet delegations to the Indian Science Congress. Welcoming the Soviet delegation, Nehru expressed the hope that "in the near future our two countries will be able to exchange diplomatic representatives (cheers) and that having done so, the door will be opened for closer contacts in many fields of beneficent human activity."[10]

A quick establishment of diplomatic relations between Moscow and Delhi was facilitated by the approach of the Soviet government, which tried to simplify the formal procedure to the maximum.

The arrangements for establishing diplomatic ties were agreed to in early April through talks between K.P.S. Menon, and A.A. Petrov, the Soviet ambassador to China. On April 2, Menon proposed to

Petrov for the issuing of simultaneous public statements by both sides for the quick implementation of the agreement for exchange of diplomatic representatives between the two countries.

An Indian government communiqué dated April 13, 1947, said: "being desirous of maintaining and further strengthening the friendly relations existing between India and the USSR , the government of India and the government of USSR have decided to exchange diplomatic missions at the embassy level".[11]

There was a similar announcement by the Soviet government.[12] The joint communiqué issued by India and the former USSR on April said, "striving to preserve and further strengthen friendly relations, existing between the USSR and India, the government of the USSR and the government of India decided to exchange diplomatic missions in the rank of embassy."[13]

This act had an enormous significance for India. The establishment of diplomatic relations with the USSR on April 13,1947, meant the Soviet recognition of India's independence even before it attained its full independence on August 15, 1947. The former USSR became one of the first very few countries that extended diplomatic recognition to independent India. This was of enormous political significance for India.

The establishment of diplomatic ties between India and the former USSR drew adverse, even alarming, comments from the West. A typical Western view was expressed by *Le Monde*, which commented that since Britain was about to leave India, "the Soviet government has more and more turned its eyes on that country." The paper went on to say:

> "It is largely the Left-wing Hindu national movement which desires close understanding with the USSR of which one of the most eminent leaders is Pandit Nehru. It is this political celebrity who is the most active advocate of the Soviet Union in India. The Soviet -Indian friendship is still only at

> its beginning ...but one need only spend a few weeks in Moscow to notice that the Indian theme appears more and more frequently in the press ..."[14]

In contrast, the Soviet media highly estimated the establishment of diplomatic relations between our two countries, describing it as an important chapter in the history of relations between the two countries. The Moscow journal *New Times* in this connection wrote that the "establishment of diplomatic relations between India and Soviet Union is an event of great international significance Soviet public welcomes the event as a testimony to strengthening friendly relations between the people of the USSR and India on one side, and as testimony of development of India in the direction of pursuing independent policy, from the other. The enemies of peace and friendship between people could not prevent the establishment of diplomatic relations between India and the Soviet Union".[15]

The Indian press also highlighted the great significance of this event. *The Hindustan Times* in this context wrote that the information about the establishment of diplomatic ties between India and the former USSR bore the testimony to the fact of the significant recognition of India's independence before its constitutional declaration.

The British Government, concerned about the fate of the Anglo-Indian relations and being careful to avoid their aggravation, was forced to reconcile with the inevitability of

The establishment of the diplomatic relations between Moscow and Delhi and gave official consent to the acredition of Vijayalakshmi Pandit as India's first ambassador to the former Soviet Union.

After the agreement for the exchange of diplomatic missions between India and the former Soviet Union was signed at Peking, Jawaharlal Nehru started his work for the immediate implementation of the signed document. He insisted that the Indian embassy at Moscow should be opened before the formal declaration of India's independence and succeeded in getting the Viceroy's consent to this. It is no wonder that Nehru chose no other than India's veteran diplomat and his sister Vijayalaksmi Pandit as independent India's first ambassador to the former Soviet Union. Independent India's first ambassador was accorded a ceremonial farewell in Delhi in early August, 1947. Talking to the diplomats, assigned with the job of opening up the Indian embassy at Moscow, Nehru said that "you are going to a friendly country from which we were cordoned off by colonial rulers. We have to make up for the lost time and strengthen our ties with the Soviet Union as we are neighbours and we have many things in common. We do not have and should never have contradicting interests".

Vijayalakshmi Pandit was accorded a very warm welcome at Moscow. The Indian embassy opened at Moscow was the interim Indian government's first diplomatic mission abroad. Though India had embassies in the US and China before this, they were considered as continuation of relations established during the British rule of India. But the Moscow embassy was the first-ever Indian diplomatic mission opened by the interim government of India, that too at its own initiative, the significance of which can hardly be overemphasised.

The establishment of diplomatic relations no doubt heralded a new era in the history of friendly relations between our two great civilisations and peoples.

Notes

1. Menon K.P. S., *Memories and Mossings*, 1979, p. 222.
2. *The Statesman*, New Delhi, 8t Sept, 1946, p.5
3. *The Statesman*, New Delhi, 1 October, 1946, p. 5
4. Sarvepalli Gopal, *Jawaharlal Nehru: A Biography*, vol. 1, 1889-1947, Cambridge, p.336.
5. Vats Bhagat, Intrigi protiv indii, M., 1971, p.125
6. Menon K.P.S. , *Memories and Mossings*, p. 222

7. Goroshko G,b. Iz istorii ustanovleniya sovetsko- indiiskikh diplomaticheskikh otnoshenii. Norod Azii I afriki, 1982, No-3, p.33.
8. UN General Assembly, Official Records, 2nd Part , First Session, Plenary meeting, 25 October, 1946, p.732. *The Indo-Soviet Journal*, December, 1946
10. *The Statesman*, 8 January, 1947,p. 6
11. *The Statesman*, 15 April , 1847, p.1.
12. *Izvestia*, 15 April , 1947, p. 4.
13. *Pravda*,14 April.1947.
14. *Le Monde* , 16 April 1947, p. 2.
15. *Novoye Vremya*, no. 16, 1947, pp.15-16.

3

Some Aspects of Regional Security in Central Asia: A Perspective from Kazakhstan

Yerbulat Seilekhanov

The issues of regional security play a leading role in the foreign policies of the states of Central Asia after independence, and it is not an accident. As the experience of political development since the collapse of the USSR has shown, the states of Central Asia did not have enough reserves of domestic resources in order to carry out on their own accepted level of stability and security in the region. A political, military, and, to a large extent, economic stability in the region were sustained by external factors, which include Russia, West and China.[1] They have played a significant role in the international systems of regional security, which the states of Central Asia were "knotted to".

Thus, from the point of view of regional security architecture, it could be claimed that in the West, it was sustained by the Organization for Security and Cooperation in Europe (OSCE) and NATO (in the framework of cooperation according to the "Partnership for Peace" programme), in the North by the Collective Security Treaty Organization (CSTO), in the East, the Shanghai Cooperation Organization (SCO). At the same time, it is clear that in the South, then and now, a sort of "security vacuum" prevails. Still, the potential threat emanating from unstable Afghanistan has not been blocked, despite the actions by the US and its anti-terrorist coalition allies. In this regard, a problem of seeking mechanisms of providing real security arises, either by the states of Central Asia themselves, or, given the interest of the states of South Asia and the Middle East in security, a wider international mechanism of interaction for the resolution of this issue.

One of such solutions would be the cooperation of the states of the continent in the framework of the Conference on Interaction and Confidence Building Measures in Asia (CICA), initiated by President of Kazakhstan N. Nazarbayev in 1992. However, given that the CICA is only at the initial stage of its development and faces certain difficulties, which hinder its potential to become a sort of European analogous structure (the OSCE), it is doubtful that it can be used at the present stage for resolution of existing security issues.

Another aspect on providing security of Central Asia in the "Southern part" would be the multilateral cooperation of the states of our region with the leading powers of South Asia and the Middle East, including India, Pakistan and Iran. Theoretically, it would be possible to consider the perspective of the creation of an inter-regional system of collective security and cooperation according to the example of the SCO. At the same time, it must be acknowledged that its creation depends to a larger extent on the prospect of normalisation of the Indo-Pak, Indo-Chinese and US–Iranian relations. In Kazakhstan, it is clearly understood that these are complicated processes, extensive as far as time and efforts are concerned, but hope is expressed that they will be successful in the end.

At this point, the resolution of the security issues through the mechanisms of bilateral relations appears to be more realistic. It is argued that keeping in mind the growing economic and military–political might and international influence of India, Kazakhstan must primarily consider this country. It is apparent that the existing interaction between our states is far from reaching the maximum potential of both the countries. The intensification and deepening of relations in all aspects of cooperation is in the sphere of mutual interest.

It is of great importance for the states of Central Asia to cooperate with Pakistan and India, with which we are connected not only by religious closeness but also through joint activities in international organizations such as the Organization for Islamic Conference and the Organization of Economic Cooperation. Moreover, the fact that Pakistan and Iran border Afghanistan and have a certain degree of influence on the current domestic political processes in that country, is also of special importance.

At the same time, in considering the choice of a country-partner, one that will be able to provide regional security of Central Asia in the South, it is important to take into consideration the geopolitical realities. From this point of view, it is important to keep in mind the interests in the region of Russia, China and the US. The prospects of the formation of a political circle, Moscow-Beijing-Delhi, that are being discussed from time to time, point to the fact that at least two of the above-stated actors at the global level (namely Russia and China) will welcome the idea of cooperating with India on the issues of security and stability in the southern parts of Central Asia. It should not be overruled that the United States will also provide its support due to its geopolitical and geo-economic interests. The Central Asian states themselves are interested that the actions in the region by external players will be harmonised so that the problems of Central Asia are not turned into a new "Great Game".

The best outcome that is in long-term interests of our foreign political players and the Central Asian states would be such that security in Central Asia has to be based on sustainable economic growth and political stability.[2]

In this regard, Kazakhstan is highly interested in political and economic stability not only at home but also in its neighbouring states. Currently, there are three pressing problems that prevail in the region and have a certain potential of instability. These include the potential risk-ridden Ferghana valley (Uzbekistan), political struggle in Kyrgyzstan and common for the whole region, the problem of power transfer. From the outset, it is important to state that currently, these do not represent troublesome issues. The situation in the Ferghana valley is under control of the authorities of Uzbekistan and there have been no new cases of instability since May 2005. The domestic political struggle in Kyrgyzstan is taking place in the framework of the democratic process, and, despite several stark incidents, it is argued that one should not expect massive clashes in the country.

The process of power transfer is a quite predictable one. The presidential elections in Kazakhstan points out to the steadfast victory of the present head of state, N. Nazarbayev; E. Rakhmonov continues to remains in power; G. Bergymukhammedov follows the course of his predecessor S. Niazov. The new president in Uzbekistan follows the course pursued by his predecessor Islam Karimov . On the whole, it should be claimed that in Central Asia, leaders continue to ensure guarantees of stability of a political course . Thus, on the whole, the risk of destabilisation in the region related to the power transfer is postponed, at least, in the mid-term period. I think that, for business and political circles, the states of the region should work with cooperation and such an outcome could be a positive indication.

At the same time, a question arises: what will happen to the region in the future? Perhaps Kazakhstan can serve as a possible example of a positive development in this relation as it is known that it is now undertaking wide democratic transformations. It could be stated that these transformations will be carried out successfully, which, in turn means that Kazakhstan has all chances of building a sustainable political system. In this regard, it is assumed that the Kazakhstan experience of political modernisation will be of interest to our regional neighbours as well. It should not be overruled that the processes of liberalisation and democratisation in Kazakhstan will then have a catalysing effect on the whole political zone of Central Asia.

The problems that threaten the national security of the states of Central Asia include the so-called nontraditional risks and threats, terrorism, drug trade and illegal migration. There is a need for coordination and cooperation of international efforts to counteract these threats, which cut across the borders. At the same time, the effectiveness of the fight against these threats depend on many factors: fullness and objectivity of determining and taking into consideration the underlying reasons and conditions that foster, or, on contrary, hinder the above-mentioned threats;

strict normative legislature of a commonly accepted type; prevalence of the state system of countering terrorism, drug trade and illegal migration; availability of technological equipment and professional training of special forces; coordination of actions and information exchange between special agencies of various countries; ability to curb financial sources of criminals; public support for the fight against nontraditional threats, etc.

Especially, an important measure of counteracting the threats of terrorism, drug trade and illegal migration must become the ways of seeking to deal with the underlying reasons and conditions that give birth to these threats. In this regard, all possible means—political, social, economic, legal, educational, informational, propagandistic, etc.—must be put to use in order to have an impact on the current situation.[3] The conduct of joint training, internships and educational courses with the aim of exchanging the experiences of the border and the policy and customs bodies of states that take part in the joint fight against trans-border threats, appears to be especially effective.

Certain steps in this regard are already underway. The bilateral Commission on Counteraction of Terrorism, serves the example of a joint effort by the Republic of Kazakhstan and the Republic of India. It is especially important to extend such a positive experience into the sphere of the fight against drug trade with the drug flows from Afghanistan representing a real threat. As the specialists in the fight against the drug trade emphasise, the production of Afghan opium and heroin is constantly growing. Particularly, in 2006, their production has grown compared to the previous year, by more than 40%; 150 thousand hectares of land accounted for opium and poppy plantations and the overall volume of the produced drugs amounted to six thousand tonnes. In this regard, the experience of the fight against the drug trade of India, located not so far from another world centre of drug production- the so-called "golden triangle" in Indo-China, would be invaluable for the states of Central Asia.

On the whole, it is expected that in order to resolve the issues of the fight against international terrorism, religious extremism, drug trade and illegal migration in Central Asia, there will be an interaction at the bilateral level. Today, efforts are needed in order to strengthen the regional security systems (perhaps the creation of new ones) with a possibility of forming an inter-regional system of their interaction.

Notes

1. Bayzakova K.//Collection of presentations of "round table" "Strategy of Kazakhstan joining 50 most competitive nations of the world: ways of implementation", Almaty: KazISS, 2006
2. Ibid.
3. Ibid.

4

Russia and India: Maintaining the Long-Range Vision

Leonid Ivashov

Recently, New Delhi has been sending signals indicating that India is dissatisfied with the level and quality of its economic cooperation with Russia, particularly in the military–technical area. Should we conclude that India has decided to turn entirely towards the West? I see no reason to think so. What we do see is New Delhi's natural reaction to Russia's shortcomings in the process of interacting with its traditional partner.

India is a major country with an independent and diversified international politics which lets it play an important role in global affairs. It would be a big mistake to assume that our strategic partnership with India should somehow preclude its mutually beneficial interactions with other countries.

Indeed, there have been worrisome indications concerning the Russian–Indian relations. In my view, two of them deserve particular attention. One is that, contrary to expectations, two documents – a broad economy and trade cooperation treaty and the atomic energy cooperation agreement – were not signed during the November 2007 visit of Indian PM Dr Manmohan Singh to Moscow. The other is the recent statement made by the Indian Chief of Naval Staff Admiral Suresh Mehta that New Delhi can reconsider the format of its military–technical cooperation with Moscow in case Russia continues to postpone the completion of the contract to modernise the former Soviet aircraft carrier Admiral Gorshkov purchased by India.

I believe that the talk about the signs of a rift in the relations between Russia and India are mostly due to the above two facts. Yet, both "signals" are quite explainable and do not necessarily mean that New Delhi is losing interest in Moscow.

As for the Indian PM's visit to Moscow, it was very fruitful from Moscow's perspective. Several significant agreements have been reached. Two of them – on the cooperation in creating a mid-size military transport aircraft (IL-214) and a 5th generation fighter -pertained to the military–technical cooperation between Russia and India. Another agreement closed the problem of India's debt to the former USSR.

True enough, in certain respects, the results of the visit fell short of the expectations which emerged following the visit of Russian President V. Putin to India early in 2007. At that time, a special task force was formed to prepare a broad economy and trade cooperation treaty. Something had to be done about the imbalance in the Russian–Indian trade: though its volume increased rapidly in 2006–2007 (approximately at 30% annually), the trend resulted mainly from the Russian export growth, particularly from the expanding sales of the Russian military-related products. As a result, the situation became unacceptable to New Delhi. According to the Russian side's data, India's trade balance deficit in 2006 reached nearly US$ 1.5 billion. Chances are slim that a broad economy and trade cooperation treaty is going to be signed until a solution appropriate from the standpoints of both sides is found.

The problem tells on the state of the Russian–Indian cooperation in the nuclear energy area. This aspect of the matter is particularly sensitive due to its relation to the nonproliferation theme. India has not joined the Nuclear Nonproliferation Treaty and has no intention to sign it in the status of a non-nuclear power. Having carried out a series of nuclear tests in May, 1998, India enacted a moratorium on further nuclear testing but did not abandon its nuclear programme.

It is well known that in 1998 Russia used the Soviet-era agreement with India to construct a nuclear power plant in the southern part of the country and made a deal to install two reactors at the Kudankulam nuclear power plant. The construction is nearing completion, and currently Russia is ready to install four more reactors in Kudankulam and to build new nuclear power plants in India.

However, there are no reasons to expect that India will accept any Russian offers uncritically. Russia is not the only seller available. There is an intense competition over the Indian markets, especially those of high-tech, weaponry, and nuclear equipment. The cooperation with India is sought by the US, France and other countries. Russia has an impressive potential to compete, but to do so we need to make serious and truly innovative offers.

In the case of the Kudankulam nuclear power plant, Russia should try to offer safer reactors and better terms than other countries do. In reality, the reactors we are trying to sell to India are obsolete and have no chance to win the competition with the US–Japanese and French ones in the nearest perspective. Experts say that a breakthrough in the area can be made possible by a joint effort to ensure the transition to a closed nuclear fuel cycle on the basis of fast neutron reactors. India is known to have a unique expertise in the use of Thorium, and Russia – Uranium-238.

The above considerations apply to a particular, though a highly important problem. As for an innovative approach to the Russia–India cooperation on the whole, I find it necessary to remind that in most cases Russia has been economically successful, particularly in the military–technical area, when it employed the entire spectrum of the political, economic, cultural, and scientific ties with the country. So, V. Putin's visit to India was paralleled by extensive contacts between the Russian delegation and the Indian scientific and cultural circles. Thanks to this approach, we made a breakthrough in the sales of naval, aircraft, and ground equipment to India. In particular, a deal was made to supply our latest T-90S tanks to the country.

We suffer a loss of vision as soon as our approach is reduced to mere commerce, to the sales of specific products and technologies. In other words, what we should consider is a large-scale complex programme of Russia–India cooperation embracing a broad range of issues. Importantly, the programme should aim at more than just particular financial results. It should be equally adequate for Russia's interests and those of our strategic partner.

The tendency to get a lot and quickly can do us an ill-favour. By the way, this is exactly what happened in the case of the Admiral Gorshkov aircraft carrier. I would say that the Russian officials acted irresponsibly in 2004 when the modernisation and sale deal was made. Overly motivated by financial considerations, they made serious mistakes. The condition of the vessel was not appraised properly, nor was the necessary amount of work estimated when the contract deadline and the total – August 2008 and $1.5 billion – were set. Now it transpired that a lot more work has to be done than initially expected, and the Russian side asked for postponing the commissioning and raising the contract cost to US$ 2.7 billion.

Naturally, this way of doing business is frowned upon in New Delhi. Once a contract is signed, the deadline must be met, or eventually the Indian side will question Russia's credibility when it comes to major contracts.

Rosoboron export cannot and should not be the driver of the Russia–India relations. India is of such importance to us as a partner that the relations with it should be broad-based and planned in offices other than those of this company, which is absolutely respectable but operates within the limited military–technical sphere.

There are many cooperation directions which still await Russia making up its mind. For instance, India with its rapidly growing economy is keenly interested in a tandem with Russia in the science-intensive sectors, but Russia sends indefinite messages in response. Sometimes

we express full readiness to cooperate, but sometimes we generate the atmosphere of a total secrecy. I witnessed the situation personally when I took part in the negotiations on the military–technical cooperation with India. Most of the time, we made efforts to sell hardware while India wanted to work together on high-tech products, be it submarines, aircrafts, or the nuclear power industry equipment.

I recall that in the late 1990s there was a chance to win an interesting contract to supply A-50 radar aircrafts to India. For some reason, Russia chose Israel as a partner for creating the radar for the plane. As a result, the contract was never signed.

My impression is that the uncertainty in our behaviour is explained by the pressure exerted by Washington. It kept telling us to slow down, warned us against spreading nuclear and other sensitive technologies, and also made efforts to occupy the niche which it asked us to stay away from.

We should have opted for closer ties with India in all aspects, regardless of what we hear from the US. One possible way to re-energise the Russia–India cooperation is to invite India officially to join the Shanghai Cooperation Organization.

I had extensive discussions with people from the Indian political establishment, including the future President and Minister of Defence, at the time when the Shanghai Cooperation Organization was at the formation stage. They showed great interest in the organisation, but India still did not join it. I think that this is largely Russia's fault as Russia did not make enough efforts in this direction. Yet, India's full membership in the Shanghai Cooperation Organization could contribute to a more stable security and cooperation system in East and South Asia, promote the cooperation between Moscow and New Delhi, and help to draw our positions on many issues of international politics closer.

5

CICA and the Contemporary World

Jandos Asanov

In the fast changing world of the twenty-first century, Asia occupies a unique place. Asia has been showing remarkable economic growth over the last few years and some quarters are already calling the twenty-first century as the Asian Century. With its rising military, economic and political clout, Asia is playing an increasingly important role in the world community. For these reasons as well as on account of the changing demography, the future lies with Asia. The centre of gravity of the world economy is slowly, but surely, moving towards Asia.

At the same time, Asia continues to face numerous security challenges which threaten not only the economic gains but also the peace and stability of the continent. Asia has experienced some of the most disastrous conflicts of the post-Second World War era. It is also an extremely diverse region with some of the largest and the smallest countries with significantly different levels of development and aspirations. There are cultural, ethnic, religious and historical differences to overcome. As we approach towards the end of the first decade of the century, Asia continues to face multiple flash points with significant conflict potentials that have been in existence for historical and other reasons. Any of these flashpoints could spark a conflagration that could undermine the peace and prosperity of the region.

In addition to the traditional military flashpoints, Asia also faces a number of non-traditional security challenges, now commonly known as *New Threats and Challenges.* While globalisation has brought unprecedented benefits in the form of rapid economic, technological and social changes, these changes have also spawned the much more sinister by-product of non-traditional security challenges. Some of the major non-traditional challenges faced by Asia today are terrorism, transnational crime, and environmental degradation, the spread of infectious diseases and trafficking in human beings, illicit drugs and arms.

Globalisation has also been blamed for increasing the economic and social inequalities and consequent tensions in certain parts of Asia. In spite of decades of positive macroeconomic development, nearly 900 million people in Asia continue to live on an income of under US$ 1 a day. While poverty itself cannot be identified as a security challenge, it has certainly contributed to the rise of some of the new threats and challenges.

Most of the non-traditional challenges have transnational linkages aided by the ease of communications and transportation. Terrorism, international crime, drug trafficking and trafficking in human beings prosper on account of transnational linkages. The emergence of new infectious diseases has a spillover effect as demonstrated by the spread of bird flu. It is, therefore, becoming increasingly clear that both traditional and non-traditional security challenges cannot be addressed in isolation and require collaborative multilateral responses for their resolution.

It was to address these very concerns by a collaborative multilateral approach that President Nursultan Nazarbaev conceived the idea of the Conference on Interaction and Confidence Building Measures in Asia (CICA) and presented it to the community of nations at the United Nations General Assembly in 1992. Till then, a collaborative approach had been confined to few sub-regional mechanisms like Association of South East Asian Nations (ASEAN), South Asian Association for Regional

Cooperation (SAARC), Economic Cooperation Organization (ECO), etc. the CICA process is unique because it aims to create a meaningful security environment covering the entire continent of Asia through dialogue, cooperation and confidence-building measures among the member states. The member states of CICA come from all parts of Asia covering nearly ninety per cent of the area and the population of the continent.

In 2007, President N. Nazarbayev in his speech at the 62nd session of the UN General Assembly underlined:

> "... speaking of Asia, we have to mention here the issue of the establishment of a continental arrangement of collective security. That has become possible due to the implementation of

> Kazakhstan's initiative to convene the Conference on Interaction and Confidence-Building in Asia (CICA), declared by me standing on this very podium, during the forty-seventh session of the General Assembly in 1992. Today, the CICA process brings together 18 states, which occupy 90 per cent of Asia's territory. Their population makes half of the people living on our planet. Time has proven the relevance of the CICA process, within which a political dialogue among Asian states is gaining momentum".

CICA is one of the youngest and most diverse regional groupings. It must be remembered that while the idea of CICA was conceived sixteen years ago, CICA as a functioning forum is very young; having come into existence when the first Summit Meeting was held on June 4, 2002. CICA is also among the most ambitious groupings, especially in terms of the range of issues it seeks to address and its heterogeneity infuses it with a potential dynamism. The fact that the CICA is in a position to reconcile the diverse concerns is reflected in its ability to adopt a comprehensive set of documents and declarations and its ability to take tangible steps for the implementation of Confidence Building Measures within such a short span of time. This bears testimony to the commitment of the member states to the CICA process.

The Third Meeting of the CICA Ministers of Foreign Affairs is scheduled to be held on August 25, 2008. The period between the Second Summit Meeting of CICA held on June 17, 2006 and the Third Ministerial Meeting has been one of the most creative periods of the CICA process so far. The Second Summit marked the birth of the CICA Secretariat, the permanent administrative body of the CICA charged with, inter alia, the responsibility of implementing decisions jointly taken by the member states. At present the diplomats seconded by the member states work in the Secretariat.

While reaffirming a commitment to the basic principles and goals of the CICA contained in the Almaty Act of 2002, the Second Summit also decided to carry forward the CICA process through active cooperation among the member states in countering drug trafficking, meeting non-traditional threats and challenges, promoting trade, environmental protection, energy security, education and tourism.

The way forward to accomplish the tasks laid down by the Second Summit was through the implementation of the Confidence Building Measures (CBMs) contained in the *Catalogue of CICA Confidence Building Measures* adopted during the Second Meeting of the CICA Ministers of Foreign Ministers in October 2004. It may be mentioned that the CICA Confidence Building Measures go beyond the traditional concepts of reducing tension and fear of war. The leaders of the CICA member states recognised that in the increasingly inter-connected and interdependent world of the twenty-first century, non-traditional security challenges were posing even greater threat than the traditional politico-military challenges. The CICA Catalogue, therefore, laid down five dimensions for the realisation of the Confidence Building Measures: (i) military–political; (ii) fight against new challenges and threats; (iii) economic; (iv) environmental; and (v) humanitarian.

After the CICA Secretariat became fully functional, the first major step was the adoption of the *Cooperative Approach for Implementation of the Confidence Building Measures*. The member states agreed that in view of the diverse profile of the CICA and realities typical to the Asian continent, it would be best to start with the realisation of the Confidence Building Measures in the non-traditional security challenges which would create sufficient goodwill among the member states.

The Cooperative Approach laid down detailed modalities for the implementation of the Confidence Building Measures. Eight member states, namely, Azerbaijan, India, Iran, Kazakhstan, the Republic of Korea, Russia, Tajikistan and Turkey volunteered to act as coordinating or co-coordinating countries for the realisation of the

Confidence Building Measures in the areas of human dimension, new challenges and threats, the development of secure and effective systems of transportation corridors, drug trafficking, national disaster management, information technology, energy security cooperation, the development of small and medium enterprises and tourism.

Kazakhstan took the lead and organised the first Experts Meeting in Astana in June 2007 to draft a concept paper and action plan for the Confidence Building Measures in the human dimensions, which was subsequently adopted by the Senior Officials Committee in October 2007. The Islamic Republic of Iran 24 organised an Experts Meeting in Tehran in December 2007 to finalise the concept paper on Cooperation among the CICA Member States in Combating Illicit Drug Trafficking and Turkey organised an Experts Meeting in Ankara in January 2008 in the field of New Threats and Challenges. The concept paper and the action plan in these two fields are likely to be adopted at the meeting of the Senior Officials Committee being held on the eve of the Third Ministerial Meeting.

Other coordinating countries have also taken specific steps for the implementation of the Confidence Building Measures. Russia has presented a draft concept paper in the area of Promotion of Business Opportunities and Information Exchange in Small and Medium Enterprise Sector; Azerbaijan has presented a draft concept paper in the area of Development of Secure and Effective Systems of Transportation Corridors; the Republic of Korea has presented a draft concept paper in the area of Energy Security and Tajikistan has presented a draft concept paper in the area of Tourism. These draft concept papers will be considered at the Experts Meetings to be organised by the respective coordinating countries. In addition, Israel will be organising a Seminar on Advanced Agricultural Development . More member states are expected to come forward to act as coordinating countries for the implementation of the Confidence Building Measures in different fields.

The member states also realised that in order to accomplish the ultimate goal of making Asia a region of peace and security, it is necessary that the CICA should have active cooperation with other Asian regional and sub-regional organisations and fora. A two-pronged strategy has been adopted for this purpose. On one side, the CICA is en route to establish an institutional-level relationship with other regional organisations. On the other hand, the CICA will be organising a conference of all the Asian regional and sub-regional organisations and fora to discuss Asian security challenges in the times of globalisation and interaction between regional entities as well as other issues.

The Third Meeting of the CICA Ministers of Foreign Affairs thus comes at a time when substantial progress has been made towards accomplishing the tasks assigned by the Heads of State/Government at the Second Summit. The Ministers will be taking stock of the progress made till now and give directions for the future. The developments and future vision will be reflected in the outcome documents of the event.

During the short period since its inception, the CICA has made big strides in its endeavour to find ways and means to eliminate the causes of mistrust, tension and hostility and create conditions for sustainable peace in Asia and the economic growth of the Asian states and their peoples. The fact that the CICA process is receiving wide acceptance, is demonstrated by the fact that two new states, the Hashemite Kingdom of Jordan and United Arab Emirates, will be admitted to the CICA during the Third Meeting of the CICA Ministers of Foreign Affairs, taking the total membership to twenty.

6

Greater East Asia and Russia's Task

Sergey Lounev and Arun Mohanty

The New Mega Trend: Winning or Gaining Old Regions into Macro-Regional Complexes

Regionalisation in its contemporary form is a relatively new phenomenon. It is not accidental, the concept of region has not been clearly defined so far and there are numerous varieties of applied classification. This concerns the scale as well as countries belonging to this or that geographical definition.

Under regionalisation, we understand most closely the political, economic and cultural mutual dependency of neighbouring countries. Two different phenomena are understood by the term regionalisation—revival of regional powers and the formation of integrated groups. During the bipolar period regional powers appeared, first of all, in those regions, where there was conflicting mutual dependency and integration took place very slowly. The opposite picture was observed in those regions where the complementing mutual dependency significantly outweighed the conflicting situation. Here began the active integration processes based on:

- The growth of economic mutual dependency and bringing economic interests closer
- The presence of a common external opponent
- The absence of a clearly dominating centre

After the collapse of the socialist system, a confrontation between the two regionalisation processes is not so much obvious. Apart from India and China, Australia, and to some extent South Africa and Egypt, can be considered as regional powers (the possibility for the emergence of other regional powers in Africa are limited) towards the end of the twentieth century, Russia became one of the regional powers. We believed that there are no chances for the emergence of regional powers in Europe and North America. The unification of Germany provided it with the opportunity to turn itself into a regional power. However, the past decade did not witness anything that would suggest the beginning of the process. On the other hand, the expansion of the European Union and the intensification of the integration increasingly dilute Germany's influence. Brazil is turning into a regional power if it has not become one already.

Globalisation and regionalisation are interlinked and at the same time contradicting tendencies because all countries are subjects as well as objects of globalisation and regionalisation. The process of globalisation is stirred, first of all, by unlimited competition, and requires a growing effectiveness of all kinds of economic activities from the subjects (that is why it negatively affects the interests of the less developed countries).

Actions in the framework of regionalisation to a large extent correspond to the political, social, and cultural interests of the individual countries. Here too, there are sufficient numbers of facts in order to view regionalisation not as interim stage on the way to globalisation, but as a final objective, which means that it would stand as an obstacle on the path of the further development of globalisation.

Incorporating "old" regions into macro-regional complexes is an interim and possible variant. A similar process gives opportunity to different countries:

- for participation in globalisation unsparingly, without experiencing pressure from
  The entire world economy;
- sharply attracting less developed countries of the macro-region, providing them with preferences and investing in their economy;
- improving business positions of more developed countries, which gets the expansion of the geographical zone of activities in a concessional form;
- Strengthening geopolitical positions, as the scale becomes far stronger, and the integration group becomes capable of defending its members collectively in a much better way from foreign competition.

In essence, the macro-regional complex manifests a prototype of one of the poles of the world system; Europe went through this path.

Perspectives for Formation of "Greater East Asia"

Probably, we can talk of "Greater East Asia" at present (North-East and South-East Asia, Central and South Asia) first of all, from the economic and cultural–civilisational points of view.

Positive factors facilitating formation of the macro-region are:

1. We can speak about full economic mutual complementarities in the given region, because complementary mutual dependency as a whole outweighs conflicts. There exist all three models of economic development: post-industrial, industrial and raw-material based. Korea (it occupies first place in the world in per capita patents), Taiwan, and Singapore would soon join Japan that has been developing a knowledge-based economy. The world city (industry) has already been shifted from Europe and North America to South Asia to some extent. One-third of the world resources have been concentrated in this macro-region (the Asian part of Russia, Central Asia, some states of South-East Asia)
2. An economic integration process has started in the region. The share of trade turnover of the East Asian countries with each other is close to half of the total turnover. One-fourth of India's foreign trade is attributed to East Asia; that too India's export to the countries of South-East Asia is growing very fast (30% in a year)[1].
   The Indian imports from these countries are growing significantly (40% growth in 2007–08)[2]. All the regional organisations (from the ASEAN-plus format to the East Asian Community) set the goal to gradually reduce tariffs in inter-regional trade and the removal of limitations on the import-up to the formation of a free trade zone.
3. The process of currency–financial integration has taken a start. Though there is a long way up to the creation of a common currency, the first steps in financial cooperation have been

taken. In May 2008 a declaration was made for the creation of a regional stabilisation fund to the tune of 80 billion USD (Japan, China and South Korea would contribute 80% and the rest would be contributed by the countries of the ASEAN), which may start functioning from next year.[3] The countries also have agreed for an exchange of economic information and increase trade accounts in the regional currency. The objective of the creation of the fund is the prevention of the repetition of the Asian crisis of 1997–98 and reducing of the region's dependency on the international currency-financial organisations, where the US and other Western countries have a dominating influence and the instability in the international financial markets, linked, first of all, to a weakening of the American economy and the dollar. The last factor is linked to the prediction by the Asian Development Bank that the economy of the countries of the region will grow at the lowest rate (true, the figure is nonetheless very high – 7.6%), and the inflation level would be higher than in the course of the last decade – 5.1%.[4] Here again, the countries of East Asia whose total hard currency reserve constitutes about 4 trillion USD, can easily increase the amount of the fund in future (the annual growth is estimated at around 600–700 billion USD).[5]

4. New forms of cooperation are also under consideration. It is contemplated to create an organisation of rice exporters in the pattern of the OPEC, which would include Thailand, Myanmar, Laos, Vietnam, Cambodia, India and China.
5. The approaches of the three Asian giants, which stand for the expansion of economic cooperation in the framework of a macro-region, seem to be positive.

The US and West Europe are serious competitors for Japan, but the Asian countries are not its competitors because their development has entirely corresponded to the concept of the "flying goose" given by the Japanese economist Kaname Akamatsu, and propounded in the 1930s (it means following a more developed country and adopting its strategy in economics after it reaches a new technological level; Japan gave the textile industry to South Korea and Taiwan, when it developed the electronics and automobile industries. When Japan concentrated on a stronger high-tech sector, South Korea and Taiwan began the development of their main sphere of activity in the preceding period, whereas the textile industry was given to Indonesia, Thailand and others). The presence of its own niche in the region predetermines a favorable perception of Japan towards the regional economic integration. China looks at East Asia as its sphere of influence and aims at the creation of free-trade zone with all countries of the region—Japan South Korea, ASEAN and India. The creation of a powerful economic international formation is profitable for China, because this will facilitate to soft economic "napolzaniye (penetration) of China to south-east Asia, and Beijing hopes for an economic leadership in the region. India could not develop a complimentary mutual dependency with the neighbouring countries of South Asia.

The Look East Policy that was declared in the early 1990s envisaged an activisation of power in East Asia. In 1995, India was given the status of a full-fledged partner of the ASEAN. In November 2002, the first ASEAN + India summit took place. India was one of the 16 countries participating in first East Asian summit held in Malaysia in December 2005. The Mekong-Ganges forum uniting India and five ASEAN countries such as Cambodia, Laos, Myanmar, Thailand and Vietnam started functioning. In 1997 the BIMSTEC consisting of India, Bangladesh, Sri Lanka, Nepal, Bhutan, Myanmar and Thailand was formed with the objective of executing joint economic projects. The Indian government agreed for the setting up of the new forum of BKIM (Bangladesh, China, India, Myanmar), not in the form of just another sub-regional organisation, but for the implementation of concrete joint projects.

The development of international economic ties is quite beneficial for the countries of the macro-region, because they led:

- to decreasing the dependency on Europe and the US;
- to expanding domestic market of the region, which is relatively narrow in certain countries.

6. There is a cultural–civilisational affinity of the countries of the region and their difference from the Western model. The civilisational ground on which socio-economic development takes place, is very wide from individualism – the very foundation of Western society to collectivism, typical for the traditional Eastern society, with the existence of great many interim variants. What is typical for continental countries of East Asia is a more traditional path close to the clear collective vector. Probably this explains the attraction for socialism in the Chinese society and countries of Indo-China.

   The middle path that envisages development in a wide field but is quite far from both the collective and individual vectors, is a characteristic trait for civilisations like Russia, Japan and India. Along with this, there exists a vast difference between their models and the Western models in terms of organisational and political, economic and social life, which brings these countries closer to the continental states of East Asia.
7. The theoretical foundation of the specifics of development of the states of the macro-region has already appeared in the macro-region. The first is the idea of Asian values, a quick

spread of which is linked to, first of all, pressure from the West on the developing countries after the collapse of the bipolar world for bringing them in close consonance with the Western model of society and economy. This was reflected in many rich countries of East Asia, which were inspired by economic success rather than the spread of vices, typical for an individualistic Western paradigm in the region: a high level of crime, the spreading of narcotics, a sharp rise in divorces, a lack of the housing problem, racial tensions in the society.

Here the concept of (Asian values) that includes strong paternalism and illiberal state was actively used— the existence of a centralised, hierarchical bureaucracy; collective mutual interaction at the national level; subordination to authority of the group; discipline, love for labour and thrift; respect for the elders (to the power also), priority importance to social accord; bowing down before education and its full development.[vi] We can accept F. Fukuyama's concept that traditional Asian cultures begin from fourth (culture) and third level (civil society) and move towards upper level, to the second (Institutes) and to the first level (ideology). But contemporary Western political thoughts try to move from above to below,[vii] that is why the existence of institutes for the traditional East is less important than preserving the deeply rooted moral codex.

8. It is necessary to consider the racial factor, on which permanent attention is concentrated first of all in India (confrontation between white on the one hand and yellow, black and brown on the other hand). The hegemony of white civilisations and cultures could not evoke strong feelings for revenge, but at present begin to appear as the first possibility.

Greater East Asia is capable of turning itself into a centre of attraction for countries of the South. Other regional powers of the South (Brazil, South Africa, etc.) from a psychological point of view are inclined to cooperate with the given macro-region rather than with the North. The earlier model of participation in international economic division of labour creates obstacles to the formation of a similar coalition. But along with the growth of importance of Greater East Asia, similar obstacles would gradually be removed.

The weaker sides of the question about the creation of Greater East Asia could be found in the external as well as political and military political spheres.

1. The sole superpower (US) will by all means create hurdles in the creation of the particular macro-region without its participation. Washington very well understands that the emergence of regional organisations as a whole places certain limits on the world leader because of a) large size; b) presence of compromising decisions, which are defended far more rigidly than in case of the concrete state; c) since laws of the international market influence the members of the integrating group directly, if world is to be full of such regional associations, the US could find itself in the situation prevailing hundred years ago when becoming the world leader in terms of size of the economy, it had occupied a semi-peripheral situation in the international system. More than that, Greater East Asia is the most priority region in the world for the US.

Most probably, Washington will use most different and traditional methods:

a. To attempt to expand economic cooperation in the framework of the entire Asia-Pacific region in a wide sense, for example, to activate relations on the lines of APEC

b. To set their own trojan horse in the institutional structure of the Greater East Asia (as it happened in the East-Asian Community, which admitted Australia)
c. Use the political and military–political ties with its partners in the macro-region for limiting regional integration.

The US has military–political agreements with Japan and South Korea, which help it to maintain a military presence in these countries and it ahs different military–political agreements with Indonesia, Taiwan, Singapore, Thailand, Pakistan and other countries. In the beginning of the 1990s, official representatives of the US advanced the thesis about the necessity of a gradual reduction of the US military's troops in Asia. But realising that Japan because of threat from China would begin its own military programmes, the US confirmed all its military obligations. In the middle of the 1990s, the US started talking of its strategy of "deep involvement in theAsian affairs".[8]

Japan, which was predicted by some researchers to be the world leader of the twenty-first century, so far could not lay a political foundation to its economic might (which is on a declining path). Japan in the 1990s became the main international investor and occupied the first place in terms of providing economic assistance. However, it does not show its readiness for political activisation (though the US has pushed it in that direction).

The example of Japan shows the unconvincing nature of the thesis that economic might would certainly be translated into geopolitical force. It is true that Japan is distancing itself from the resolution of global political and military problems on the one hand, because of the traumatic shock received at the end of the Second World War (for the first time in its history, it was occupied and hit by nuclear bombardment) and on the other hand, the concentration of all efforts for raising its economic potential.

2. At the same time, there is a sharp rise in the Japanese fear about China. There are acute problems between the two countries:
   - perception of history (Diametrical approaches to the events of the Japan–China war 1937–45);
   - Territorial differences (attraction of China towards the Senkaku islands);
   - Future of Taiwan;
   - The question of human rights;
   - Illegal immigration from China to Japan
   - China's unwillingness to go for a compromise on different political issues; · Negative attitude of China to the US–Japan union;
   - The Japanese apprehension about the possibility of a massive internal crisis in China;
   - A sharp rise in the Chinese potential as a regional superpower, which may take resort to military steps for establishing its hegemony in the region, and the possibility of Beijing formulating a concept of "Greater East Asia" without Japan, in case of a further strengthening of the economic and political role of China in South-East Asia.

   Japan occupies fifth place in the world in term of its total military might (though its military expenditure constitutes 1% of the GDP, which is one of the lowest among all developed countries). However, it lags far behind China in this respect. Only the US can give the guarantee for Japan's security, including in the nuclear sphere; considering Russia enjoys much more blissful relations with China.

3. There are many factors that limit relations between China and India:

a. The Pakistan factor: India considers China as Pakistan's ally and continuing military cooperation, particularly in the nuclear sphere, between China and Pakistan evokes utter concern in India.
b. Neighbouring countries (India is very much concerned regarding the development of military infrastructure by China in the Indian ocean zone, particularly the activisation of its military cooperation with Myanmar and getting direct access to the Bay of Bengal; China's military–political and political contacts with the countries of South Asia and that China is not satisfied by certain anti-Chinese content of India's increasing ties with the countries of East Asia);
c. Military problems (both countries are highly concerned that the military potential, particularly in the sphere of nuclear-missile potential of the neighbour would be used against it);
d. Territorial question (Indian–Chinese negotiations move ahead very slowly, first of all in the western sector; China does not recognise the creation of Arunachal Pradesh, including regions considered disputable by China;
e. Activities of Tibetan emigrants in India;
f. Economic competition;
g. Weakness of contacts in cultural–ideological and scientific–technological spheres;
h. Competition between the two countries, which is the basic factor linked to the majority of factors that negatively impact the Indian–Chinese interaction.

4. Other countries of Greater East Asia consider China not only as a prospective economic partner, but also as security threat (in terms of being dependent). In this connection, they use different methods: from trying to engage China in the common structure of the Asia-Pacific region with the objective of

dialogue development and getting opportunity for a collective pressure on China up to the attempt to pursue the policy of balancing and strengthening mutual ties with other regional (India, Japan) and outside powers (first of all the US, and to some extent, Russia and Australia).

Thus, we observe multi-dimensional processes in the political and economic spheres: an obvious and good prospective for the economic integration of the macro-region and a quite significant tension in the political and military–political relations.

In any case, the economic cooperation will continue, and the possibility for creating functional economic integration-specific unification can be assessed at 50–60%.

The macro-region has:

a. economic inter-dependency and supplementarity and there is a convergence of economic interests;
b. there is no clearly dominating centre (at present, China is not entirely the dominating power in East Asia, which would be contained by other states)

   However, it should be mentioned
c. About the absence of a common enemy in Greater East Asia (the US is perceived cautiously, so is the development of ties with it).

The possibility of formation of a political integration entity is minimum in the near future. Apart from that, there is a tendency to halt the traditional process in East Asia of development of relations in the security sphere, first of all, on a bilateral basis. The perspective for creating multifaceted cooperation in the sphere of security has emerged. However, that will be created on a wider basis than Greater East Asia. US would remain as main actor in the macro-region in the political and military–political spheres. To some extent, the six-party negotiations on the Korean issue would be the prototype of such an organisation.

The Global Perspective for the Macro-Region

From the economic point of view, Greater East Asia has turned into a main macro-region of the world. Major industrial productions have been concentrated here. According to the size of the GDP in terms of purchasing power parity, China has surpassed Japan (4.42 trillion USD on the basis of PPP) and entered the second place—7.04 trillion USD on the basis of PPP in 2007). India has occupied fourth place (almost 3 trillion USD); South Korea with an 1.2 trillion USD GDP, Indonesia with an 846 billion USD GDP have come closer to this group. The GDP of these five countries (16.5 trillion USD) is bigger than the economy of the EU (14.45 trillion USD) and the US (13,86 trillion USD)[9] Considering the dynamics of the development, it would move further away from Europe and the US.

From a political point of view, the region is not unified and the US is a much more important actor with its significant potential for the rectification of external policies of the countries of the region.

Energy Problems and Regional Transformation

There exist quite contradicting inter-relations between the energy problems and regional transformation in the macro-regional complex "Greater East Asia". Considering that a majority of the countries of the region chose an industrial vector of development, their energy requirement would permanently grow. According to the International Energy Agency (Paris), the average annual growth rate of energy consumption up to 2025 in India would be 2.6%, China—1.8%, Japan—0.3%, and towards 2030 India and China would consume 45% energy resources of the world.[10] Own resources in East and South Asia are already insufficient.

More than that, there is a dependency in energy supplies on one region of the world, i.e., the Middle East. 76% of the oil imports of the countries of the Asia-Pacific region come from the Middle East. Japan meets 88% of its energy requirement through imports from Persian Gulf. The Middle East accounts for 60% imports of China and almost the entire import of India. A similar situation demands the diversification of oil imports, because the Asian giants are extremely vulnerable, because of the growth of instability in the Middle East. In this context, the inclusion of the Asian part of Russia and Central Asia to the macro-region and a comprehensive development of energy links permit the Asian states to get:

- diversification of oil and gas import, that permits to raise energy security;
- ensuring significant independence from actions of the world leader;
- getting reliable partners in a long-term perspective;
- growth of commercial profit;
- improvement of ecological atmosphere;
- deepening of regional integration;
- development of cooperation with the Asian countries would give Russia the following advantages:
    - development of the utterly neglected infrastructure of eastern Siberia and the Far East;
    - raising the living standards of the population;
    - Setting up continental cooperation;
    - Turning the Russian macro-region into a real gate to the Asia-Pacific region;
    - Diversification of directions of energy exports.

Along with this, there exist two tendencies in the policies of the states of Greater East Asia.

1. There are forces trying to create macro-regional energy integration (realisation of the variant discussed above);
2. The US push to create a division between energy importers and exporters has been able to achieve some success in this game. In December 2006, the first meeting of the energy ministers of the major oil-consuming countries (the US, China, Japan, India and South Korea) took place in Beijing. A similar division of importers and exporters would have a negative impact on the integration development of Greater East Asia.

At the same time, it is observed in the macro-region that there is firstly, a competition for access to the energy resources and secondly, an attempt for joint action.

China, Japan and India often perceive each other as competitors. India organised the first Indo-African conference on oil in Delhi as a reply to the China-Africa Cooperation Forum held in Beijing in November 2006. The Indian experts and journalists do not make a secret that India is very much interested in getting access to the Central Asian resources and considers China as the main competitor (India considers Russia as a perspective partner in Central Asia). The economic competition in this area has not turned into political competition, and there is a consciousness of mutual interests. China and India have started cooperation in concrete energy projects in third countries. The state companies of both countries signed a special agreement for cooperation in January 2006.[11]

The Role of Different Powers in the Formation of the Macro-Region

China (1) is destined to play key role in the formation of reater East Asia; however, the policies of US (2) and Japan (3) will have vital significance for the transformation of the macro-region. The role of the remaining countries is less important. The position of

Russia (4) in the contemporary stage is not very strong (because of an absence of consciousness about the priority of development of ties with Asia, though its potential is very high). The Far Eastern and East Siberian regions are already integrated into Asia, with which they had had stronger economic ties than with the European part of Russia. India (5) can be number two player in Greater East Asia in the future. However, the economic ties of India with countries of the region at present are at a very low level, though developing quite fast. The economic ties of India with Japan bear a political character to a greater extent than any real economic content. It is to a great extent linked to India's orientation towards the domestic market which predetermines the known economic isolation of the country.

Transnational Threats in East Asia

Firstly, the eco-systemic crisis is one of the main challenges to the macro-region. China and India are the main polluters with polluted soil, water and lower layers of atmosphere (the US is higher layer of atmosphere). The Asian giants chose an industrial path of development, but this has rigid ecological limitations. Till recently, the main usual source of energy consumption in China and India was coal. China and India occupy the first place in the world according to this indicator: 120 million t flying joli is formed in China every year and 80-100 million t in India. As a result, acid rain falls in both countries producing extremely negative consequences for health and is also threatening for the neighbouring countries. Besides, other countries (Japan, South Korea, Philippines) have fixed acid rain in their territory because of environmental pollution, resulted by coal burning in China. It is the coal industry in China and India that calls for a special concern of the international community.[12] China occupies the first place in the world in terms of throwing (more than 10,4 million t, more than 25% from world garbage), India occupies the third place after the US (more than 2.5 million t, 6.35 of the world garbage).[13] The given situation leads not so much to conflicts than to the striving of the countries of the macro-region to extend help to each other in the ecological sphere, because it does not recognise national borders.

Secondly, a similar coordination of efforts requires a stop to the spread of epidemics that regularly appear in Asia.

Thirdly, there exist significant differences between the Islamic states of the region and countries of the Middle and Near-East. In the majority cases they actively fight with Islamic terrorism, and are allies on the issue of China and India, which suffer from Islamic radicalism. Pakistan is isolated here; however, this country probably will not find place in Greater East Asia.

Lastly, similar favourable approaches are characteristic of the governments of the countries of the region and in relation to ethno-confessional conflicts, this is natural because a majority of the countries are multinational and poly-confessional.

Greater East Asia and Russia

The process of re-establishment of Greater East Asia as principal world economic centre and a sharp rise in the role of the largest countries of the continent are of vital importance for Russia from the point of view of global changes. The North is not interested in a full-scale and partner-like integration of Russia into its structure. Remaining in the state of periphery of the North, with massive supplies of all possible resources (raw material, finances, most qualified working force, etc.) will lead to only a gradual degradation of the country. The strategic objective of the West in relation to Russia is the preservation of the status quo: it needs a weak Russia, but not chaos; the development of a raw-material industry, but not high-tech industry; the destruction of military power, but not complete destruction at the given stage , etc. the comprehensive development of mutual links with Greater East Asia would provide Russia the possibility to strengthen its position as a world centre , dramatically increase the flexibility of foreign policy and foreign economic relations, evade the ultimate decline to raw-material-based development and get significant commercial benefits.

Russia's entry into the East Asian Community is Moscow's most important task. To accomplish that it is necessary to work with, first of all, India and China, keeping in view the strategic partner-like relations with the Asian giants and their interest in the development of a dialogue with Russia. Their joint action can influence the approach of Japan (which is scared that Russia's entry into the organisation will strengthen the position of China, but with having no possibility to openly oppose the Russian membership because of the declaration for the need to develop cooperation on the entire territory of Asia), Australia (its influence can be weakened, positioning it as US Trojan horse and country that does not belong to Asia) and several countries of South-East Asia.

At the same time it is no doubt necessary to conduct dialogue with these countries.

Here, we are not talking about Russia's choice of amount of engagement in the activities of the macro-region, because Russia is already participating in s full-fledged economic integration-based cooperation with the countries of Greater East Asia: from the economic point of view, the Far East and East Siberia are already oriented towards Asia much more strongly, than towards the other parts of Russia. Moscow is bound to put these processes under full control and to certain extent change them (departing from clear raw-material-based vector of development) so that it does not lose these economic regions in the future.

A simple re-orientation of raw-material export to Asia does not bring significant changes and only raises its manoeuvring capacity. It is necessary to convince the Asian countries about the primary need of development of the internal continental regions of Asia. The world investments go only to the coastal zones of Asia and the development of the internal and much more backward regions of Eurasian powers have to be undertaken by themselves, either individually or jointly, whichever is significantly more beneficial.

a. Here, it is possible to implement the idea about the prospects of cooperation between Russia and the Asian countries (first of all with China) in the agro sphere. At present, the countries of Greater East Asia are self-sufficient in food products and even sometimes, export them. Nevertheless, ecological problems can change the situation and compel the Asian countries to search for new ways of ensuring foodgrains. Russia can be a natural partner in resolving the issue.
b. The forest resources of Siberia and the Far East are an important area for cooperation. It is necessary to stop the export of raw materials and involve Asian investors for the development of the Russian wood-processing industry and paper-pulp industry. The large companies of the developed countries would hardly evince any interest in enterprises located so far from the zone of their interests, but the neighbouring Asian countries, interested in supplies to the internal regions, could be the consumers of finished products.
c. There is a lot of scope for cooperation in the processing industry. It is possible to unite Russia's high-tech with the Indian, Japanese and South Korean engineering thoughts (there is similar cooperation with India in the defence sphere) and the Chinese production with its qualitative and cheap labour force. The product made as a result of this cooperation would have a huge market: Greater East Asia has the highest, long-lasting rate of growth in the world; there the purchasing capacity of the population grows permanently. Such a cooperation and volume of markets can attract additional foreign investment. In case of

the realisation of this scenario, a paradoxical thing might take place: reforms in Russia with the objective of getting closer to Europe stage by stage would be implemented on the basis of the development of political and economic links with the East.

d. It is necessary to emphasise the oil and gas industry. It is extremely important for Russia to diversify the directions of energy export. The European Union is scared of the dependency on Russia on the issue and is permanently looking for an alternative to Russian commodities. However, Russia must search for new routes for the oil and gas pipelines—in the eastern and southern directions to avoid the dependency on one buyer, Europe. Besides, the most prospective thing would be the transportation of not raw materials, but the products processed on Russian territory. Russia has to choose a many-sided cooperation so that it does not the become hostage of the concrete state.

   a. For the Russian Federation it would be beneficial to expand the participation in the creation and expansion of infrastructure (from auto highway and metropolitan), construction, modernisation and reconstruction, machine-building and metallurgical enterprises, objects of nuclear industry, thermal and hydro-electric, oil and gas pipelines on the territory of the countries of Greater East Asia (first of all this concerns India, China and the countries of South-East Asia).

   b. Cooperation in building international corridors like the "East–West" (from South-East Asia to Europe through Russia) and "North–South" (from India and Iran to Europe through the Russian territory). Preliminary assessments showed that the given transport corridors would drastically reduce transit time and transport expenses. Russia can receive significant dividends by playing the role of the "Transport Bridge" between Asia and Europe and significantly modernise the infrastructure close to the regions through which the corridors would pass.

c. It is prudent to continue the development of the military–political cooperation with the countries of Greater East Asia from the point of view of arms sales. If limits on the arms export to India and China have been set, the market potential of South-East Asia is yet to be adequately utilised.

Greater East Asia is becoming an extraordinarily priority region for Russia, with the perspective of turning the principal direction of foreign policy. Russia's place in world system and its status as a world power would depend on how best it can integrate with this macro-region.

Notes

1. Правда, в 2007/2008 фин. г. рост составил только 15%.
2. Сайт Department of Commerce – http://dgft.delhi.nic.in/ Export Import Data Bank.
3. «*Vzglyad*» («Look», Moscow). 07 May 2008.
4. *The Standard* (Hong Kong). *03 April 2008.*
5. *Russian Business Consulting Daily* (Moscow). 06 May 2008.
6. Inoguchi, Takashi (1997), "Asian Values and Democracy in Asia", Tokyo the United Nations University.
7. Fukuyama, Francis (1995), "The Primacy of Culture", *Journal of Democracy*, Vol. 6., No. 1.
8. См., например, J. S. Nye, Jr. (1995), "The Case for Deep Engagement", *Foreign Affairs*, vol. 74, N 4,.
9. Официальный сайт ЦРУ – http://www.cia.gov/cia/publications/factbook/geos/ch.html; http://www.cia.gov/cia/publications/factbook/geos/ja.html; http://www.cia.gov/cia/publications/factbook/geos/in.html; http://www.cia.gov/cia/publications/factbook/geos/ks.html; http://www.cia.gov/cia/publications/factbook/geos/id.html; http://www.cia.gov/cia/publications/factbook/geos/ee.html; http://www.cia.gov/cia/publications/factbook/geos/us.html.
10. "International Energy Outlook 2003", Paris, International Energy Agency, 2003.
11. *The Hindu*, 13 January 2006.
12. "Global Environment Outlook. Geo4", United Nations Environment Programme Valetta (Malta): Progress Press Ltd, 2007, p. 101.
13. "International Energy Outlook 2006", Paris, International Energy Agency, 2006.

7

Geopolitics at Work: The Georgia—Russia Conflict

Peter W. Schulze

A. From Frozen Conflicts to Military Protectorates

The guns are silent. The smoke has settled and both war parties have more or less withdrawn to the approved lines of a ceasefire agreement, brokered by the European Union. In addition and somewhat surprisingly, the assessments in the media war which erupted after the hostilities and fully blamed Russia as an aggressor have changed too.

There is not enough time to list the episodes of the escalating conflict, which started well before the demise of the Soviet Union and led to an outside monitored ceasefire agreement which has constantly been broken by both sides.

August 8, 2008 marked a radical change in the relationship between Georgia and the Russian Federation since 2004. The low warfare situation of provocations, accusations, shootings, economic embargos and a creeping policy to turn South Ossetia into a military protectorate of Russia erupted fully into a full-blown military conflict. The Georgian President, Mikhail Saakaschvili, waged a "Blitzkrieg" on South Ossetia.[1] Georgian troops pushed forward to conquer Zkhinvali, the capital of South Ossetia and to block the strategically important Roki Tunnel, so that the Russian troops could not enter the war zone with heavy equipment.

Both the aims were not achieved. The Russian military intervened 12 hours after the Georgian military offensive.[2] The Russian troops pushed the Georgian army back. And like the recent campaigns in the Balkans in 1999 as well as in Gaza in 2009 have demonstrated, the overarching goal of the military operations is to destroy systematically by air and tank attacks most of the offensive military equipments of the enemy. This includes dual useable infrastructure, i.e. means and routes of transportation, port facilities and of course, all military hardware and equipment which can be used for new offensive purposes.

In addition, to provide the conflict from escalating once more, a "cordon sanitaire", a buffer zone of roughly seven kilometres was created and fortified around the South Ossetian border to disengage both sides and allocate additional security.

At the end of August 2008, both the Russian chambers of Parliament, i.e. the State Duma and the Federation Council, as well as the Russian President Dmitry Medvedev signed and ratified a declaration announcing South Ossetia and the other separatist region, Abkhazia, as sovereign states. By December 2008, bilateral security and cooperation agreements were concluded, allowing Russian troops to be stationed in South Ossetia and Abkhazia. Apart from not being internationally recognised, both regions, Abkhazia and South Ossetia, can now be defined as Russian protectorates. Such a move, the recognition of both separatist bodies as sovereign states, implied a fundamental change in Moscow's view on the principles of international law. Fearing problems at home, the post-Soviet state had never recognised separatist entities. However, the West's intransigence in the case of Kosovo and with the conflict in Chechnya under control, Moscow entered new terrain – much to the dismay of its partners in the Shanghai Cooperation Organization (SCO) and in the CIS countries.

Russia's military intervention put an end to Saakaschvili's masterfully played policy of "brinkmanship", which frustrated the northern neighbour with numerous small incidents of provocation. And as expected, the Kremlin overreacted in return. Saakaschvili could blame the Russians over and over again for using disproportional means, due to an economic embargo for Georgian products and the closure of transport lines. The spiral of confrontations went out of control in 2008.

Now, after the war, the brinkmanship game is over for good. Nevertheless, the Kremlin did not achieve all its targets in the short war. Obviously, the Georgian forces were defeated, the issue of the "frozen conflicts" was solved and Saakaschvili humiliated. However, the real goal to topple the Georgian President was not accomplished. Even the sovereignty of South Ossetia and Abkhazia is somewhat an ambivalent victory, because this act paradoxically shields Tbilisi against Russian pressure in the near future. No other country of the world community, apart from Nicaragua, followed Moscow's step. And indeed, despite the refusal of the NATO summit in December 2009 to grant Georgia and Ukraine access to the Membership Action Plan, it became clear that the Western community would do the utmost to protect Tbilisi against external threats.

Once it was clear that Moscow would support South Ossetia, the outcome of the war was entirely predictable. Therefore, it is most astounding that bizarre speculations and rumours accompanied the war and did not die even after its end. And also this was remarkable that contrary to the one-sided judgement in the Western media which solely blamed Russia for the offensive and for using disproportional means, was the media coverage and the consensus among Russia's political elite, regardless of its attitude to the Kremlin, which was extremely supportive of the Kremlin's action.[3]

Amidst all the speculations, one set of questions still troubles experts' minds: who won the bluff game – the Medvedev–Putin team or Saakaschvili? In other words, everyone had long expected a military conflict, but the question remained open as to when and who could trick the other side best into taking the blame.

This appraisal takes into consideration that both sides knew well about the respective buildup of military hardware and manpower thanks to satellite reconnaissance and instructors working in the Georgian army. Ever since the Washington administration discovered the strategic relevance of Georgia as a transit country for energy, the Baku-Tbilisi-Ceyhan pipeline became operative in 2005, and for its geopolitical value for monitoring and securing the US interest in the greater Middle East operation/concept, the Bush-administration supported unconditionally Georgia's request for membership of the NATO. This was indicated by the resolution to render support for Georgia's membership application by both the House of Representatives and the Senate in February 2007.

In November 2003, soon after the "Revolution of Roses" which led Mikhail Saakaschvili to power, Washington assisted the modernisation of the Georgian military, which by this time was poorly equipped, trained and clothed. Military and technological aid was transferred and in addition 2,000 Georgian soldiers were commissioned to participate in the Iraq campaign. Within four years, trained by American and Turkish instructors, the Georgian military became a formidable force in the region. In addition, Israeli technicians upgraded the Soviet hardware, i.e. planes and tanks, to NATO standards.

To sum up, Washington knew perfectly well that Saakaschvili was preparing for war. Such military movements were of course depicted by satellites and by the instructors working with the Georgian units. Further, it seems to be utterly impossible that the Russian buildup on the North Ossetian border went unnoticed by the US spy satellites vis-à-vis the Russians knowing about the Georgian war preparations. No doubt, similar technological devices and undoubtedly teams of informers operating inside Georgia gave respective signals.

Placed in this context that Washington knew about the Georgian and Russian military buildup and that Moscow waited for the Georgians to strike first, only the European Union and NATO seemed to have been left out of the picture. If we accept such a scenario for a moment, it throws open fairly astounding questions.

The most important ones that need to be answered are the following:

1. Did Washington share the obtained information about the Russian military buildup on the Northern border of South Ossetia with Saakaschvili?
2. Did Washington withhold such information in order to encourage Saakaschvili's war campaign despite the looming Russian counterattack?

3. Did Washington try in vain to stop Saakaschvili from launching the attack on Zkhinvali? This would imply that Washington lost its control over the Georgian President.
4. Did both Washington and Tbilisi underrate the decisiveness of the Kremlin to launch a massive counterattack?
5. Did the Bush administration and the Georgian President jointly play a hazardous game, in which it was assumed that Saakaschvili would be propelled into a win–win situation, regardless of the outcome of the conflict?

Rewarding answers, even six months after the war, are not in sight. However, given the information about the Russian forces being in place, it would have been quite bizarre if the Georgian President would have thought to win a military campaign against Russian forces. Therefore, three issues remain crucial: first, was the information shared; or second did the Bush administration or leading figures within this administration assure Saakaschvili that the US would support him? And third, did the US administration pursue other goals, i.e. linked to the election campaign, as the Russian Prime Minister Putin suggested?[4] In this respect, Saakaschvili would have been a tool in a much larger play.

Nevertheless, the assumed win–win situation demands some time for discussion. Widen the game of brinkmanship to open warfare: Saakaschvili would indeed move into a comfortable win–win situation, shielded from personal consequences despite a military defeat. First, the West would have never allowed him to be toppled as president. Second, the war would reunite the Georgian people against the external aggressor and quell opposition against him. Third, the West would rally behind Tbilisi and Saakaschvili. Fourth, the war would have been won ideologically and even more important, Tbilisi would not lose parts of its territory.

And indeed, the core areas of Georgia remained untouched, the opposition was silenced and the Western media portrayed Georgia as an outpost of Western civilisation and democracy in a sea of autocratic regimes. And miraculously, after all the painful and fruitless struggles to regain control over Abkhazia and South Ossetia, these trouble spots were meant to be gone once and forever. Consequently, the accession path to NATO would open. That is why the Bush administration immediately jumped on the chance and pushed for the NATO membership of Georgia and Ukraine.[5] However, at the Meeting of the NATO Foreign Ministers at the NATO HQ, in Brussels, from December 2–3, 2008, a fast track membership approval of Ukraine and Georgia to the NATO was blocked by the European member states and the Bucharest decision from April 2008 was re-enforced.

B. The Conflict's Purgative Power: The International Dimension

While the regional dimension of the war lost its menacing character, the conflict acquired an international dimension from the beginning. The Russian counterattack which led to the temporary occupation of the core territories of Georgia alarmed the international community. The General Secretaries of the UN, the EU and the USA condemned the disproportional use of power, and demanded together with an immediate ceasefire, the withdrawal of the Russian forces to the positions held before the war.

As argued above, the Kremlin did not need, nor did ask for, a military conflict with Georgia. But Moscow welcomed the opportunity to portray its willingness to punish the Georgian President for his anti-Russian politics. By doing so, the Kremlin aimed at drawing a clear line for the US-led influence in the CIS countries. The message was clear and meant containment: to limit the Western influence in the territorial area which stretches from the Baltic Sea to the region between the Black and Caspian Sea—an area called "Zwischeneuropa" (the Europe in between the Russian Federation and the European Union). Too weak economically, and too heterogeneous politically, the states of that region are unable to organise cross-border cooperation or to look after security and peace by their own means. During the last decade there were two waves of NATO expansion towards the East and a successful completion of the eastward extension of the European Union, which relies for its economic, political and military strength on those institutions close to the Russian border and sphere of influence. While the EU's eastern move did not alarm the Kremlin that much, because Moscow underrated the EU still as a predominantly economic power without political or military muscle, the NATO's expansion was met with strong opposition. The NATO's sphere of influence borders now on the Black Sea and a third round of extension was well under way, aiming at Ukraine and Georgia.

Since 2004, with the advent of the "Orange Revolution", this area is in turmoil and plagued by domestic power struggles, which have resulted in internal political instability and are often incited by outside forces. The area oscillates between the European Union and Russia, while the US is pulling its own strings at the back, pursuing its interests without sharing information about policy goals.[6] And open or covered attempts by Moscow to "roll back" the US-led onslaught or to achieve "regime changes" in the states which were feared to have been fully pulled into the US sphere of influence failed miserably, damaging Russia's international standing.

In this respect, Moscow needed a convincing score, a victory, regardless of how the international opinion would react, to demonstrate to the neighbouring CIS countries that either the US cannot support them, and/or that Russia, after the years of neglect for the area, is now ready to fight for its interest in the post-Soviet space.

Signals of such a shift were visible in Moscow's course of foreign and security policy. They had already been given earlier to the international community. A change in paradigm, based on a newly acquired strength due to the massive windfall profits from energy exports which had filled the Federal Reserve since 2003, was in the making. Vladimir Putin's address at the International Security Conference in Munich, February 2007, served as the first alarm bell. The address did not imply a fall back to the Cold War attitudes. Quite the opposite, cooperation was the focal point and interest of the Russian leader, however under changed conditions. Putin asked the Western powers to recognise the reality of a changed international environment, which unravelled in front of their eyes and saw Russia's return as a great European power. Accordingly, Putin asked for a treatment of Russia on equal terms in order to enhance cooperation, and to meet challenges to common security and interests. Members of the Russian government, like Foreign Minister Sergei Lavrov, did reiterate this position over and over again.[7]

The Caucasian conflict saw all three key geopolitical players in action, i.e. the EU, Russia and the USA. And of course, their motivations and interests differed quite substantially. However, as indicated, the management of the conflict prefigured in some way the shifts in international power constellations that may let us foretell the future working of a multipolar world – at least for the overall European space.

Let me enhance this thesis with a few suggestions:

1. The European Union staged a dramatic and successful comeback in authority and reputation during the Caucasian crisis. Let us remember: the EU was barely visible and immobilised in its policies towards Eastern Europe after the

ambitious project of a European constitution failed in 2005. And even the fate of the watered-down Lisbon Treaty is still in doubt due to the Irish referendum. However, suddenly the EU appeared nearly out of the blue to manage the Caucasian crisis. The answer is not easy and may contain two reasons. Definitely, despite the temporary weakness of the EU, its authority and potential power was never in doubt in Moscow's foreign policy circles. The Kremlin slowly but steadily accepted and feared the EU as a geopolitical rival in this part of the European space. In addition, it seemed to be pure luck, that the presidency of the EU was held by the French President Sarkozy. His political skills and authority were at hand at the right time to conclude a ceasefire, stop the war and hammer out a de facto peace arrangement which allowed all parties to save face. Russian President Dmitri Medvedev was well advised to accept the compromise and to pull the Russian troops back according to the Six-Points Agreement reached between the EU and Russia. As a result, Russia demonstrated its willingness for a lasting conflict resolution and the EU stated clearly its interests in shaping the fate of the "Zwischeneuropa". In addition to its needs to be stated, contrary to Russia, the EU had very little means to pressurise Russia in accepting the compromise solution. Russia knew the limits of its power quite well.

2. While active in the preparation of the conflict, Washington and the Bush administration were almost entirely blocked from its solution. This was of course partly due to the presidential election campaign. But there are other, more structural factors which kept the US out of the picture. First, changes in the international environment point to an early end of the unipolar and US-dominated world order. Second, the US seems to suffer from a phenomenon which first appeared at the end of

the "imperial presidency" of Richard Nixon, i.e. of "imperial overreach". The Bush-administration got stuck in a plethora of barely solvable conflicts and issues which it helped to generate by irresponsible policy actions. And, in addition, being to a high degree responsible for the Caucasian war, Washington could neither be part of, nor a partner in the endeavours to look for a solution. This situation may not change under the new Obama presidency, because a paradigm shift has also happened in the US: the global economic and financial crisis has moved the domestic issues to the top of the agenda in the foreseeable future.

3. As stated, Russia's return as an active great power to the international scene will limit the range and manoeuverability of the NATO and the European Union to shape the political and security landscape of Europe. Georgia was a test case; the real problem for Russia's European relations will arise with the future of Ukraine.
4. Russia's policy towards the "Near Abroad" has undergone a fundamental change. During the 1990s nearly all projects of closer cooperation among the CIS countries failed. Even Putin's pet project to stem the EU's eastern move by creating the "United Economic Space" (together with Kazakhstan, Ukraine, Belarus) in 2003 in Yalta broke down due to events in Ukraine. Ever since, the CIS space has not been abandoned as in the 1990s when the Russian state had no means there in order to engage. Since 2004, Moscow has tried to bring such countries into closer political, economic and security cooperation which could or would not embrace the Western calls for pluralism, democracy and the rule of law.
5. As indicated earlier, the zone of potential conflict between Russia and the European Union stretches from the Baltic Sea to the space between the Caspian and the Black

Sea. The states in that space lack any preconditions to look for the security and welfare of the region by their own means. They are pulled in opposite directions. And the external powers of attraction, i.e. the EU, Russia, and also the USA, exert considerable influence on their internal political stability. In my view, there are four different scenarios for the near future that are possible: first, the area and its states will be completely dominated and split up between the EU and Russia; second, Russia and the EU will come to some mutual understanding to contain their rivalry and work commonly with these states on an equal basis. Third, a murky status quo will be preserved in which each side avoids policy actions that could be understood as hostile and could provoke countermeasures in return. Fourth, the issue will be solved by the creation of a new European Security Architecture in which Russia and the European Union, including the NATO will form a real strategic partnership for peace and security in Europe.

The purging power of the conflict in the Russian–European relations appeared shortly after the war ended.

Russia fulfilled the Six Points Agreement and as a reconciliatory signal, the EU invited Moscow again to discuss the future shape and content of their Partnership and Cooperation Agreement (PCA) which had expired in 2007. It is only to be hoped that the cardinal mistake of the first PCA, not to define the role of Russia in Europe, will not be repeated. Despite all the bubbled foam about a "strategic partnership" emanating from Brussels, and even from some national governments, the relation between the EU and Russia has always lacked clarity. This confusion was of course shared on the Russian side as well. Brussels did not know how to deal with Russia and vice versa. There was no strategy on either side and it was sometimes utterly unclear whether Russia was perceived as a potential enemy, a rival or only a competitor. The integration of the former COMECON countries into the EU added new fuel to complicate the issue.

At least for NATO, such doubts did not exist, explaining the two rounds of expansion to the East. And NATO even reopened, in 2009, the temporarily disrupted function of the NATO-Russia Council. And, the new US President seems to be more inclined to invite rather than to alienate the country in meeting challenges both the countries and the international community face in the future.

And miraculously, suddenly the high–flying idea Medvedev announced during his first visit to Berlin, in June 2008, namely to work for a new Peace and Security Order which would encompass the whole of Europe, seems to attract even some Transatlantic circles.

May be the process that Gorbachev had tried to set in motion, striving for a "Common European Home" which then led to the Charter of Paris, in its nature a peace constitution for the whole of Europe, can be revived again.

Notes

1. Golts, Alexander, "The Failure of Realpolitik", *The Moscow Times*, 12 August 2008. Golts, Journalist and military expert, who is definitely not a supporter of the Kremlin's foreign and military policy, draws a parallel between the Georgian attack on Zkhinvali and the case of Sarajevo during the Bosnian conflict. "Whatever the Georgian army has done is no different from the purported war crimes for which former Bosnian Serb leader Radovan Karadzic is now standing trial in The Hague. Serbian artillery stationed on the hills surrounding Sarajevo systematically destroyed the separatist capital. This is exactly what the Georgian army has done by taking positions overlooking Zkhinvali". See as well Bomsdorf, Falk (Head of the Moscow office of the Friedrich Naumann Stiftung): Der Krieg im Kaukasus kennt fast nur Verlierer, Report, 13 August 2008.
2. Russia did not need the war, but could not avoid it either. The Kremlin was put into a chess-like position. It had no choice but to move to counter the Georgians. But Moscow waited until it became clear as to who started the war. However, this led to speculations about a power struggle between the hawks and the doves in Kremlin politics. One of the

leading right-wing voices in Washington, Robert Kagan, who became the foreign policy adviser of the former presidential candidate John McCain, immediately tried to whitewash Saakashvili and to put the blame on Russia. "The details of who did what to precipitate Russia's war against Georgia are not very important. (...) This war did not begin because of a miscalculation by Georgian President Mikheil Saakashvili. It is a war that Moscow has been attempting to provoke for some time". Kagan, Robert, "Putin Makes his Move", *The Washington Post*, 11 August 2008, A15.

3. Shevtsova, Lilia, "The Kremlin's New Containment Policy", *The Moscow Times*, 18 August 2008, "The war has intensified a conservative backlash in Russia. The country is now highly unified against the West".
4. Interview with Prime Minister Vladimir Putin in Sotchi, by Matthew Chance for CNN.com/Europe, 29.08.2008, available at: http://edition.cnn.com/2008/WORLD/europe/08/29/putin.transcript/index.html (last visited 13.03.2009): "If my suppositions are confirmed, then there are grounds to suspect that some people in the United States created this conflict deliberately in order to aggravate the situation and create a competitive advantage for one of the candidates for the U.S. presidency. […] I have said to you that if the presence of U.S. citizens in the zone of hostilities is confirmed, it would mean only one thing: that they could be there only at the direct instruction of their leaders. And if that is so, it means that in the combat zone there are U.S. citizens who are fulfilling their duties there. They can only do that under orders from their superiors, not on their own initiative."
5. Chairman's Statement of the NATO Meeting of the NATO Foreign Ministers, NATO HQ, Brussels, 2-3 December 2008 (available at http://www.nato.int/docu/pr/2008/p08-154e.html (last visited 13.03.2009): "NATO Ministers briefed their Georgian colleague regarding the decisions on Georgia and Ukraine taken during the North Atlantic Council meeting on 2-3 December 2008. In that meeting, NATO Ministers reaffirmed all elements of the decisions regarding Ukraine and Georgia taken by NATO Heads of State and Government in Bucharest. They noted that Georgia has made progress, yet has significant work left to do. Therefore, they decided to provide further assistance to Georgia in implementing needed reforms as it progresses towards NATO membership."
6. For a more detailed analysis see: Bahr, Egon: Geleitwort, in: Schneider-Deters, W., Schulze P.W., Timmermann, H.: *Die Europäische Union, Russland und Eurasien*, 2008, 19-25.
7. Lavrov, Sergej: Die Kaukasus-Krise und die Ukraine, in: *Frankfurter Allgemeine Zeitung*, 15.09.2008, 8.; See also, Schulze, Peter W.: Russlands Rückkehr als Machtfigur der europäischen und internationalen Politik, In: *Internationale Politik und Gesellschaft* 3/2007, 114-131.

Oli crum acta vo, Catquo consuas tandam estem noxim horum furbefenate diem terum diem auc fex sciis bontiam ocum, diu que tem ina diocum et optemus interum nos egiliu similii ssusuam iam iam octus hostam ia ne omnos M. Marehem iu quo hostiac tem quodista quo adeoraet vatus publis avocum abeffre constum terri por inatquit re, quem inprae morena, con Etritiam patriam aut no. Ercenat urnimis prortil iquit. Quos constra vertus autessatimis ne acci peressedi iam num unculicae turniam.

Quem ompra? Sericis orbit perfin senat, consi publibu teatisquitum pervid Cupplius dicipse inatus, pra tuus avo, caequem stum terum eterdici simus consto iu vilibut vit vigna, nonin dicae ad artius. Ti. Is at, di fue cre iaet iae tum aut L. Verum dit. Ena, qua ad sper ina consuscrum publi perum iurore tabendemquid iam mus con dit vast grat, que perfeco nsigit, quituam opone cepes, mantus Catus intiu quid iam. Ta vius es egerori butus, alabentrum re patil telut audefati, senarissua in patienatqui crum mo me publiis facchui demover fentemum.

Edo, ora? In senatiam maxime publica vis bonsimus? Nos inat, atquam sena, Cateata re nondum consuam dum iu mo tem opublienam dius ercentemus? Upiorte prarbemnem nonfere iae compost? Tur per quonsignox sigitis, me achus renimis. Nost dio publint iquiterit pata quodiu maiorsul hora, Palinculego contraetrae, scit, ut Catustilin tum vehenderem tem interid consiliur, potiam audam sterum prestum ac is hebatquo conia teres et publintil cuperrips, cote fit, sulius, concerraelum it L. Maet; niam tus ia conen telinit; nihintem es clutemuntri fora, nice audem linatiam cercepo tiaedessedo, quod re, sediescenat, num, consimurnin vis horunum inatquon patum vis inpris veris, sentilis, nium niam nequit videfac tortum issignatuam tuus, nihica ius hores no. Habemo morum resceri pera, derferi oricaet, propubl isquam se, nos, et ne corisse diissentere is mo mo est ac tum. Oltorbem praet L. Sp. Mulintra, es silicer ficasdam. Simante multod ius; Cat, diu il viliesc essuliciis ce atoravendum es viri, cepertus at vivivir isultum acre consultum optientisse teritanum in sa rei senatque in hac rena, nonsuli stris; nia conoximus conc vili, niamdi, nihilic aperacchum sendiem habena, dicione quonsuam, sente tea nos, es auconsum fir linte dii fui cupiciam interfent.

Ove, nequa no. Romnequ itemque quemus li, num proribus, no. At Cat. Ihilibes bonsi factus nonsulicas vivasdam illa nos, mo non Itam publice moenatodi pritriocrei perum omnius prionsunum crebus, Ti. Publien arbis. merbite rfectalin temnon tus aucitelius, ocum, poraectum sularibenter ad fur, temenatiam coniu sendelica; C. Vivirmissit vitus Mae consis C. Ahactabus, ceporsum coeniam interec tamque no. Ris auro Cati publis.

8

International System: Descending to Chaos or Looking up to New Opportunities?

Kortunov S.V.

The growing global financial crisis seriously pushes the issue of the control of processes related to the world economy and international politics. The scale of the crisis is compared with the Great Depression of the 1930s by many, while some of them compare it with the situation that Europe faced in the fourteenth century during the "New dark era". Sergei Karaganov believes that this is the beginning of a new era in world history.

Russian President Dmitry Medvedev too drew attention to the global crisis in his address to the Federal Assembly on March 5, 2008. He particularly recalled the Caucasus crisis, which "cast doubt on the effectiveness of international institutes in ensuring security" and practically destabilised the foundation of global order, and the global financial crisis that began as a local emergency phenomena in the national market of the US received a global character. According to the Russian President, these two different issues have "common features and common origin". President Medvedev linked it to the unilateral actions of the US.

The objective of the article is not to analyse the reasons and consequences of the global financial crisis. This analysis is being done by experts on world economy, international relations and international finance. We would rather dwell on the issues of international security system, whose decline coincided with the maturing of preconditions for financial crisis— immediately after Soviet disintegration and break-up of the bipolar architecture of international relations. The origin of decline of the contemporary system of international security lies in the degradation of its foundation – the Westphalian peace of 1648.

The world history till the confirmation of the Westphalian system, which means the international system of national states, was a history of dominance and confrontation between different empires. Differences of opinion about empire that it is an absolute evil is at best a benevolent mistake, and a deliberate lie at the worst.

First of all, if we take the world history as a whole, the empire is a significantly more stable state as compared to the others, including national states, which has been justly stressed by the great Russian historian V. Makhnach. Secondly, if we take periods of dominance in world politics by full-fledged empires, which according to Makhnach include only four like the Roman empire, the Byzantine empire, the Holy Roman empire and the Russian empire , each one of them acted as important factors of stability in separate regions as well as in the system of international relations as a whole. The fall of these empires was followed by war and military conflicts that pushed the world into chaos.

The dividing line between the era of empires and the era of national states was the Westphalian peace concluded by the European powers in 1648 after13 years of bloody war in Europe. This war was a world war of that period. For all practical purposes, all large European countries such as Sweden, France, Germany, Netherlands, Denmark, Check, Britain, Spain, Italy, and to a lesser extent Poland and Russia, were involved in this war.

The Westphalian system strengthened certain rules of the game on world order, which are working so far with known amendments and modifications:

- The Westphalian system did not ban, rather permitted war, including aggressive invasions, which was declared as a lawful right of a sovereign state;
- The Westphalian system did not prevent, rather facilitated, a stipulation of the right of the strong in international law;
- The Westphalian system confirmed the principle of non-interference in internal affairs of sovereign countries following the axiom formulated by J. Boden in international law—"sovereignty is absolute and permanent authority of the state over the citizens".

Because of this, in the seventeenth, eighteenth and nineteenth centuries, nobody could think it right to interfere in the internal affairs of European tyranny, which openly violated human rights and citizens' rights on a massive scale. Even in the first half of the twentieth century, Western democracies could not interfere in the internal affairs of fascist Germany and communist USSR. The international community silently looked at the unfolding genocide of Jews in Germany or the mass repression in Stalinist USSR. Moreover, it did not have any lever of influencing these regimes.

The situation to some extent changed in the last three decades of the past century because human rights became an instrument of struggle against the former USSR. This began with the decline of the Westphalian system of international relations.

Beginning from 1648, the Westphalian system of international relations went through six modifications, each one of which was a result of large-scale warfare. The first such warfare after the thirteen-year war was Napoleon's invasion, which was much larger in scale. This ended with the defeat of Napoleon by the coalition of European powers with the dominant role of Russia that made most significant contribution in the victory over Napoleon. The Vienna Congress convened in 1815 confirmed the next division of the world and formed a "Holy Union" under Russia's practical leadership. The union fell in 1830, largely because of Austrian and British intrigues.

The Positive and Negative Sides of a Unipolar World

The bipolar world that emerged after World War II presented a world of limited sovereignty (with the exception of two superpowers) and in this capacity essentially contradicted the Westphalian system. The unipolar world that emerged after the Soviet disintegration stood with a greater contradiction to the Westphalia system, because there was only one country—USA—that enjoyed full sovereignty. Of course, this world did not reflect a Pax Americana (a long-time dream of the American rightist conservatives) and even a world hegemony of the USA.

Rather it was an attempt to assume world leadership with the help of "soft power".

The growth of the economic potential of China, India, Russia, South Africa, the European Union, Brazil, Mexico and other countries towards the end of the twentieth century and the beginning of the twenty-first century did not create preconditions for the formation of a multipolar world, because the US remained as the economic, political and military leader. US dominated in four important spheres: economic, political, military and even in cultural sphere to some extent (through mass media, Hollywood, internet, etc).

The world order under formation during 1991–2001 could be called as polycentric unipolarity. The essence of this world order lay in the realisation of a historical project on the basis of economic, military–political and ethical–legal commonality of the countries of the West and the spreading of these standards to the entire world. Naturally, this evoked acute resistance in the entire world, including the activisation of "asymmetric reply" in the form of transnational terrorism. The other peculiarity of the project was that it did not have the foundation based on agreements. Its foundation was built on chain precedents, which were essentially unilateral decisions and concepts of the USA such as – The doctrine of "expansion of democracy" of 1993; – The concept of NATO expansion (1996) – The new strategic concept of NATO, according to which the NATO's responsibility zone expanded beyond the Northern Atlantic:

- The doctrine of preventive attack;
- The doctrine of democratisation of the Greater Middle East.

The unipolar world (rather the attempt to build it) existed for 10 years from 1991 to 2001.The beginning of its fall was heralded by the event of the terrorist attack on the USA on September 11,

2001, which was backed by very serious forces that wanted to deliver a powerful blow on the US concept of the new world order , and show as baseless the US declaration for world leadership in the twenty-first century.

They achieved this objective in many ways. The role that the US wanted to assume came under doubt. Serious defects appeared in all systems of the US security including in foreign intelligence and internal security. The huge military and economic power of the superpower (the US accounts for 40% of the world military expenditure and 20% of the world GDP) turned out to be inadequate because it could not protect its ordinary citizens in major cities from a small group of terrorists.

Here, two things are very clear. First of all, a serious crisis is existing but post-confrontational mechanisms and concepts of international security are no more effective. Secondly, a complete unpredictability of principles, parameters and content of a new system of international relations are under formation. At the same time, at present, we can state the fall of the unipolar world with a certain degree of certainty. This means the fall of that system of international relations, which was under formation after the end of the Cold War. The mechanism of the collective security of the CIS could not be used, which may lead to its ultimate degradation. The NATO's potential also seemed useless to meet the most serious challenge of the twenty-first century. Now, the NATO leadership understands that its potential was built to fulfil absolutely different tasks rather than fighting the menace of international terrorism and other new challenges and threats.

The 9/11 event delivered a powerful blow to the UN and other organisations of the international security system, for example, the Organization of Security and Cooperation in Europe, which is rendered useless in the new historical situation. The USA sent clear signals that it needs neither the UNSC, nor the OSCE, or other international organisations and is capable of ensuring a legal basis for its action whatever it might be. Still worse, members of the international community including Russia practically accepted this. As a result, today, the entire world including the Middle East once again got convinced that humankind had entered a new era in which the central element is neither principles of wisdom and humanism like in the past, nor even the norms of international law, which makes the world more fragile and unprotected.

The world order based on international law was practically destroyed in 1999 by the NATO invasion on Yugoslavia. Therefore, the action of international terrorists against the USA on September 11, 2001, strictly speaking, took place in the situation of a destroyed world order when there was nothing to violate from the legal point of view. In other words, the terrorists acted on the basis of the real precedent of 1999, by and large approved by the international "civilized" community. In the meantime, the military action of an anti-terrorist coalition led by the USA took place in the conditions of an absence of world order based on international law.

At the same time, we see that a large majority of countries in the world of the twenty-first century do not fight for their sovereignty; rather, they consciously give it either to the US (countries such as Poland, of eastern and central Asia, the Baltic region, Georgia and others) or to supranational structures of Germany, France, countries of the Benelux, Portugal, Spain and others. Except the US, which is the bearer of complete national sovereignty in the contemporary world, there are only four countries such as Russia, China, India and Iran which insist on national sovereignty. Does it mean that the world is witnessing the formation of a neo-Westphalian system? Or is the world passing through the Westphalian era of national states, and would return to the empires' era, only at a new level?

Nobody has the answer to this. Nevertheless, it is evident that the US, Russia, China, India and Iran have to be turned into new empires, which is unlikely, because none of these countries fully correspond to the major criteria of empire. Most importantly, none of these countries, even the US, wants to be an empire in the sense of bearing the responsibility of an empire's burden.

The Crisis in the International Security System

The fall of the Westphalian world order led to a serious crisis of the whole system of international security, built with so much of hard work after 1945. The danger of interstate military conflicts and its uncontrolled escalation is growing at regional and local levels. First of all, this concerns such regions like the expanded Middle East, Transcaucasus, Central Asia, South-East Asia, and the Korean peninsula. The perspective of aggravation and increase in a number of domestic conflicts looks to be likely. The first of this concerns the Near and Middle East, an area of potential confrontation in the Balkans and also in the post-Soviet space (Fergana valley, Crimea, Trans-Dneister, Abkhazia, South Ossetia, Jhabakhetia, Nagorno- Karabakh) and in some countries of Africa. As a result, there is a rise in destabilisation and chaos in the world.

The conflict potential as a whole is rising, and a huge significance of power is being imposed upon the international community. The practice of unilateral and negative action, from the point of view of international law by some countries, as well as the attempt towards an unceremonial imposition of one's own position while ignoring the legitimate interests of the other partners inflict a serious damage to stability.

Now, it is evident that practically all mechanisms for maintaining international security, created after World War II and during the Cold War (the UN, NATO, the Organization of Security and Cooperation in Europe and others) are not adequate to meet the challenges and threats of the beginning of the current century. The attempts to reform these organisations have not been successful. As a result, there is a sharp decline in controlling international crises and processes.

The countries of the Asia-Pacific region, first of all China, are playing an ever greater role in the world. This facilitates a rise in the existing and emergence of new contradictions in the world and strengthens the competition with a possible military component.

National and socio-economic problems are flaring up in different regions. There is a danger of damaging international stability as a result of regional conflicts, arms race at the regional level, the spread of weapons of mass destruction, terrorism, narco-business and other security challenges.

The rise of national and religious extremism, particularly in some regions of the Islamic world, is a dangerous challenge to regional and international stability.

The competition for energy resources that assumes significance among the factors influencing the military–political situation is getting aggravated.

The struggle for resources promotes arms race. The concern for maintaining control over its own resources pushes the countries to raise their defense potential. The consumer countries are playing with the idea of using military–political instruments for ensuring access to those recourses through force.

An uncontrolled arms race can be seen in the world. Today, it has reached a qualitatively new level and its scale in certain regions has reached the peak of the Cold War period. This takes place in the backdrop of the degradation of global and regional regimes of control over weapons. A fast militarisation is taking place in the world, particularly in its conflict zones. The absence of international procedures of control over the conventional arms trade leads to its fast spread, even among criminal structures.

There is rise in the threat of the emergence of so-called destabilising weapons, nuclear warheads with low capacity, strategic rockets with non-nuclear war heads, etc.

The growing destabilisation of the international relations and the US policy for "compelling to peace" and "imposition of democracy" are among reasons for a new global arms race. The arms conflict in Iraq and former Yugoslavia initiated by the US clearly demonstrated the hopelessness of an international guarantee for security and compelled the other countries to defend their sovereignty through strengthening their defence forces. It is not only openly the anti-US states that are engaged in arms imports but also states like Malaysia, Vietnam and the United Arab Emirates which have not their own defence industry. One more factor for the arms race is the closing of the "nuclear umbrella", under which the satellite countries of the USSR and US felt secured and the weakening of the containment role of the nuclear arsenals of the later-nuclear countries. In certain cases, all this compels many countries to opt for their own force on the issue of defence.

At the same time, the US is the leader in arms race in quality and quantity. There is no doubt about the leader in the race as the US military budget constitutes half of the world expenditure on defence. The US military budget in 2007 constituted 700 billion US dollars (the Russian military budget is about 70 billion US dollars). The US military expenditure has a strong innovative character. The US would spend 75.7 billion US dollars for developing and testing new weapons systems. The Pentagon has asked for 51.1 billion US dollars for building an anti-missile system, and the military use of space and nuclear weapons. New types of weapons are under development on the basis of geophysics, ionosphere, EMI-weapons and others.

The following tendencies should be noted in case of the nuclear factor:

- In spite of a serious improvement in the international situation and the minimum probability of a large-scale war and military conflicts between leading powers, a cardinal decrease in the nuclear weapons' role in the international politics is not evident (this tendency can be changed, may be after 15–20 years. If the nuclear weapons proliferation gets strengthened, the rise of its role in the nuclear age is quite possible). Unprecedented terrorist acts and the changing priority in threat perception lead to the dangerous decline of the threshold of nuclear weapons use, the rise of the probability of its use and a possible uncontrolled escalation. This is facilitated by a further proliferation of weapons of mass destruction and their means of transportation.
- The accumulated technological progress and results of testing of separate components of the anti-missile defense system bear testimony of the possibility of a mid-term perspective (5–10 years) for the deployment of a limited anti-missile system, whose density would keep on growing permanently in the subsequent period. It is unlikely to threaten the Russian interests in next 15–25 years, particularly if Russia continues to modernise its strategic nuclear potential. The realisation that the US anti-missile defence system would facilitate a "retargeting" of the nuclear forces of other countries and from US objects to possibly Russian objects, which would destabilise the strategic situation in the world.

The magnitude of these challenges is reinforced by a "centralized" regime of control over the weapons, which ensures the predictability of a military–political situation, and an adequate strategic warning that could remove the danger of unexpected attack, which would be degraded further. The tenure of two important bilateral Russia–US agreements in the sphere of limitation and reduction of strategic weapons would come to an end in 2009 (START) and 2012 (an agreement on the reduction of strategic and offensive potentials). The inspection under the agreement on medium and small-range missiles has been stopped as a result of the completion of the 13-year period of inspection activities (however, a ban on the production of small and medium range missiles still continues). Most probably as a result of the NATO expansion towards the East, the agreement on the conventional forces in Europe would be buried. There is no hope that a new agreement with the US and NATO in this sphere would be signed. Notwithstanding the ratification of the CTBT by three nuclear powers—namely Russia, Britain and France—there is no hope that it would come into force (because of the positions of the US, China, Israel, Iran, India, Pakistan, North Korea and some other countries possessing nuclear technology).

The agreement on the reduction of strategic and offensive potentials is most probably the last agreement on arms reduction signed between the US and Russia. A further reduction of nuclear arms would take place at best through parallel unilateral steps, and possibly without mutual agreement.

Since the US would not be able to leave Iraq in the next 3–4 years, it would hardly be able to execute other large military operations of this scale. At the same time, in the case of Iran, the possibility of use of military force in the form of attack on nuclear objects and other military and infrastructural objects cannot be excluded, which might sharply destabilise the situation. More than that, the attack can be launched by the present or future administration, which would be forced to run out of Iraq and be thereby compelled to use force in order to compensate for the defeat. In any case, the military conflict in the Middle East is similar to the Israel–Lebanon conflict involving two to three countries including Israel and Iran. This can start as Israel's fight against transnational terrorist organisations, hiding in the territory of certain Arab countries. Moreover, as long as the Americans remain involved in Iraq, the active actions of similar organisations would grow. When the US leaves Iraq after 3–5 years without achieving democratisation and stability in the country, tens of thousands of militants, trained during the Iraq war for terrorist activities, would find themselves without any engagement. This "terrorist international "would spread its activities every where, including Russia. Further radicalisation of the Islamic community would exacerbate the global terrorist situation. A further growth in the anti-US and anti-Western mood is inevitable along with an increasing impression about the US's failure as the world's policeman. The US would pass through a post-Iraq syndrome like the post-Vietnam syndrome. As a result, the security vacuum in the world would grow. Thus, the development of the situation would pass through a worst-case scenario: chaotic Iraq, a rise in militant Islamic terrorism, the inability of the US to confront it while retaining the desire to demonstrate to the world that it is not a "paper tiger".

The Islamic world has so far presented itself as a virtual civilisational subject. Hundreds of millions of Muslims are united by religion but split by political thoughts, related to the nature of political power, own religious history and that of the regions and others. However, in a strategic perspective, the Islamic community presents itself as a powerful resource for resistance to the formation of the new world order, if its formation continues without taking their interests into account. Besides, if the Islamic world is not respected properly, it might come to be dominated by Islamic extremism, which is fraught with the "clash of civilizations"(it is not clear as to what does "respect to Islam" mean). The most terrible perspective is the capture of power by Islamists in Pakistan as a result of a military coup or through a legitimate election procedure. Then, the nuclear arsenal would be under their control.

The widening gap between the super-rich and super-poor countries leading to the marginalisation of not only separate states but also entire regions in the world and the growth of the Weimar syndrome in the Islamic world will facilitate an escalation of activities of transnational terrorist organisations, including in Greater Europe that includes Russia. In any case, the level of international terrorist activities would remain, at least, as high as it was in 2001–2006. Most likely, this level would grow in the coming decade, if coordinated radical steps that would include military and certain other actions are not taken.

This is linked to another problem which is the practical inability of the international community to resolve the issue of so-called failed or failing states.

If responsible members of the international community during the next 3–4 years do not take significant steps to meet the above-mentioned challenges and threats or at least reduce their acuteness, those challenges and threats would rise. Only a part of those issues could be addressed as a result of the unprecedented economic growth of the world. The solutions to those issues have to be found. If they are not addressed on time, more significant efforts and resources are required for their solution.

Another three to six nuclear powers would appear in the world by 2020. In the case Iran becomes a nuclear power by 2015 (this is likely to happen), this would set the mechanism for the ultimate failure of the NPT. In the worst-case scenario, some more countries would join the nuclear club in the subsequent 10 years. These countries might include countries that have opted in favour of a non-nuclear status (first of all South Korea, Japan, Taiwan, Libya, Syria, Egypt, Saudi Arabia, Algeria, Turkey, Brazil and Argentina).

Thus, after 8–12 years Russia and the world might face a nuclear crisis—there would be proliferation of nuclear arsenals in other countries, including states with unstable regimes, in which the conditions for the safe preservation of the nuclear weapons and the requirements for excluding a nonsanctioned access and application of this weapon would be at the lowest level. Along with a real possibility of nuclear terrorism, all this might pose such threats not only for regional security but also for global security so much so that ecological, energy and other challenges and threats would be relegated to the back seat.

Regarding the East and the West, you can rule out the emergence of challenges but a direct military threat from these directions is not very likely. True, if the mechanism for a real partnership between Russia and NATO is not created, the alliance would remain as a closed-door military bloc and would not be transformed into an effective system of the Euro-Atlantic, and consequently, global security. Therefore, the deterioration of relations between Russia and the West recently, and the increasing alienation between them, poses one of the major threats to national security.

The region of the Greater Middle East might witness serious destabilisation, which could be caused by two-thirds of local wars like the Israel–Lebanon war of 2006 summer. Israel and Iran are likely to be drawn into this war.

In the Far East, China in all likelihood would activate the effort to conquer Taiwan, which might evoke the most acute crisis in the Chinese–US relations and the Chinese–Japanese relations. This kind of development can hardly correspond to the Russian interests because it would mean a sharp destabilisation of the entire Asia-Pacific region with unpredictable consequences.

If the regional systems of security cannot be built in Greater Europe, the Asia-Pacific Region, and more importantly, in Central Asia and the Middle East, along with the strengthening of the mechanism of global security under the UN, then the resumption of international relations of sharp competition between new centers of power typical of a polycentric system cannot be ruled out. They would compete for dominance over regions having a vital significance for Russia and even for certain regions of the Russian Federation.

Foreign Policy Concept of President Medvedev

The Russian President D. Medvedev promulgated his new foreign policy concept of Russia on July 12, 2008. Along with his speeches on international issues, this concept can be considered as a new stage in the foreign policy activities of Russia. The question is whether this document corresponds to the above-mentioned risks, challenges and threats of national and international security.

The new concept contains three key theses – emphasis on an all-round strengthening of international law as the basis for inter-state relations and the formation of international security system, a stress on the UNO and its Security Council as an international organisation that has no substitute, having a unique legitimacy and task of reduction of the role of force in international relations while reinforcing strategic and regional stability.

President Medvedev in his address to the Federal Assembly on November 5, 2008, once again raised the issue of building a "new global security architecture" and appealed to the international community to concentrate on the following directions of practical activity.

First of all, to continue work for strengthening the legal foundation of international relations: "Particularly generally accepted norms and principles of international law should determine the rules of the game in world affairs. Developing the habit of matching the action with international law would facilitate the reduction of the factor of crude force, and would be the confirmation of a collective image of action. Otherwise we will confront with international chaos and practical impossibility of preserving the international order".

Secondly, try to form a polycentric international system.

Thirdly, to establish universal diplomatic methods of regulating crisis situations.

Fourthly; to conduct a permanent dialogue for the fast formation of new rules of international financial architecture.

Of course, all these tasks are noble and full of high moral and spiritual thoughts, which should be welcome. However, how this reflects contemporary reality is a different issue.

The history of international relations, for example, bears testimony that international law is not only the sum of certain abstract, though noble, principles of conduct in foreign policy; rather, it is a fixation of the existing co-relation of forces in the international arena.

It is quite clear that after the Soviet break-up in 1991 the world witnessed a new correlation of forces, which did not reflect the main components of the Yalta–Postdam system of international relations. In these conditions the documents signed in 1945 could not be the only source of international law, and to insist on that is meaningless and counter-productive. The unilateral actions of the US, particularly in Yugoslavia and Iraq, can be criticised. However, it should be understood that they reflect the destruction of that international law that fixed the correlation of forces created 60 years ago. An appeal to this international law (which has been done 22 times in the new foreign policy concept) is a symbol of weakness, not force.

It is also meaningless to stress the exclusive role of the UN in contemporary conditions (it has been done 23 times in the new foreign policy concept) in building a new system of international security. The effectiveness and prestige of this mechanism is declining from year to year because of objective reasons. The anachronism of its procedure including the procedure to take decisions in the Security Council is quite evident. The attempt to reform this organisation has completely failed at this stage.

Lastly, it can be admitted that the call for the reduction of the role of force factor in international relations cannot have a political perspective. Rather, a tendency to have a greater role of this factor including the factor of military power is quite evident. In the contemporary world, an adequate reaction to crisis and conflict is not enough. One has to learn to manage it jointly. This means the transfer of accent to various preventive measures. In the long term, it is about rearing people in the spirit of a world culture, and a dialogue between people, as well as tolerance.

Thus, it is necessary to note that all the three major theses of the new foreign policy concept, confirmed but the third President of Russia's appeal to strengthening the norms of international law, the prestige of the UN and the reduction of the importance of the force factor in world affairs -unfortunately, these cannot be realised in the contemporary conditions. Consequently, that cannot serve as a convincing symbol of the foreign policy potential of Russia. In the absence of a real force, including the military force, such a foreign policy inevitably would lead to endless complaints. Noble calls for the "humanization of international relations" without the support of soft and hard power, are not capable of being a realistic basis for the growth of international influence.

This is convincingly proved by the events of the summer of 2008 in the Caucasus. Forcibly entering into the territory of South Ossetia, Georgia, with US patronage, did not care about international law. The UN Security Council, refusing to condemn the aggression, proved itself to be a helpless and barely useful body. Russia tried its best to prevent the war till the last moment and was forced to take adequate steps for defending its peacekeepers and the people of South Ossetia from Georgian aggressors. Thus, military force once again became the supreme arbitrator in international politics. Using military force, President Medvedev to an extent reviewed the foreign policy doctrine declared by him on July 12, 2008, which ran counter to reality.

At the same time it was clear that many proposals of D. Medvedev are timely because they compel to reassess the role of international law in a wide historical perspective. It is necessary to resolve the issue of the correlation of law and force. The role of law, its moral authority and the moral authority of international relations, including that of the UN, were adversely affected by the known events of the preceding period, first of all by the actions of the US in Yugoslavia and Iraq. This raised suspicion that the international law in essence bears only a declarative character and is not a source of force. Right, at present, is sanctioned by force. If there is force, there would be law. This kind of situation is not permissible. The developed countries of the world have to show respect to international law, and they have to change themselves for this. It should be understood that the international community of the twenty-first century is not a world of centres of force, but a world of mutually respectable people and cultures. There is a need for new geopolitically adequate, new geopolitical morals, based on international law, which should also be reassessed .

What should be done?

The first decade of the twenty-first century forms the basis for making certain conclusions regarding the fall of the old world order.

First of all, it should be firmly noted that efforts to establish the American world order have been defeated, at least in the present stage. This kind of world order does not have any perspective as a tendency of world development that has no alternative. Further attempts to impose it on the world will confront still more resistance from other objects of international relations.

The role of Europe in forming the new world order is relatively declining, while the role of Russia in this sphere is growing. The role of China is not absolutely clear. However, the concept of a multipolar world, as evident after the events at the beginning of the twenty-first century, is impermissibly a simplification of the real tendencies of international development.

The key region of the world defining global security is Eurasia. What is significant is that Russia as a Eurasian country cannot be second-class partner, if its active participation in fighting international terrorism in that important space is expected.

All this does not mean that new world order from today onwards would be formed in the paradigm of the Russian–US interaction. First of all, the US would continue to strive for dominance in global affairs as the single leader. Secondly, Russia is still weak in an economic and military sense for acting like an equal power centre with the US in building a new system of international relations. Russia in its politics would orient towards Europe, China and the Islamic world. This kind of multi-vector policy through successful diplomacy can make Russia quite valuable and it may become an indispensable partner of the international community.

Besides, the possibility of Russia and the US coming closer because of their unequal military–political weight should be considered as limited. Both sides so far, have been guided by tactical and pragmatic considerations, while pursuing their own objective. It is unlikely that any kind of strategic union or even an equal partnership can emerge from this kind of cooperation. The solution of this issue needs a serious mutual movement towards each other, which does not exist so far.

It is desirable to engage the US administration in a wide political–strategic dialogue as proposed by President Medvedev in his address to the Federal Assembly on November 5, 2008. In order to achieve this goal, it is required to have a joint search of means for minimising the risk stemming from an objectively existing situation of mutual nuclear containment. However, considering the US attitude towards bilateral and multilateral control over nuclear weapons, mutual agreements can hardly be expected. This means that Russia does not have any other option but to continue its independent nuclear policy, which is permitted under the agreement on the reduction of strategic and offensive nuclear weapons potential and the non-functioning agreement on the CTBT. In the new situation, Russia can independently determine the qualitative and quantitative structure of its nuclear force, on the basis of land-based ICBMs with multiple heads, which ensures a guaranteed preservation of the nuclear containment potential from attack by the US and other countries in any kind of development in the military–political sphere. Russia has the economic potential for this.

In order to form a real and effective system of international security corresponding to risks, challenges and threats of the twenty-first century, it is necessary to have a new revolution in values, a new renaissance of "justice", "equality" and "fraternity" of the people, and the development of such concepts as "market", "freedom" and prosperity, self-expression and other liberal ideas.

There has to be hard battle for winning the "hearts" and "minds" of people, in which the most decisive role would be played by the propaganda of values. This presupposes the involvement of millions of people in dialogue in the framework of which there has to be interaction and mutual enrichment of all cultures and civilisations.

Developed and rich countries of the world are capable of building such a structure of international relations in which each the state and its people would have the opportunity for ensuring prosperity and dignified living standards, own prosperity and self-expression. There is a need for a well-conceived programme for changing the present world order and the entire philosophy of international relations. Russia can and should say its weighty word in course of formation of a new, just and human world order.

9

The Battle for Water in Central Asia and Regional Potential for Cooperation

Stanislav Chernyavsky

The former Soviet Union and Iran accumulated a huge experience of legal interaction over long years on different questions, including the use of water resources of the Arakas and Kura Rivers and also the natural resources of the Caspian Sea. These healthy traditions continue in our times as well, though the length of the border between the Russian Federation and the Islamic Republic of Iran got reduced significantly. New independent states that emerged after the Soviet collapse in southern Caucasus and Central Asia strive to follow the legal practices of the past years of maintaining good relations with Iran.

Along with that, as noted in the Fifth World Water Forum held from March 16 to 22, 2009 at Istanbul, the significance of water resources for resolving the task of development and economic growth have increased so much that the need for a consistent correction of positions of the concerned sides on the use of water resources is obvious. (1)

The paper dwells on the specific nature of the water resource balance of Central Asia, the relations of states of the region to the perspectives of interactional beginnings and major obstacles in the way of taking strategic decisions. The paper makes an attempt to formulate proposals about the possibility of finding a political consensus by the countries of the region on the issue of use of water resources.

The Specific Character of the Water–Energy Balance in Central Asia

The water resources of the countries of Central Asia are not distributed equitably. The region is clearly divided into rich states with water resources like Tajikistan and Kyrgyzstan on the one hand and countries like Uzbekistan, Turkmenistan and Kazakhstan dependent on them for water, on the other. While Kyrgyzstan controls the basin of the river Syr Darya, Tajikistan controls the Amu Darya.

The Syr Darya is the longest and second largest in terms of rivers in Central Asia. It has a length of 3,019 km and a basin area of 219 thousand square km. The major part (75.2%) of its water resources is formed in Kyrgyzstan, 15.25% in the territory of Uzbekistan, 6.9% in Kazakhstan and 2.7% in Tajikistan.

The big river, Amu Darya, has a length of 2,540 km, with a basin of 309 square km. Like the Syr Darya, the Amu Darya loses much water for irrigation purposes downstream. Its main stock (74%) is formed in the territory of Tajikistan, 13.9% of the water is formed in Afghanistan and Iran and 8.5% in the territory of Uzbekistan.

Tajikistan occupies the third place in the world and the second place in the CIS after Russia in terms of satisfying water requirements. For example, the annual hydro-energy potential of the Republic constitutes almost 600 billion kWh. Apart from that, Tajikistan has significant reserves of drinking water in the Lednikakh (more than 60% reserves of Central Asia). The Nurek hydroelectric station built during the Soviet period with 3 million kWh regulates nearly 4% of the water necessary for Uzbekistan and partly for Turkmenistan. (2)

Afghanistan which uses not more than 2 billion cubic meters of water for irrigation purposes in its part of the Amu Darya basin contributes to the issue of water resources in the region. Potentially, it can take up to 10 billion cubic meters of water which would have negative consequences for Turkmenistan and Uzbekistan.

China's plan for transforming the Xinjiang-Uyghur autonomous district into the largest trade and economic centre of Central Asia that would lead to an increased use of water resources evokes serious concern. As a result of the realisation of the Chinese plan for building a canal on the Cherny Irtysh, which would be completed by 2020 and the rise in water use would become 1 billion cubic metre, could lead to serious problems in water supply to some regions of Russia.

The process of decreasing the Irtysh began in 1990 when the Bukhtomirski dam was constructed in Kazakhstan, which has one of the sources of the Irtysh—the Zaysan Lake. If China builds another water reservoir, that would accelerate the process of making the river smaller. As a result, a water-fence (*vodozabor*) supplying water to large Siberian cities could be over the water.

The water-energy issue of the Central Asian region is fraught with a high conflict potential. Up to 90% of the water resources are spent mainly in the agricultural sector which is included into the economic turnover. With a growing population, the demand for water by 2015 could rise by 20% compared to the first half of the current decade. In other words, the water resources in Central Asia in the coming years would decrease in absolute terms, and the preservation of the contemporary level of annual consumption of water of around 5–6 thousand litres per head could become a unfulfilled task. Simultaneously, owing to an even distribution of the forming sources, 80% of the regional Vodostok and some large hydro-technical installations are concentrated in the territory of Kirgizia and Tajikistan. Each of the mountainous countries use less than 10% of the general quantity of water for own consumption and strive for significant material compensation from the side of "equal" consumers—first of all, Uzbekistan and Kazakhstan.

A growing competition on this basis of hydro-energy and agrarian priorities for the trans-border water use obstructs the transition to a rational exploitation of the water resources.

The hydro-energy stations of Kyrgyzstan and Tajikistan, regulating the main regime of water supply, are oriented as before, towards the requirements of the agrarian sector of the neighbouring countries. If they would work for energy production rather than for irrigation, it would mean that a most intensive exploitation of the water reservoir would take place not in summers but in winters. Kyrgyzstan and Tajikistan would have a significant growth in energy production and possibly export its large supply. The maximum exploitation of the water reservoir in summers is not profitable either for Kyrgyzstan or for Tajikistan. However, it is vitally necessary for their plateau neighbours, which continue to receive water from the territory of the mountainous countries practically free of cost. Though Uzbekistan is situated in the focus of the main contradictions of regional water use to whom the main complaints of Kyrgyzstan and Tajikistan are addressed, Turkmenistan and Kazakhstan are trying to strengthen their potential through one-sided steps, and are also slowly being dragged into the conflict.

The specifics of the water energy balance of Central Asia have caused a serious debate about the use of market mechanisms of management of regional interaction in this direction. Nevertheless, that did not lead to a significant closing of interests of the agrarian and energy sectors of the regional economy. All questions concerning the water–energy balance – the accumulation of hydro-resources for their further use during the irrigation period, the use of reserves of water for hydroelectric stations and potential projects for the expansion of water use in each of the Central Asian countries – are used as levers of pressure on neighbours.

For example, the press release by the Tajik embassy in Kyrgyzstan in February 2009 blamed Uzbekistan for stopping the transit of energy supply from Turkmenistan under the pretext of technical reasons. Speaking in December 2009 in the 15th Conference on Climate Change in Copenhagen, Tajik President Emomali Rahman proposed to conduct a complex excercise of the influence of the system of water use on the ecological situation of the region.[3]

Uzbek Prime Minister Shavkat Mirziev in February, 2010 demanded from Tajikistan to conduct a detailed and independent exercise on the construction of the Rogun hydroelectric station, because the building of such a huge object could damage the fragile ecological balance existing in the region, which would be similar to the consequences of the Aral lake catastrophe.

S. Mirziyev declared that "the threat increases in connection with that more and more accidents are taking place in hydro-energy objects on Toktogyl and Nurekhydro station, built more than 35 years back and where no planned repair work has been done, presenting a real threat for the entire region". (4) He gave the example of the accident that had taken place in Sayanoshushenskoi hydroelectricity station long ago.

The delay in achieving agreements between the CentralAsian countries is linked to the political context of the concerned dialogue. In the backdrop of a low level of life standard of the population, a systemic crisis of water use is not viewed as a direct challenge to political stability by the ruling circles of the Central Asian states. The hypothetical variants of aggravation of situation in connection with the want of water or electricity traditionally would be "readdressed" to the neighbouring countries. Strategic risks, particularly an accelerated reduction of all kinds of natural sources of water, an unprecedented loss in the sphere of water use, deteriorating ecology (Aral, the melting of ice that led to desertification, the salting of soil), price rise on energy and some other problems are considered in the system of taking decisions but carry a facultative character. The necessary material means for resolving the issue are absent. According to international assessments in 2005, a total loss of all the countries of the Central Asian region connected with an ineffective management of water resources constitutes 1.7 billion USD or 3% of the GDP, which is not perceived as a catastrophic indicator. In other words, the contemporary imbalance of the water complex of Central Asia does not feel the pressure of temporary parameters for achieving resolution, and a discussion on the optimisation of the regional water use could continue beyond short-term perspectives.

At the same time, the situation of a chronic imbalance of the regional water–energy complex leads to the deterioration of the perspective agreements. The growing competition for hydro-energy and agrarian priorities of the Central Asian countries create conditions for an automatic expansion of the exploitation of water resources by all countries of the region, and consequently, a reduction in the time for the disappearance of the natural sources.

Thus, the water resources of Central Asia form a complex of challenges of strategic and tactical nature, whose resolution demands significant material expenses and a principled change of approaches to water use. So far, the situation has continued to develop in the regime of "deferred catastrophe"—and there too, a possibility for reducing the crisis lies in the domain of management-related decisions.

Here, it is necessary to consider that it concerns not the spectrum of concrete contradictions but a conflict of national programmes of development of all the Central Asian states.

Differences in the Approaches of the Sides to the Integration Process

The implementation of measures on sustainable development of the hydroelectricity and irrigation system in the countries of Central Asia requires a huge capital investment. Considering the socio-economic situation in the countries of the region, it is improbable that they can resolve the problem individually. That is why the necessity for uniting the efforts is obvious, notwithstanding the contradictions.

Energy and water are an objective basis for integration in Central Asia. An inter-state cooperation in this sphere is a necessary condition for raising food independence, energy self-reliance and the expansion of export potential and the concentration of investment resources. However, decisions taken in the framework of the Eurasian Community about the formation of mechanisms for tapping the potential of the Syr

Darya and the Amu Darya and the management of water and energy regimes of these transborder water arteries have so far not been realised.

Along with an acute competition on the consumption of the transborder water stock existing between Uzbekistan and Kirgizia and Uzbekistan and Tajikistan, there are differences of opinion between Kazakhstan and Kyrgyzstan and Uzbekistan and Turkmenistan. A difference of opinion appears between Kyrgyzstan and Tajikistan from time to time. A reduction in the difference in the opinion between Kazakhstan and Kyrgyzstan, and also between Uzbekistan and Turkmenistan is important, but is not the absolute condition for bringing progress to multi-sided agreements. Tajikistan and Kyrgyzstan, poor in hydrocarbons, constantly demonstrate their readiness to reduce the quantity of water for agriculture. There also, a resolution of any new conflict is achieved at the last moment. All the countries of the region demonstrate their right to water, which remains as a free resource with unresolved presentation in the energy equivalent.

The interstate calculation on energy supply is the main hindrance while resolving the water issues. Here, Uzbekistan maintains a harsh *zhestko* position. It goes for compromise with its neighbours with difficulty. Contradictions between key water suppliers (Tajikistan and Kyrgyzstan) and its main consumers (Uzbekistan , Kazakhstan and Turkmenistan) did not lead to the formation of sustainable coalitions on the water issue, which compounds its conflict situation. The orientation of countries of the region towards different legal models of resolution of water resources is a dangerous signal. While Kyrgyzstan and Tajikistan give emphasis to the Dublin Convention of 1992, Uzbekistan stresses the interactional principle on the regional level.

It can't be said that the leaders of the Central Asian countries did not make any effort for resolving the issue of water use in the region. An international conference held at Nukuse on September 20 declared the support for the ideas of equal rights and interstate cooperation on water issues. The five presidents of the region confirmed their "obligation on full cooperation at the regional level on the basis of mutual respect, good neighbourliness and decisiveness" on the water resources issue in the Nukus declaration. It was followed by the Bishkek declaration of the heads of the states on May 6, 1996 in which the necessity for "accelerating the drafting of new strategy for water distribution and economic methods of management in the sphere of use water and energy resources" was recognised.

The agreement on the cooperation in the field of preservation of surrounding atmosphere and rational use of nature signed in 1998 emphasises the necessity for the creation of a water–energy consortium in Central Asia. However, the formation of the water–energy consortium of the countries of Central Asia has not taken place so far. The differences about the share in the consortium, the lack of a desire for compromise, the crisis of trust and regional political competition obstruct the realisation of the project.

Fifteen years were required for the working group of four interested countries – Kazakhstan, Uzbekistan, Kyrgyzstan and Tajikistan – in their meeting at Bishkek in April 2006 to present the project of inter-state agreement on the joint use of the water–energy resources of the Naryn–Syr Darya cascade of water reservoirs of which Toktogulski is the largest. All the sides have not made any progress on the issue.

In September 2006, a non-formal summit of leaders of the Central Asian states was held at Astana where the issue of the regional use of water resources was discussed. No practical decision was taken there. The participants once again emphasised the need for joint decision on the issue of water distribution and consumption at the interstate level.

Removing the contradiction between the countries of Central Asia through multi-party coordination seems to be improbable. To achieve a balanced agreement while preserving the existing volumes of water consumption is impossible.

At the same time, any project to change the natural or economic factors requires not only large investments but also a minimum three to five year period for realisation.

In the mid-term perspective, the contradictions in water use of the Central Asian region would remain as a political factor. Moreover, the continuation of existing uncertainties promotes competition betweendifferent groups of the national elite. A part of the ruling circles preserves a negative attitude towards the Russian investment resources. In other words, a conflict potential regarding water use closely unites the internal political and external political challenges of development in Central Asia.

Obstacles in the Way of taking Strategic Decisions

The experience of multi-sided cooperation on the issues of water use in the Central Asian countries bears a contradicting character. Part of the experts think that certain issues concerning a just distribution of water resources of the transborder rivers of Central Asia have been resolved at a bilateral level, and a resolution of the others would be achieved in the near future in the framework of the Eurasian Economic Community. In reality, the situation is not all that optimistic.

The water–energy issue is quite relevant for the Eurasian Economic Community. The Sochi Summit of the Eurasian Economic Community held in August 2006 took a decision for drafting a concept of effective use of water–energy resources of Central Asian region.(5) A high-level group has been formed for working out a coordinated mechanism in the sphere of the water–energy resources and a road map has been approved.

The "roadmap" of perfection of the mechanism of interaction of member-states of the Eurasian Economic Community on the issue of water–energy resources presents a plan of stage-by-stage creation of joint market conditions in the process of integration of sectors of water management and energy of the economies of the states of the community.

The main principle of cooperation should be the continuity of the water–energy regimes of the basins of rivers with the regime of energy consumption and investments in the region. The strategy
drafted in the framework of the Eurasian community stipulates the following objectives and tasks:

- Drafting and realisation of coordinated measures in the sphere of rational use of the water–energy resources;
- Taking measures for fulfilling the inter-state agreements and accords, also agreements between subjects of the member-states of the Eurasian Economic Community on issues linked with the use of water–energy resources;
- ensuring optimal correlation between irrigation and energy regimes on the working of water reservoirs;
- Attracting investments for the realisation of existing water–energy objects of interstate significance;
- Creation of stimulus for attracting investment;
- Creation of conditions for production cooperation in water management and energy spheres.
- Formation of new inter-state management and executive bodies with the status that permits executing decisions in the framework of the Eurasian Economic Community,which is the key task.

The creation of a regulating body is required by the reasons of investment. Russia is the largest investor in the hydro-energy sector of Tajikistan and is considering the possibility of investment in Kyrgyzstan. Of late, the participation of Iranian companies in the hydro-energy sector of the above-mentioned countries has significantly increased.

The regional tension caused by water use and being closely linked with energy, creates a potential political risk for investors. In this connection, the arrival of foreign investments should be linked with the regulation of the water–energy regime of transborder rivers in the framework of the agreed to structures.

The formation of a coordinating body on the management of water–energy resources stipulated the creation of the following structures: high-level groups for preparing mechanisms for the water–energy regulation and the international water–energy consortium – an executive economic and technological body on the realisation of norms of agreements and decisions of the high-level group.

The High-level Group has been Constituted and has had Several Sessions

However, the international water–energy consortium has not been formed so far. There are objective reasons for that, as creating a water–energy regulating body is no easy task. The main obstacle for forming a constantly functioning and effective structure in the framework of the Eurasian Economic Community is the absence of political will on the part of the Central Asian leaders to overcome the differences. Nevertheless, a transborder character of water resources and a close interlinking between the water and energy supply in the region dictates the necessity for working out of a coordinated regional policy in the sphere of energy and water use.

In spite of the mentioned projects, there is a spectre of problems, which requires a balanced resolution. The vulnerable moments include first of all, the efforts to achieve a hard normative resolution of the whole complex of questions of creation of a regional water–energy balance. Secondly, it requires a high level of orientation towards big business about the optimisation of its participation in the realisation of the project. In this connection, the ruling elite of the Central Asian states are scared of turning into a virtual master of the water–energy resources, which would be regulated by national mechanisms.

Apart from this, resolutions accepted in the format of technocratic decisions, do not consider many real domestic political risks, with which the Central Asian leaders are confronted with. In each of the countries of Central Asia, groups of interests are formed which emphasise getting the corporate advantages in present conditions as well as in the process of integrational changes. This situation along with inadequate readiness concerning institutions would continue to exist in the course of a long period. The firmness of administrative vertical, multilateral agreements in the format of presidential commands would evoke dissatisfaction from the "middle layer" of the ruling circles and lead to clan-based competition in the higher echelons of authority. The observation of quotas, tariff and seasonal plans for regional water use would thus depend not only on the technical contradictions of transition to market calculations for water and energy, but also on a balance of domestic political forces in the Central Asian countries, first of all in Uzbekistan, Kyrgyzstan and Tajikistan.

The difficulties of a multilateral resolution of the Central Asian water-use include differences in the positions of the external political partners of the countries of Central Asia about the directions of investment support. Investment projects, proposed under the patronage of the US and the European Union do not reflect the requirements of building "horizontal" trade -economic links between the neighbouring countries and in the mid-term perspective would lead to the strengthening of differentiation of national strategic interests of the states of the Central Asian region.

In the framework of the project of the partnership on the development of greater Central Asia, advanced by the US State Department, Washington strives to get involved in the process of energy issue resolution in the region, which means an influence over water use. US companies participate in the building of electro-transmission in the southern direction (Afghanistan and Pakistan), and provide consulting services to Kazakhstan, Kyrgyzstan and Tajikistan.

The forum on electro-energy regulating bodies formed under the Programme of Central Asian Regional Economic Cooperation (CAREC) is engaged in the implementation of projects, directed towards the formation of a common energy network in the region. The programme of CAREC was initiated by the Asian Bank of Development in 1997 for the realisation of projects in the sphere of energy, transport and trade in Central Asia. (6)

Azerbaijan, Afghanistan, China, Kazakhstan, Kirgizia, Tajikistan, Uzbekistan and Mongolia, and international donors such as the Asian Development Bank, the European Bank of Development and Reconstruction, the IMF, the Islamic Bank of Development, the PROON and the World Bank participate in the CAREC programme. One of the major priorities of the CAREC is to support the effective and rational use of energy and water resources in Central Asia. Apart from this, the World Bank and investors from the EC, US, and Japan are ready to take part in the creation of a Water-Energy Consortium (WEC) of the countries of Central Asia. The experts of the World Bank have prepared their concept of the creation of the WEC.

It cannot be ruled out that a further institutional strengthening of the WEC would lead to its transformation into a full-fledged regional organisation, and could be a significant resource for the penetration of the outside countries into the markets of the Central Asian countries.

Difficulties characteristic in the conduct of a strategic line of the Eurasian Economic Community in the sphere of the water–energy balance of Central Asia, bear a long-term character. More than that, many things linked to their challenges would appear in the agenda and in case of activisation of the search for multilateral agreements under the format of the SCO. Nevertheless, the initiative of Islam Korimov, advanced in the Bishkek Summit of SCO (2007), first of all, significantly prolongs the status quo on the water issue and secondly, transfers the hydro-energy issue into the domain of national resolution. A new negotiation process with the participation of China permits the expansion of the spectre of sources of material means for the modernisation of irrigation systems. On the one hand, the conditions for restraining an extensive growth of regional water use are strengthened, and on the other hand a weight of arguments in favour of the conservative variants of transferring the hydro-energy of mountainous countries to the export rails is also strengthened. However, the SCO's involvement in the process of establishment of a water–energy balance in the region is not a decisive step towards achieving a strategic breakthrough. The orientation of the ruling circles and the export community of the countries of Central Asia towards different legal models of resolution of transborder water use remains formal and an informal obstacle for the achievement of multilateral agreements in the short-term perspective.

The Possibility of achieving a Political Consensus

An objective want of water resources and competition in the sphere of water use in Central Asia has of late obtained special significance. Serious efforts for resolving the water issue in the multilateral format permitted preventing the escalation of local conflicts, but did not lead to overcoming major inter-state contradictions on the water issue, in spite of the projects of linking it with the energy issue.

The Central Asian water issue has a Russian projection. Russia as the leading country of the Eurasian Economic Community and the country whose companies are planning to build large hydro-energy projects in Central Asia, is a participant in the regional water management process. In order to resolve practical issues in the sphere, particularly linking water–energy regimes of the basins of the rivers with regimes of consumption of energy and investment, Russia is interested in finding political consensus among the countries of the region.

It is clear that Russia with these objectives in mind should distance itself from the functions of a single arbitrator of the regional contradictions, rather facilitating an involvement of foreign investment into the sphere of water use and ecology, keeping aside expensive forms of cooperation with the Central Asian states. It is important to pursue a policy for stage-by-stage achievement of bilateral agreements of states of the region on a stable resolution of the regime of the Syr Darya and the Amu Darya, highlighting ecological and social arguments.

It is high time to work out a project of joint balance of the water–energy resources of the region for a complex development and use of hydro-energy resources of the basins of the rivers of the Syr Darya and the Amu Darya. It is important to confirm the coordinated regimes of the water use of the basins of these rivers and works of the electro-energy system, define the framework of financial cooperation and the involvement of foreign investments.

The joint construction of hydroelectric stations, inter-system lines of electricity transmission, and the modernisation of energy equipments and irrigation systems in the region also would facilitate the reduction of conflict potential in the sphere of water use.

The experts, specialists not only in the sphere of hydrology and ecology but also in the field of international relations, can make a positive contribution to a mutual understanding and the building of real cooperation. The Russian expert community has highly assessed the outcome of the international conference "Euro Asian Economic Community: Issues of Food Security" held in Moscow on May 19-20, 2009. It has also positively viewed the outcome of the third conference held at the Tebriz University on October 14-16, 2008 on the water resource management in Iran.

Notes

1. Global UN report about state of water resources,assed from www.un.org.
2. Vodno-energeticheskiyeresursitcentralnoiazii:problem ispolozovaniya i osvoeniya. Eurasian Bank of Development, Otraslovoiobjor., 2008, 24 April, assessed from www.eabr.org
3. The speech of President of Tajikistan E. Rahmon in the 15th conference of sides of framework convention of UNO about climate change / www.president.tj/rus
4. *Pravda Vostoka*, 3 February 2010
5. www.evrazes.com/view/561
6. www.carecinstitute.org

10

Contemporary Japan-Central Asia Relations

Elaheh Koolaee and Mandana Tishehyar

Introduction

Japan, one of the most important economic powers in the world, has played an important role in worldwide investments, especially in the developing countries, during the last decades. In fact, economic policies have an important role in Japan's foreign relations with other countries and regions.

Like many other countries in the world, the concept of foreign policy in Japan has been interrelated with its geopolitical situation from many centuries. This element causes some constant variables and factors challenging the Japanese foreign policymakers. The most significant factor is the deficiency of natural resources in Japan and its dependence on importing raw materials from abroad.

So, the Japanese oil companies and major merchants have much more influence on foreign policymaking than the political parties, military institutions and public media in this country. Inevitably, Japan's economic development and energy security are definitely interrelated. The realistic approach to international relations of the Japanese politicians is based on improving their national interests by considering energy security.

The collapse of the USSR and the emergence of new independent countries in Central Asia gave new opportunities to the Japanese investing companies. However, because of the changing structure of the international system and also the politico-economic characters of these countries, the Japanese politicians have revived their foreign policy in this region to find a new basis for improving their national interests.

In this article, after a short historical review of Japan's foreign policy transformation, the process of Japan's relations with Central Asian countries and the existing challenges and opportunities will be analysed. Thereafter, Japan's new foreign policy trends for developing these relations will be discussed.

Japan's Foreign Policy after the Cold War

The collapse of communism in the Eastern bloc at the beginning of the 1990s was one of the few historical phenomena that influenced all of the political, military, cultural and economic dimensions in the world. In this new era, the industrialised countries' pattern developed as the main way for providing security on the national, regional and international levels. The development of liberal democratic values and the free market model brought the interdependency between the developed and developing countries to a new global dependency.

The end of the Cold War, however, encouraged the rebirth of Japan's Asian Policy with a change in the international environment during the 1990s. Like many other countries, Japan has changed and improved its foreign policy aims and the Nakasone doctrine suggested a new form of diplomacy based on:

1. Improving relations with all countries but keeping special security relations with the US as the focus point of Japan's foreign policy;
2. Looking up to Japan's influence on the international stage, and seeking support for a permanent seat in the UNSC;
3. Active participation in international struggles for decreasing world instability such as the proliferation of mass destruction weapons and the lack of democracy in developing and underdeveloped countries;
4. Cooperation in the process of improving economic development and social stability in the developing countries by making investments and transporting technology;
5. Participating in the process of developing internal markets in different countries to further the world economic growth, strengthening the free trade system and improving Japan's economic growth;
6. Developing global environmental cooperation and helping refugees;
7. Beginning a new trend for cultural and scientific exchanges with other countries (Safavi, 109 and 148)

Indeed, Japan has tried to gradually change its position from a marginal passive observer in international affairs to an influential actor which is relatively active in global interactions.

Japan's Foreign Policy in Central Asia Region

a. *Politico-Economic Characters of Central Asia Region*

The popular Silk Route[1] that led to the development of ancient civilisations such as the Chinese, Egyptian, Mesopotamian, Persian and Roman has again emerged as a means of strengthening the ties in the East, and this time it is Japan joining the crew. (Hamid, 29 August 2006).

The Caspian Sea basin has long been a source of oil and natural gas. The fire-worshipping Zoroastrian religion was founded on the western shores of the Caspian as Zoroastrians built temples around local pillars of fire fed by the escaping natural gas. The two great pre-World War I oilfields were in Texas and the Caspian Sea region of Imperial Russia. After the war, when civil war raged between the Russian Whites and Reds, the British forces landed in Batumi in a failed attempt to influence the future of the Caspian Sea oil. During World War II, Adolph Hitler also launched Operation *Blau* to capture the Caspian Sea oilfields.

The struggles for achieving to the natural resources and potential capabilities of the heartland of the world had been forgotten after the falling of an "Iron Curtain" around all of the Central Asian region and the Caucasus for about 70 years during the domination of communism on the whole of this part of the world.

Central Asia regained global strategic importance in 1991 when the vacuum left by the collapse of the Soviet empire allowed the energy companies around the world to compete for the region's vast oil and gas resources.

With the collapse of the USSR in 1991, the Soviet republics of Central Asia, Kazakhstan, Kyrgyzstan, Tajikistan, Turkmenistan and Uzbekistan, became independent for the first time in their history (Rashid, 10 April 1997: 22).

Central Asia's plentiful oil and natural gas reserves have made the region an increasingly important area for world energy security. The five former Soviet Central Asian countries hold nearly 4% of the world's natural gas reserves, and both Uzbekistan and Turkmenistan are already major natural gas producers. The Caspian Sea appears to be sitting on yet another sea—a sea of hydrocarbons.

Although Russia still controls much of the region's oil and natural gas export routes, new export options are under development, and energy exports are likely to prove a major driver behind Central Asia's future economic growth.

In the Soviet era, Moscow's dominant influence over Central Asia was beyond dispute. But the emergence of the five independent Central Asian republics in 1991 has brought competition from other great powers which also hope to exert their influence in the region, including China and the United States. Moscow, Beijing, and Washington all want influence with the new states for economic, political, and military reasons (Blua, 10/26/05).

Zbigniew Brzezinski, the former National Security chief under Carter, in his important article which was published in the September/October 1997 issue of *Foreign Affairs* and entitled "A Geostrategy for Asia" wrote: America's emergence as the sole global superpower now makes an integrated and comprehensive strategy for Eurasia imperative".

He believed that a glance at the map also suggested that a country dominant in Eurasia would almost automatically control the Middle East and Africa. Foreshadowing Brzezinski, the imperial strategist Halford Mackinder, in a 1904 paper, 'The Geographical Pivot of

History', maintained that the Eurasian land mass and Africa, which he collectively termed the world island, were of decisive significance to achieving global hegemony. According to Mackinder, the barriers that had prevented previous world empires, particularly the limitations in transportation, had largely been overcome by the beginning of the twentieth century, setting the stage for a struggle among the great powers to establish a global dominion (Fourth International World Socialist Web Site, 1998-99).

But this is not all fact. On the other side of the coin, there are the Central Asian countries, whose centrally planned economies, economic and political reforms have preceded slower than elsewhere in the Commonwealth of Independent States (CIS).

Each of the Central Asian countries remains economically tied to Russia and Central Asia's lack of export pipelines, in addition to its remoteness from markets, makes it have a limited development of natural resources. Thus, all the Central Asian states face the dilemma of finding export outlets for their energy supplies at world market prices while also securing inexpensive energy from their neighbours for their own impoverished people. The export pipelines, especially for natural gas, are still needed in order to facilitate further increases in Central Asia's energy production.

The landlocked position of the countries mentioned severely limits the choice of markets. In principle, the region's oil and gas could be exported by pipeline to the growing markets of Japan, China, India and Pakistan, but the capital cost would be extremely high and some transit routes, for example through Afghanistan, would mean a risk of disruptions due to political strife. An alternative transit route would be through Iran to the Persian Gulf. At least for the region's oil, this may be the most economical outlet. From Iranian ports the oil could then be shipped to the growing Asian markets (Noreng, April 11. 1998).

The risks involved in pipeline projects should be analysed from at least three angles: the transportation problems, the great power involvement and the potential instability of the regimes in place. These three dimensions are interlocked. The transportation problems invite interference from neighboring states for both economic and political reasons. Hence, the solutions affect the great powers involved. The potential instability of the regimes in place makes them seek allies outside the region. Hence, the internal politics of the new states of the Caspian Region and Central Asia also affects the great powers. These interlocking dimensions of political risk make the region perhaps the world's most complex environment for the oil industry (Noreng, April 11, 1998).

The political risk should induce oil investors to apply a higher-than-usual risk premium when assessing investment opportunities in the region. This risk premium in addition to the cost of transportation could mean that oil and gas development in the region is economically less attractive than what appears from the geological potential.

b. Japan's Entry into Central Asia

After the collapse of the Soviet Union and the creation of the newly independent republics of Central Asia and the Caucasus, one of the first countries to explore the commercial and energy potential of the region was Japan (Nissman, 1999-2000).

Japan recognised the Central Asian countries as soon as they declared their independence in December 1991, and established diplomatic relations with them in January 1992. Japanese embassies in Kazakhstan and Uzbekistan were opened in January 1993 (Yuasa, src-h.slav.hokudai.ac.jp/coe21/publish/no16_1_ses/04_yuasa.pdf).

First of all, the availability of abundant energy resources from the nearby Russian Far East and the return of the Kurile Islands, referred to by the Japanese as the Northern Territories, were subjects closest to Japan's interests. However, Japan tied the issue of energy investment in the Russian Far East to the return of the disputed islands. This led to frosty ties between Moscow and Tokyo, prompting the latter to focus its attention increasingly towards Central Asia instead.

Central Asia was an attractive option for a number of reasons. Japan was attracted to the region's oil and gas deposits. Aid to Central Asia was also intended to show the Russians that more funds could be forthcoming if they returned the disputed islands to Japan. In addition, there were doubts over Russia's uncertain future outlook, the aging infrastructure and difficulty in penetrating to Russia's highly-protected energy industry.

Japanese government officials also romanticised about the links between Japan and the people of Central Asia. Japanese Foreign Minister Michio Watanabe reportedly found it difficult to distinguish between Japanese and the locals in Central Asia on his first trip to the region. The Japanese also reminisced about the 60,000 Japanese war prisoners deported to Central Asia by Stalin when the Red Army invaded Manchuria in 1945.

c. *Japan's Eurasian Diplomacy*

Japan's foreign policy is directed toward three considerations: the US-Japanese relations, Japan's international standing and prestige through the promotion of multilateral institutions of cooperation and relations with its two great power neighbours, Russia and China. In this sense, the new Eurasian initiative complements all three objectives clearly.

Such a rationale drove the Japanese engagement in the region from 1992 up to 1997. After 1997, Japan's Central Asia strategy underwent reassessment. By 1997, Japan still lacked commercial progress in the region despite having good diplomatic relations with the Central Asian regimes. While keeping its position as top donor for the economic development of Central Asian countries, Japan's lack of strategy toward Central Asia has been pointed out (Hickok, 2000).

The feasibility of Central Asia as an alternative to Russia and the Middle East in meeting Japan's energy security needs appeared to be overestimated by the Japanese and exaggerated by the oil and gas-rich Central Asian states. In addition, talks with Russia over the disputed territories yielded no result. This led to a domestic criticism that Japan lacked a clearly defined strategy in engaging Central Asia.

Despite the policy setback, it became increasingly clear that Central Asia is a region of growing geopolitical significance and that Japan's participation adds to the region's stability. In 1997, for the first time, the Japanese ambassador to Russia stated in an interview that Japan should help the Central Asian states develop because these states play a role as the buffer region in the Eurasian continent for the maintenance of peace.

Once Japan defined a clear purpose in Central Asia, it devised a sophisticated response marking the beginning of a new diplomatic phase in Central Asia. In fact, the Eurasian Diplomacy concept, therefore, became a guideline with a wider geographic range, which was an exceptional case for Japanese foreign policy after World War II (Yuasa, src-h.slav.hokudai.ac.jp/coe21/publish/no16_1_ses/04_yuasa.pdf)

Also Prime Minister Ryutaro Hashimoto outlined a new Eurasian foreign policy in 1997. Under the "Eurasian diplomacy", Hashimoto pointed out three directions for cooperation:

1. Political dialogue aiming to enhance trust and mutual understanding;
2. Economic cooperation as well as cooperation for natural resource development aiming to foster prosperity;
3. Cooperation to build peace through nuclear non-proliferation, democratisation and the fostering of stability.

With this respect, Japan would help towards regional integration within Central Asia itself with plans to improve communication, transportation and energy networks in the region. While acknowledging the expanding influence of Central Asian and

Caspian oil and gas resources on the world energy supply, Hashimoto stated that Japan's economic engagement with Central Asia would be based on the development of the energy sector, not as an end for Japan, but as a means to foster prosperity in the region.

However, that was clear that all the infrastructure improvements, transport and communications improvements that have been promised by Itochu, British Petroleum and others were directed towards producing and transporting oil and natural gas, and the infrastructures- such as highways – are to follow the pipelines.

However, investors only want profit, and any kind of stability that guarantees those profits is acceptable to them. They do not care if the country is ruled by totalitarian or democratic methods. Turkmenistan is totalitarian, and is very attractive to investors because there is a lack of civil and ethnic conflict. Although the Turkmen people have been promised the benefits of Turkmenistan's large natural gas resources, no observers have seen any evidence of these benefits (Nissman, 1999-2000).

This is a real fact that the driving force behind Tokyo's heightened interest is natural resources. Japan, which depends on the imports of oil and gas, is seeking to reduce its reliance on oil from the Middle East. Tokyo wants to diversify both in terms of what it buys and where it buys it from. It also wants to increase its use of nuclear energy –for which it must import uranium (Fogarty 28 August 2006).

On the other hand, because of the lack of security and economic stability in the Central Asian countries, Japan's presence in this region is mostly limited to sending economic donors and Japanese companies did not invest there because of a high rate of risks during the 1990s.

In sum, Japan understood that with its small population, vast distances away from viable markets, and its landlocked geography, the Central Asian states needed to deepen their level of cooperation with one another so as to create a local regional market economy. This would help lessen dependence on its export economy and provide more incentives for foreign companies to enter the region because of the bigger markets available for foreign investment. Such a regional blueprint would thus generate greater stability and wealth within the region.

The Central Asian republics responded positively to this new initiative in 1998 and 1999 with visits by top-ranking Central Asian officials to Japan.

Another area of converging interests is the focus in deepening Central Asian regional integration. In working for a stable Central Asia, Japan attempted to bring Afghanistan into the Central Asian fold as the inclusion of Afghanistan would create a potentially larger market in the Central Asian region while instability in Afghanistan could impact the region negatively. In November 2005, Afghanistan was admitted into the Central Asia Regional Economic Cooperation (CAREC) grouping organized by the Japan-led Asian Development Bank (Len, 17 February 2006).

Since the 1990s, the Japanese government has seen itself as being able to play a brokering role [in Afghanistan]. The Japanese government played a very important role in putting together an international coalition to deal with the post-conflict situation in Afghanistan (the japannews.net, June 5, 2006).

Japan also realised the importance of measures against terrorism in Central Asia as a priority for international security, especially after a group of Japanese geologists were taken hostage by the Islamic Movement of Uzbekistan in 1999 and the US operations in Afghanistan and Central Asia after the 9/11 terrorist attack. (Yuasa srch.slav.hokudai.ac.jp/coe21/publish/no16_1_ses/04_yuasa.pdf)

d. Central Asia plus Japan Dialogue

A Japanese policy of engagement in Central Asia materialised firstly in Japan's Central Asia plus Japan Dialogue initiative announced by Foreign Minister Yuriko Kawaguchi in 2004—the distinctive feature and competitive advantage of which is to encourage Central Asian regional integration and to enhance the capacities of these countries to deal with regional problems by regional means.

In the inaugural meeting held in Kazakhstan in August 2004, participants also discussed the importance of intra-regional cooperation aiming for stability and development of the Central Asian region as a whole and also for cooperation between Japan and Central Asia in the international arena. It was stated that the need for development of market economies and democratisation will be stressed through future dialogues (Len, 17 February 2006)

During Foreign Minister Kawaguchi's visit to Central Asia in the summer of 2004, she proposed the goals of the CAJ dialogue. In August 26, she gave a policy speech entitled "Adding a New Dimension: Central Asia plus Japan" at the University of World Economy and Diplomacy in Tashkent. Based on the concept of Eurasian diplomacy, she emphasised Japan's attitude towards Central Asia as follows:

> "It goes without saying that there are many changes we have no control over. The sweeping changes to international security as a result of 9/11 are only one example of this, and suddenly, Central Asia finds itself in the middle of a dramatically shifted regional strategic environment. I can tell you emphatically that Japan has no selfish objectives towards Central Asia. A country that does not engage in the use of force and a country with no

political, territorial, or other potential sources of conflict with the countries of Central Asia, Japan is a natural partner for Central Asia, and the foundations have already been laid. In reflection of Central Asia's geopolitical importance, Japan has a major interest in securing peace and stability in this region, as it affects the peace and stability of the entire Eurasian continent" (http://www.mofa.go.jp/region/europe/uzbekistan/speech0408.html)

She also suggested the future enlargement of the dialogue geographically towards Afghanistan. This subject was partly realised when the Foreign Minister of Afghanistan participated as a guest at the second ministerial meeting of the dialogue in June 2006.

The Japanese and Central Asian envoys in their meeting also approved an action plan that stressed the need for enhanced cooperation in fighting drug trafficking and poverty. The plan also called for cooperation in fostering human rights and political dialogue. The five also agreed to boost regional trade and improve Central Asia's infrastructure (the japannews.net, June 5, 2006).

The first theme is seen as an attempt to enforce the plans made during the announcement of the Central Asia plus Japan forum in 2004, which envisaged the provision of education to a considerable number of students and professionals from Central Asia in the Japanese educational institutions. This step is also connected to the overall task of encouraging democratisation, human development and various reforms in Uzbekistan through providing education and engaging the younger generations of policymakers.

This direction of the Japanese foreign policy was further supported by Kawaguchi's successor in the post of Foreign Minister Aso Taro, who in a June 2006 speech stressed the regional holistic approach to Central Asia, support for regionalism and promotion of democracy and market economy in the region.

Such attempts by Japan to assert a more active Central Asian diplomacy, under the rhetoric of strengthening the capacities of the regional states in dealing with their own problems, are seen by many as a part of the Japanese efforts to limit the Russian and Chinese attempts to subvert the Central Asian countries. Whether or not this is the intended Japanese policy or that these are wishful interpretations, remain uncertain (Dadabaev, September 06, 2006).

Taro succeeded and developed these principles and pillars of the dialogue. For example, in his policy speech entitled "Central Asia as a Corridor of Peace and Stability" on June 1, 2006, he stressed the following guidelines governing Japan's diplomatic relations with Central Asia:

1. approaching the region from a broad- based perspective;
2. supporting an open regional cooperation;
3. Seeking partnerships rooted in universal values (democracy, a market economy, the safeguarding of human rights, and the role of law) (Yuasa, src-h.slav.hokudai.ac.jp/coe21/publish/no16_1_ses/04_yuasa.pdf).

He also said that the region was the scene of increasing competition among world powers. This, he said, was where Japan could play an important role because it believes that Central Asia should not be "forced to submit to the interests of outside countries as a result of a 'New Great Game' and that 'the leading role must be played by none other than the countries of Central Asia themselves'". (Fogarty, 28 August 2006).

The first -ever visit by the Japanese Prime Minister Koichiro Koizumi to Central Asia in 2006 also symbolised the continuation of the Japanese effort to formulate its foreign policy towards this energy-rich and strategically important region. While the visit of the Japanese leader undoubtedly was welcomed by both the regional leadership and the public as historic, the success of Japan's foreign policy in Central Asia also depends on a range of other factors such as the continuity of these efforts after the change of leadership in Japan, the perceptions of the Japanese foreign policy by Russia, China and the US and finally by the essence and outcomes of this policy (Dadabaev, September 06, 2006).

Conclusion

The old Silk Road that had connected Japan to the Central Asian countries still has a romantic effect on Japanese cultural and artistic works. Japan's willingness to seek a more active role in Central Asia is also motivated by specific geopolitical concerns.

Japanese politicians understand the strategic importance of this region located between Russia, China and the Middle East and they are aware of its role as a buffer zone between the great powers.

The Japan that dreamed to create a 'Great Eastern Community' before World War II, now is trying to realise this idea by forming new economic blocs in Eastern and Central Asia and connecting them to each other.

More than anything else, Japan prefers to play the role of a 'Model State' for modernising these countries. So, the main focus of Japan's Eurasian diplomacy is based more on attracting its Asian cousins than other parts of Eurasia such as Caucuses, Ukraine, Belarus, Moldova and the Baltic States.

Tokyo's policy is preventing itself from competition on oil and gas projects and is also trying to establish economic stability in the Central Asian countries. This vision helps these countries to look at Japan as an important regional actor and a good economic partner.

In such a space, Japan has to play the strategic role of a balancer. On par with the Japanese interest to the region, there is a considerable expectation of the Central Asian leadership towards

Japan. For them, Japan is traditionally considered to be non-threatening to the region because of its peace-forwarding foreign policy, its distance from the region and certain cultural and lifestyle similarities. In particular, the leaders of regional countries would like to see a more active encouragement by the Japanese government to direct investments by the Japanese corporations and companies, especially in the fields of energy resource development and transportation.

Also, the hope for Japanese support through the Central Asia plus Japan scheme in strengthening regional integration and creating a common market in the region is very high. On their side, the Central Asian leaders continuously and consistently express their support for Japan's bid for permanent membership in the UN Security Council, and join in support of Japan's concerns about the situation on the Korean peninsula (Dadabaev, September 06, 2006)

On the other hand, the Western countries believe that Japan would be a useful partner for spreading liberal democratic values and helping to change authoritative models governing the Central Asian countries.

Nevertheless, Japan, through the Central Asia plus Japan initiative, mitigates the aspirations of the SCO. Its presence in the region helps dilute the influence of the SCO—a result that the Central Asian republics, the United States and Europe all prefer. Japan's role is particularly important in light of the SCO's growing confidence, as reflected in the recent inclusion of India, Pakistan and Iran as SCO observers (Mongolia attained observer status in 2004) and the establishment of the SCO–Afghanistan Contact Group.

It is still questionable whether China and the region's other major player – Russia – will let Japan have a greater role in Central Asian affairs. Beijing and Moscow are the two leading forces behind the

Shanghai Cooperation Organization, a regional grouping that also comprises the four Central Asian states that are members of the CAJ dialogue (The japannews.net, June 5, 2006).

In that sense, it is perhaps not entirely different from the 'Great Game' that we saw [in Central Asia] at the end of the nineteenth and the early twentieth centuries.

While the objectives of the Central Asia plus Japan initiative complement those of the SCO member states, Japan also plays a positive role in the region as a balancing force against the SCO. To be realistic, however, it is unlikely that the initiative will ever have the same weight and presence as the SCO does. Since China and Russia are geographically part of the region sharing borders with the Central Asian states, their level of engagement is more intrinsic. Furthermore, Russia and China share with the Central Asian leaders the same threats and vulnerabilities with regards to terrorism and violent Islamist movements. In addition, the two giant neighbours have been the most outspoken supporters of the authoritarian Central Asian regimes (Len, 17 February 2006).

However, at the geopolitical level, clearly the struggle for influence and investment in the Caspian Region and Central Asia does not have to be a zero-sum game (Noreng, April 11, 1998).

Interestingly, Japan's activities in Central Asia reveal a subtle foreign policy that is able to accommodate both Eastern and Western value systems. In the eyes of the Central Asian regimes,

Japan has come to represent a viable Asian role model and partner for their modernisation programme. For the West, Japan has come to represent their liberal democratic values, as opposed to China and Russia who insist on an indigenous—and usually authoritarian—approach toward government. In fact, the Central Asian regimes and the West both recognise Japan's contribution to the region especially because of Japan's potential to counter-balance the Russian and Chinese influence in Central Asia.

This is a different role for Japan that could be a beginning of fundamental changes in Japan's diplomacy system providing heightened interactions in the new era of international politics.

Notes

1. The Silk Road or the Silk Route, the geographical term coined by Ferdinand von Richtofen in 1877, is essentially an 8,000 km land stretch that connects various Central and Eastern Asian Countries.

References

Arvanitopoulos, Constantine (2006), "The Geopolitics of Oil in Central Asia", *Thesis Journal*.

Atkin, Muriel (1997), "Thwarted Democratization in Tajikistan" in *Conflict, Cleavage and Change in Central Asia and the Caucasus*, Karen Dawisha and Bruce Parrott (eds), Cambridge: Cambridge University Press.

Barham, John (March 3, 1998), "East-West Pipeline: Oil and Gas to be Transported through Turkey", *Financial Times*.

Blua, Antoine (October 26, 2005), "Central Asia: Oil, Diplomacy, and Military Might", RFE/RL.

Dadabaev, Timur (September 06, 2006), "Japan's Central Asian Diplomacy and its Implications", *Central Asia-Caucasus Analyst*.

Diuk, Nadia and Adrian Karatnycky (1993), *New Nations Rising*, New York: John Wiley and Sons.

Fogarty, Philippa (August 28, 2006), "Energy Key to Japan's Central Asia Ties", *BBC News*.

Grau, Lester W. (May-June 2001), "Hydrocarbons and a New Strategic Region: The Caspian Sea and Central Asia", Foreign Military Studies Office, Fort Leavenworth, *Military Review*.

Hamid, Shoeb (August 29, 2006), "Japan interested in Central Asia", *merinews*.

Hickok, Micheal Robert (2000), "The Other End of The Silk Road: Japan's Eurasian Initiative", *Central Asian Survey*, Vol. 19, No. 1. *http://www.mofa.go.jp/region/europe/uzbekistan/speech0408.html*

Len, Christopher (February 17, 2006), "The Growing Importance of Japan's Engagement in Central Asia", *PINR*.

Mushakoji, Kinhide (1976), "East Asia, the United States, and Japan: Four Proto-Scenarios" in Morton A. Kaplan and Kinhide Mushakoji (eds), *Japan, America and the Future World Order*, NY: The Center for Policy Study, the University of Chicago.

Navab Safavi, Esmaeal (2001), *Jaigahe Japan Dar Jahane Moaser*, [Japan's Position in Contemporary Era], Tehran, CPIS. (Persian)

Nester, William R. (1990), *Japan's Growing Power over East Asia and the World Economy*, New York: Martin's Press.

Nissman, David (1999-2000), "Azerbaijan and Japan: New Allies?", Azerbaijan Country Review.

Noreng, Gystein (April 11, 1998), "Oil in the Caspian Region and Central Asia – the Political Risk of the Great Game Continued", *Contribution at a conference held in Boulder*, USA.

Ochs, Michael (1997), "Turkmenistan: The Quest for Stability and Control", in Karen

Dawisha and Bruce Parrott (eds), *Conflict, Cleavage and Change in Central Asia and the Caucasus*, Cambridge: Cambridge University Press.

Oldfather, Milishia et. al. (1996), *Shenakhte Japan*, [Japan's Knowing], translated by Ahmad Birashk, Tehran, Kharazmi. (Persian)

Pempel, T.J. (1998), *Regime Shift*, London: Cornell University Press.

Rashid, Ahmed (1994), *The Resurgence of Central Asia*, London: Zed Books.

Rashid, Ahmed (April 10, 1997), "Power Play", *Far Eastern Economic Review*.

Sadria, Mojtaba (2000), *Teorie Tazad dar ravabete beinolmelal*, [Theory of Conflicts in International Relations], translated by A. Borojerdi& G. Ahmadian, Tehran, CPIS. (Persian)

The japannews.net (June 5, 2006), "Central Asia: Regional Countries, Japan Agree on Action Plan", *RFE/RL*.

Varedi, Mohammad (1995), *Japan* (Green Book), Tehran, CPIS.

Yuasa, Takeshi, "Japan's Multilateral Approach towards Central Asia", srch.slav.hokudai.ac.jp/coe21/publish/no16_1_ses/04_yuasa.pdf

11

The Silk Route and Kazakhstan: A Historical Perspective

Sattar F. Mazhitov

The multi-vector foreign policy of modern Kazakhstan is directed, first of all, to the establishment of cooperation and partnership with other states of the world. The balanced foreign policy has proved the solvency and efficiency in the maintenance of national interests of Kazakhstan as an independent state.

Since the first days of independence, being a country located on the Great Silk Route, Kazakhstan has paid attention to the problems of its revival, which goes back to the second millennium AD. The search of arguments in this direction became one of the priorities for Kazakhstan. Firstly, efforts have been directed on the judgements of cultural aspects of the revival of the Silk Route. The initiative of Kazakhstan has been maintained by authoritative international organisations. The UNESCO discussed a problem of revival of the Great Silk Route in Paris in 1987. The World Tourist Organization has been studying this problem since 1994. The Decree of the President of the Republic of Kazakhstan "About the State Programme of the Republic of Kazakhstan: Revival of the

historical centers of the Silk Route, preservation and successive development of cultural heritage of the Turkic states, creation of an infrastructure of tourism" was issued on February, 27, 1998. The World Bank invested 440 million dollars in Kazakhstan for the restoration of the historical monuments of the Great Silk Route in 2000. Assessing the project, the General Director of UNESCO, Federico Mayer said:

> "The Silk Route taking place through steppes, seas and deserts, represented a magnificent opportunity for an establishment of contacts and dialogue, promoted opportunities for mutual enrichment of outstanding civilizations. The purpose of the project of complex research of the Silk Route is to promote the nations to realize the necessity of new dialogue today, to take an advantage for an opportunity of mutual understanding which has historical value and mutual enrichment of the civilizations located along this route".

From the beginning of the twenty-first century, the problem of revival of the Silk Route began to be filled with the real political and economic maintenance, including a wide spectrum of questions on regional cooperation and national security. The theme of the partnership of Kazakhstan and India has a special importance as the most authoritative in the Central Asia, and has a complex of mutual interests and real opportunities for these countries.

A retrospective approach to the historical past justifies that Central Asia represented and presents the rich and unique integration model of nations, languages and cultures without any distinctive border. Centuries of a developed specialisation of economic life based on the native-landscape combination of nomadic and agricultural economy allowed the speaking about the region as a vertically organised complex, which let the population of the steppe and valley to shift to full self-sufficiency in the case of necessity. In modern speech, it means that there was formed a self-satisfaction market.

There is an optimal opportunity to reveal the substances of the problem of partnership between Kazakhstan and the Central Asian countries on the revival of the Silk Route via the analysis of the following blocks of problems.

Block 1.
The contemporary condition of cooperation of Central Asian countries as the basement of the dialogue on the revival of the Silk Route

The leading role of Kazakhstan in Central Asia is connected to the new approaches of the all-European concept to the Central Asian region. It was confirmed also by the last visits of the President of Kazakhstan Nursultan Nazarbayev to Mongolia and China in August 2008.

The theme "Silk Route and Kazakhstan: Historical Perspective" obtained a huge importance in the Third Forum of the mayors of the cities on the Silk Route which was held from September, 2–4, 2008 in Almaty. In the framework of this forum a seminar was held on "A New Silk Route: From the Great Tradition to Contemporary Standards of Tourism and Cooperation". Representatives from 27 countries took part in that forum. The objective of the forum was the development of the integration between cities, promotion of the innovative ways of finance and tourism along the Silk Route, improvement of a mutual understanding between the people and a harmonious development of the given region.

Holding a Forum of the Mayors of the Silk Route Cities in Almaty was symbolic, and especially important for Central Asia, because there was a deeply integrated common geopolitical space, a three-dimensional community, which had set the historical destiny of the region's population during several ages.

The given Forum was held after the Third Meeting of the Ministers of Foreign Affairs of the partner-countries of cooperation on interaction and trust-building in Asia. The First Forum on the problems of security and cooperation in the Central Asian–Caspian region was held in the framework of this mechanism. The President of the Republic of Kazakhstan N. Nazarbayev in the hall of the Intercontinental Hotel on August, 25 stressed in his speech about the role and mission of the CICA in Central Asia, and its role in the "long term maintenance of security in the Asian continent". Along with this, an emphasis was made on the perspectives of this organisation including the role of Kazakhstan in establishing the dialogue between the West and the East.

The meeting of the CICA heads of states and governments in Asia on the initiative of Kazakhstan is a high-level summit on strengthening mutual security and trust and represents a unique instrument of international relations. The territory with a three billion population and producing one quarter of the world GDP should have an authoritative international organisation which is able to resolve conflicts on the local level, not allowing for the external continental upheavals. On this occasion, Kazakhstan was the ideal platform for initiating a dialogue, since the country did not have a burden with a negative luggage in international politics.

This only increased its positive image with such issues such as the renunciation of the weapons of mass destruction. Without any negative thoughts, sovereign Kazakhstan managed to be on good terms with the countries, capable of playing a creative intermediary role for establishing peace, stability and business relations in Asia. So, for the nations which have been suffering from a constant collision with their neighbouring countries for many years, the CICA gives an opportunity to conduct a dialogue without arbitrations that often have their own interest in maintaining the conflict situation.

The exclusive importance of CICA for the Central Asian region is explained not only by the fact that from the moment of forming the USSR, the five union republics were fully isolated from the internal world by the authorities of the Soviet empire. Before its collapse, a number of contradictions on a wide spectrum of political, cultural, economic and religious problems were in a latent form and put under the carpet by the totalitarian regime. But, before the Soviet times, Central Asia represented itself as a space of the moving dispersal or extended centres of attraction, depending on the situation of the region.

An Intergovernmental Joint Commission on trade–economic, scientific–technical, industrial and cultural cooperation with a number of Silk Route countries is the most important instrument of development and intensification of the bilateral cooperation in various spheres.

Interaction develops between the analytical circuits of two countries. So, the Kazakhstan Institute of Defensive Research under the President of the Republic of Kazakhstan signed memorandums of mutual understanding with the Indian Central Asian Foundation (ICAF). The Department of International Relations of the Kazakh State University named after Al-Farabi signed the memorandum of understanding with the Centre for

Central Asian Studies of JNU and ICAF. In the autumn of 2006, the Institute of History and Ethnology named after Ch.Ch. Valikhanov of the Ministry of Education and Science of the Republic of Kazakhstan, signed a memorandum of understanding with the Kashmir University through the intermediary Center of the Central Asian Research.

Block 2.
Conditions and formats of partnership of Kazakhstan and India on revival of the Silk Route

The process of integration of the post-Soviet independent states in the world community that began by the end of the twentieth century, has outstripped the ways for each of them. Thus the main conditions of recognition of this or that state on the part of the world community are the main priorities and imperatives of the stability of political development. Kazakhstan also has shown the world an example of a sovereign state emerging from the condition of threat of an economic collapse. These and a number of other advantages have allowed Kazakhstan to become a full-fledged member of the world community.

A different approach is necessary to understand the modern realities of the post-Soviet regions of Central Asia. The approach according to which these regions were considered as part of the former USSR is nowadays obsolete. The general approaches to these regions as components of the CIS states do not save the situation. The accent of attention on the "narrowness of the national markets" has not justified itself as a whole.

Nevertheless, the states of Central Asia and, first of all Kazakhstan, face all negative consequences of a growing competition between the world centres of power for influence in the region. Both external and internal factors affect the Central Asian integration.[1] The following concerns their number:

- *Various models and speed of economic–political reforms in the countries of Central Asia;*
- *Essential differences in national legislations;*
- *Distinctions in priorities and interests of the national elites;*
- *Non-similar external orientation at a conceptual level;*
- *The factor of external influence;*
- *Incompleteness of process of formation of system of interstate relations.*

Along with the above-mentioned factors, one of the main reasons for the failure of the Central Asian integration project is that the organisational registration of those or other regional interactions as a rule, do not follow the process of practical use of relations, but outstripped them. Being integrated, the governments have preferred to lean on rigidly structured relations or the unions. And, accordingly, integration institutes developed initially as formal structures, are deprived of real substance. It was some kind of "outstripping projects".

The existing unsatisfactory condition of the process of the Central Asian integration leads to the following consequences:

- *Weakness of integration becomes the factor for jeopardising social stability in the Central Asian states;*
- *Absence of coordinated policy of the states of the region on the issues of integration leads to the growth of interstate conflict potential;*
- *Process of decomposition and degradation of the isolated economies of the states of the region amplifies an initially interconnected character;*
- *Outside the effective regional structures, the states of Central Asia cannot strengthen their positions in the world political and economic arena.*

At the same time, it is necessary to recognise, that apart from the ambiguity of approaches of the countries of the region on regional integration issues, there are objective factors, which can become a basis of partnership and integration in Central Asia, including between Kazakhstan and India. Particularly, the following:

- *The identical strategic purposes (market economy, democracy, the secular state);*
- *Potential economic dividends from participation in regional and through them in global economic projects;*
- *High security of region power, mineral and agricultural raw material;*
- *Favourable geopolitical position;*
- *The general threats of security*

Prospects of the Kazakh–Indian relations are bright from the view point of geopolitical interests of Washington in Central Asia. In 2005, when the member-countries of the SCO demanded the withdrawal of the American military bases from Uzbekistan and Kyrgyzstan, the USA chose a new regional strategy that seeks the creation of a "the Greater Central Asia" (GCA), almost as an alternative to SCO.

In the opinion of the State Secretary of the US, C. Rais, the centre of the GCA will be, "safe and the prosperous Afghanistan which connects CA with South Asia". As the Head of the Department of State considers "the new Silk Route, the big reformatory corridor will be created connecting republics of the Western Europe with democracies of Southern and Eastern Asia". Thus, it is emphasised that the USA would like to consider the development of the Central Asia "in coordination with growing economy of East Asia, the American unions in Japan and South East Asia". C. Rais declared in Astana in October 2005: "In this plan the USA is fully prepared to help Kazakhstan and its Central Asian neighbours for their integration into the global economy".

Within the framework of realisation of the programme of "the Greater Central Asia" the USA plans the creation of an energy supply system, that seeks to direct the energy resources of Central Asia (oil of Kazakhstan, gas of Turkmenistan; hydro -resources of Kyrgyzstan and Tajikistan) towards Afghanistan, Pakistan and India for meeting their growing needs. In particular, within the framework of the Programme of Assistance to the Regional Energy Market (REMAP), the Agency of the USA on the international development (USAID) plans to assist the main producers of electric power in the Central Asia, especially Kyrgyzstan and Tajikistan, in transferring the electric power to the south through Afghanistan and Pakistan.

The disintegration of the USSR led to the formation of an imbalance of power in Central Asia. First of all, it concerned Russia, India and China for which the danger of Islamic fundamentalism has grown. Islamic fundamentalism poses threat to internal stability, territorial integrity and safety of the borders of these states. In such a situation, "ignorance of our realities has caused the formation of a negative image of Kazakhstan as an Islamic state possessing the nuclear weapon and posing danger to world community. This negative factor affected us along with our future partners".[2] Kazakhstan and its neighbour Kyrgyzstan have a mission in preventing negative tendencies in "an Islamic zone" in these conditions. Therefore, it was important to present Kazakhstan as a secular state in which the religion is separated from state, and any attempts to manipulate the issue of religion for the achievement of political aims will be resolutely stopped. Concerning the revival of Islam, our position is that it will be carried out within the framework of the general development of culture and spirituality of Kazakhstan.

Taking into account the growing economic clout of the countries *of the Asia-Pacific region,* many experts recognise its dominating role at a global stage in the twenty-first century. Kazakhstan, located on the crossroads of the transport arteries of Eurasia and possessing significant a economic potential, presents significant interest in a deep cooperation with them, first of all with Japan, India, the Republic of Korea and Pakistan. From the point of view of foreign trade and diversification of the international political relations, cooperation with Malaysia, Singapore, Thailand, and Indonesia is important for Kazakhstan.

High dynamics of economic and political processes gradually transform this huge region into one of the prospective centres of the world community. So, during the last decade, the rates of economic development of these countries appreciably surpassed the average world standards with an annual gross national product growth touching 5–6 %, and foreign trade on the average registering 9–11 % per annum. As a result, the Asian region has about 60% of the world production and about 40% of international trade at present and by 2015 it is expected that out of the 12 largest economies of the world, five will be Asian.[3]

Block 3.

Role of the Silk Route in the definition of prospects of the Kazakh–Indian partnership

The value of the Silk Route in its modern understanding lies in a number of concrete actions for deepening the Kazakh–Indian cooperation and partnership. Their practical realisation in many respects depends both on the resolution of the problems of revival of the Silk Route, and its future.

The Kazakhstan researchers mark six perspective directions of economic cooperation between Kazakhstan and India:

1. *Sphere of information technologies.*
2. *Oil-and-gas sphere.*
3. *Development of a transport corridor "the North–the South" from Aktau on the Caspian Sea via Iran up to the Arabian Sea.*
4. *Development of bilateral cooperation in the field of small and middle business.*
5. *Development of trade and economic relations with India.*
6. *Development of tourism.*[4]

On the prospects of the Kazakh–Indian partnership on fulfilling the doctrine about the revival of the Silk Route, it is important for strengthening this partnership. For Kazakhstan, the political stability, the advanced nature of the economy, potential for allocating sufficient funds for construction of large transport corridors , huge mineral resources and direct neighbourhood with Russia and China are advantages.

At present the Silk Route has turned into a route for the movement of human resources. The revival of the economy of the two countries has highlighted a problem of the optimum use of their potential. According to the Embassy of India in Almaty, nowadays, 1,500 Indian citizens are registered in Kazakhstan. Students make about 40% of them. The Indian citizens are concentrated in such cities of Kazakhstan as Almaty (about a 1,000 people), Astana, Karaganda, Atyrau and Semei.

The innovations connected to the industrial application of achievements of science and research require the creation of joint educational structures. It is necessary to note that the Indian component is limited in the educational branch of Kazakhstan. It is limited to allocation of grants for Kazakhstan by such organisations of India like the ITEC and ICCR. Meanwhile, the presence of joint Kazakh–Indian educational institutions on the training of experts in IT, international tourism, banking, management, film-industry, etc. is a topical question in the educational sector of Kazakhstan.

At the same time, the political scientists of Kazakhstan note that a level of relations between Kazakhstan and India, despite their high potential, is not very high. Particularly, there is no legal foundation of the mutual relations of a strategic character.[5] Meanwhile, this moment is the determining factor for the promotion of cooperation between the two countries on the revived Silk Route.

Thus, the above-mentioned facts form the basis for the Kazakhstan–India partnership in the contemporary conditions. At the same time, this foundation provides an impulse for the mutual participation of Kazakhstan and India in resolving the problem of revival of the Silk Route. Both states have a common understanding of the problem. The revived Silk Route would be a guarantor of world stability and the resolution of global issues.

Today, the Silk Route experiences the third revival in its history. After 500 years, each of participants of this form of dialogue and partnership has understood the ways of its revival in own way. Its primordial essence and the maintenance – partnership for the sake of prosperity, harmony and mutual survival in conditions of global problems of humankind-will be constant.

Notes

1. Burkhanov K., Sultanov B., Ayagan B. Sovremennaya politicheskaya istoriya Kazakhstana. – Almaty, 2006. PP. 216-219.
2. Nazarbaev N.A. Na poroge XXI veka. – Almaty, 1996. P.205.
3. Tokaev K. Diplomatiya Respubliki Kazakhstan. – Almaty, 2001. P.118.
4. Ibid.
5. Perspektivy ukrepleniya kazakhstansko-indiiskogo partnerstva. – Almaty: The Kazakhstan Institute of strategic studies attached to the President of the Republic of Kazakhstan, 2006. PP. 13 -14.

12

Kazakhstan: A Land of Peace and Prosperity

Kairat Umarov

In today's world, Kazakhstan is associated with continuous growth and sustainable development. The reason is that over the last 8 years, my country has been enjoying a 9–10% growth at an average in a row, which is among the highest in the world. It is true that at the early years of its statehood, Kazakhstan was in deep economic crisis as a consequence of the former USSR's collapse. However, owing to successful economic reforms and sound public policy, the country has overcome the hardships and is fast catching up with the Eastern European countries in terms of per capita income. Its GDP per capita in 1991 was US$ 400; now it stands at US$ 7 thousand.

Kazakhstan has been reshaping itself owing to the consistent and proactive policy of President Nursultan Nazarbayev whose vision has transformed the country into a modern, progressive and economically viable state.

In this success story, two factors have played a major role. First, the adoption of the"Long Term Development Strategy Kazakhstan 2030" (Kazakhstan 2030) and second, the subsequent economic reforms.

The Strategy allowed us to charter our prospective course of development upto 2030 by identifying seven priorities to concentrate on:

- National Security;
- Domestic political stability and consolidation of the society;
- Sustainable economic growth;
- Healthcare, education and wellbeing of the people;
- Development of energy resources;
- Improvement of infrastructure;
- Professional Government.

The following review of progress over the last 10 years in achieving the set priorities of the Strategy gives a glimpse of how successful Kazakhstan is in the pursuit of prosperity and development.

National Security

The topmost task of any country is to ensure its national security, which means, in the first place, protection of the territorial integrity and independence. In the long run, it could be best achieved through living in peace with the neighbouring states and in the comity of nations as a whole. Therefore "Kazakhtan 2030" attaches great importance to this objective, which we persistently follow in our external policy.

Thanks to its peace-loving and consistent foreign policy, Kazakhstan today has completed the delimitation of its borders and is strengthening good-neighbourly relations in the region. Kazakh initiatives such as the CICA (Conference on Interaction and Confidence Building Measures in Asia) uniting presently 18 nations and the Congress of World and Traditional Religions aim at promoting regional and international peace and security. We are the founding members of influential regional organisations such as the CSTO (Collective Security Treaty Organization) and SCO (Shanghai Cooperation Organization), having a great positive impact in ensuring national security.

Given the emergence of non-traditional threats such as terrorism, extremism, drug trafficking, illegal trafficking of arms and nuclear materials, Kazakhstan modernises its national armed and security forces and expands its international cooperation so that it is better prepared to handle the new challenges more efficiently. Kazakhstan has established a number of Joint Working Groups with our partners, including India.

Furthermore, Kazakhstan is the first country to renounce its nuclear arsenal, the fourth largest in the world, and the host nation for signing the treaty on the establishment of the nuclear weapons-free zone in Central Asia, which greatly contributes to global peace.

Kazakhstan is committed to further ensuring the international security through non-violent means, which also serves best our own national security.

Domestic Political Stability and Consolidation of the Society

It is a well-established fact that internal political stability is key to the successful development of a nation. For Kazakhstan, which is a multi-ethnic and multi-religious country, the domestic stability is achieved through a peaceful coexistence of ethnic and religious groups making up the nation and the consolidation of the society on the basis of universal human values: development of democracy, protection of human rights and freedoms, establishment of rule of law.

The Kazakh Government has been successful in ensuring a stable domestic environment. In its 17 years of history, Kazakhstan has not seen any internal conflict or clash along ethnic or religious lines. We believe that Kazakhstan's case in promoting religious tolerance and freedom of religions is worth studying. In fact, the great asset we have for development is the diversity of culture, talents and mindsets of our people consisting of over 130 ethnic groups with 40 religious outlooks. We have 130 cultural centres, more than 10 ethnic theatres and over 101 schools, where the medium of instruction is an ethnic language. Kazakhstan's media speaks 13 languages. As a strong follower of secularism and inter-ethnic harmony, we believe in the principle of unity in diversity.

Despite their race or ethnicity, the Kazakh citizens' fundamental rights are well protected by the Constitution. Minorities have a say in the Government policy through the Assembly of the People of Kazakhstan, which has evolved from an advisory agency to a national body with a quota of seats in the Parliament.

Thanks to its strong credentials in the religious accord, Astana is host to the Congress of World and Traditional Religions, gathering many spiritual leaders from around the world, including India, to bring mutual understanding and tolerance among different faiths.

Kazakhstan is a democratic country, where free and fair elections are held, providing opportunities for its citizens to choose their destiny. There are seven political parties and over 5,000 NGOs in the country. More than 8,000 media outlets are registered in the country, with 80 per cent of them being privately owned. Freedom of speech and prohibition of censorship are the true attributes of the Kazakh democracy.

To further the democratic reforms, constitutional amendments were adopted last year, changing the form of government from Presidential to Presidential–Parliamentary, which brought about the increasing powers of the legislative branch.

In November 2007, Kazakhstan was elected to the Chairmanship of the Organization for Security and Cooperation in Europe in 2010. Thus, Kazakhstan has become the first in the post-Soviet space to lead the organisation. This fact speaks for itself of the democratic accomplishments of my country.

Political reforms and democratic transformation have been instrumental in achieving domestic stability and consolidation of the society. However, we do not stop at that. The Kazakhstan 2030 Programme sets an objective of establishing a common national identity to further unleash the creative power of our people in building a unified and prosperous nation.

Sustainable Economic Growth

The main aim of the Strategy lies in sustaining economic development. A peaceful environment, internal political stability and investor -friendly climate, which have been provided under the Kazakhstan 2030 Strategy, have contributed towards achieving this aim and brought about a significant progress on the economic front. Over the last 11 years, the GDP has grown from US$ 22 billion to 100 billion—almost five-fold. The Kazakh economy has attracted US$ 70 billion of foreign investments, which account for 80% of all investments made in Central Asia.

Kazakhstan's international assets have exceeded US$ 40 billion. The external trade has increased six-fold and reached US$

80 billion. The Banking, Insurance and Pension sectors are robust. Today, Kazakhstan is a functioning market economy with a 90% of ownership in the private sector.

Kazakhstan is set to obtain even more ambitious tasks. For example, it is planning to enter the ranks of the 50-most competitive economies in the world within a decade. The strategic vision provides for creating jobs, generating wealth and ensuring prosperity to the people of Kazakhstan by the year 2030. As highlighted by President Nursultan Nazarbayev in his state-of-the nation address in February 2007, Kazakhstan is set to emerge as a "regional locomotive".

Now, the focus is on the development of the knowledge economy, with the transfer of technology and increase of our own R&D capabilities. From being a raw material and agriculture-based country in the erstwhile USSR, Kazakhstan is fast moving towards building a post-industrial, high-tech, English-speaking economy with capabilities in aerospace, biotechnology, IT and peaceful atomic energy.

Healthcare, Education and Well-Being of the People

As far as the social well-being of the people is concerned, tangible improvements have occurred in the quality of their lives lately. According to the World Bank, Kazakhstan belongs to the bracket of middle-income countries.

We are conducting massive reforms in the healthcare sector to improve its efficiency. To further the convenience of our people, in the next three years, 150 healthcare facilities and 300 remote area clinics will be constructed.

The Constitution guarantees free-of-charge state-financed education upto high school level. Every citizen has a right to get free high education on a competition basis. In order to develop human resources, we are promoting interaction with international partners. We are facilitating establishment of offices or educational centres of world's best universities and institutes in Kazakhstan. Under the Presidential Program *Bolashak* (Future), the best 3,000 students are provided scholarships to pursue their education in the world's leading universities. The Government also invites best professors from around the world to lecture in Kazakh higher educational institutions. The purpose is to impart world standard education for Kazakh students and to train highly qualified managers and specialists to efficiently run the growing economy.

German economist and statesman Erhard said: "the greater freedom enjoyed by the economy, the more social it is". It is confirmed by Kazakhstan's example, where market liberalisation and rapid economic growth has made it possible to expand substantially the social targeting of government expenditures. The unemployment rate is as low as 7%. The social security of maternity and childhood is ensured. From 2008, the amount of the state allowance for the birth of a child will be doubled. Salaries have increased significantly. The pensions are paid up to the world standards.

In the mid-term future, we aspire to ensure the national standard of life quality at the level of the developed countries.

Development of Energy Resources

Since energy security is on the agenda, it would be of interest to outline Kazakhstan's energy policy.

Owing to the efficient government policy, we have successfully avoided the "Dutch disease" and are efficiently using the oil and gas income, accumulated to US$ 21.5 bn in the National Oil Fund, to invest in high-tech sectors.

By 2010, the estimated oil extraction will be 70 million tonnes; in 2015, it will reach 130 million tonnes, while the domestic consumption will be below 25 million tonnes.

In 2010, 40 billion cubic metres of gas are expected to be extracted and in 2015 it will reach 80 billion cubic metres.

Based on the expansion of energy potential, the Kazakhstan Government puts emphasis on the export of downstream, petrochemical and gas-processing products. Due attention is also given to the diversification of the export routes of hydrocarbons.

By 2017, Kazakhstan is expected to enter the ranks of the 10 biggest energy exporters in the world.

Kazakhstan fully recognises its responsibility in ensuring the global energy balance and security. Speaking at the 62nd UN General Assembly meeting on September 26, 2007, President Nazarbayev proposed to adopt the Eurasian Energy Supply Stability Pact aimed at fostering a long-term energy cooperation in the region.

Oil

Currently, hydrocarbon reserves are found in 241 fields. A total of 142 companies are operating in the sector: 20 joint ventures, 48 foreign companies and 74 local companies.

In total, US$ 40.6 bn have been invested in the sector. Most of the investments were for extracting hydrocarbons.

One of the country's top priorities is the efficient development of its Caspian offshore energy resources. In 2003, Kazakhstan adopted the State Program of Development of the Kazakhstan Sector of the Caspian Sea (KSCS), main purpose of which is to boost the environmentally safe oil and gas production, to generate revenues to aid the diversification and modernisation of the whole economy, making it highly competitive and non-dependent on the oil and gas sector.

A further growth of onshore production output is linked to the intensified development of such oilfields as Tengiz and Karachaganak. Research has shown that major gains in explored reserves and in hydrocarbons production are expected to take place in the Caspian offshore area. According to the world practice, it normally takes 8–10 years to get to the commercial offshore production stage.

The Program covers the period up to 2015. It takes into account the increasing importance of the offshore O&G reserves, and integrates the principles of rational subsurface use and environmental safety requirements. The Program envisages turning the KSCS into a major hydrocarbon production zone in Kazakhstan.

In addition to the O&G development in the KSCS, the Program provides for the development of associated industries, social and environment-protection measures.

The last 30 years have shown a trend of global GDP growth at a rate of 3.3% per annum, with the growing demand for oil as the major energy source at a rate of 1% per annum.

According to international experts, with the current trends maintained, the global explored oil resources will only last for the next 40–50 years. The inclusion of the KSCS resources into the global explored reserves has become a major component of the global energy strategies.

The proximity to such dynamically developing nations as Russia, China and India opens up numerous opportunities for Kazakhstan's hydrocarbon exports. To ensure the entrance to the markets of these countries, it is vital to develop and widen the pipeline system.

The way in which the KSCS resources will be developed will be based on the uniform allocation of blocks to subsoil users in northern, central and southern parts of the sea.

The Government will be in charge of defining the blocks to be offered for tenders, and the order and conditions of the tenders.

As the KSCS oilfields get developed, the need for the diversification of export routes will keep growing. The enhancement of export routes implies a multimodal transportation of hydrocarbons, with an efficient combination of the capabilities of pipeline, railway and sea transport.

Below is the list of existing and planned routes for the transportation of hydrocarbons from the KSCS oilfields:

- Main oil pipeline Uzen-Atyrau-Samara (Russia). Given the expected growth of oil production in western Kazakhstan, it is planned to build up the pipeline carrying capacity gradually.
- The Baltic Pipelines System is a promising route to increase Kazakhstan's oil supply to the markets of East Europe and the Baltic States.
- Caspian Pipeline Consortium (CPC): given the attractiveness of the Mediterranean market for high-quality grades of Kazakhstan's oil, the CPC is a major export route. In this connection, it is planned to expand the carrying capacity of the pipeline to 58 million tonnes by 2008, and to 67 million tonnes by 2011.
- The Caspian Sea port of Aktau: Oil transfer capacities of the port and of its branches in the bays of Bautino and Kuryk can be increased to 8 million tonnes per year.
- The current transport systems will be sufficient for the export of domestically produced oil up to 2009.

When in 2009 the oil production in Kazakhstan hits the target of 92 million tonnes per year, including 21 million tonnes at the KSCS, it will be necessary to construct a new export pipeline. When production hits the mark of 140 million tonnes per year, including 54 million tonnes at the KSCS, it will be necessary to construct the second new export pipeline by 2012.

In this context, the following oil transportation routes are being considered:

- Aktau–Baku (Baku-Tbilisi-Ceyhan (BTC) pipeline).

According to the plan, at the initial stage, the BTC will be able to transport 23.3 million tonnes of Kazakhstan's oil a year initially and later, 35–56 million tonnes a year. The approximate cost of the first stage of facilities is 1.8 billion USD.

- Western Kazakhstan –Western China Project. The planned construction of
- The Kazakhstan–China pipeline will allow the transport of more than 20 million tonnes of oil a year to the Chinese market from the Caspian region.
- Kazakhstan-Turkmenistan-Iran Project. According to preliminary research, this route is economically viable for the export of Kazakhstan's oil to the Gulf countries. The project envisages that the oil pipeline will start in Western Kazakhstan and run via Western Turkmenistan to northern Iran. It could be also used for oil supply to India at a later stage.

Gas

Kazakhstan is currently using the Central Asia-Centre gas pipeline, which runs along the eastern coast of the Caspian Sea and is integrated with the Russian gas transportation systems. The pipeline is intended for the transit and export of Central Asian and Kazakhstan's gas.

In view of the plans to increase its own production of natural gas up to 50 billion cubic meters a year, Kazakhstan is getting ready to step up its export potential and consider alternative ways to deliver Kazakhstan's gas to Europe through the territories of Azerbaijan, Georgia and Turkey, in line with the policy of diversification of its export routes.

A trilateral agreement between Kazakhstan, Russia and Turkmenistan on the construction of the new Caspian gas pipeline with the capacity of 30 billion cubic meters a year was signed in December 2007. The Agreement is aimed at securing safe transport capabilities of the participating states in exporting their growing production of natural gas and envisages mutual undertakings to create favourable conditions for the economic effectiveness of the project. Its implementation will start in the second half of 2008.

Uranium

The world demand for quality uranium fuel is in sharp increase. Kazakhstan has been an important source of uranium for more that fifty years. Approximately one-fifth of the world uranium reserves are deposited in Kazakhstan. The total Kazakh reserves of uranium are over 1.5 million tonnes, over 1.1 million tonnes of which can be mined by the in-site leaching method. Some 50 uranium deposits are known in six provinces. In 2001–2006, uranium production rose from 2,000 to more than 5,000 tonnes per year. Further active mine development is underway with a view to reach an annual production of 15,000 tU/yr by 2010 that will make Kazakhstan the biggest uranium producer in the world. The State-owned National Atomic Company Kazatomprom is the sole organisation for uranium mining, reprocessing, export and import operations in Kazakhstan.

Renewable Energy Sources (RES)

An analysis of the global energy development shows that the share of the RES will continue to grow in the future. According to some forecasts, it can reach 65% of the total energy production by the end of the twenty-first century.

Kazakhstan has an enormous RES potential which surpasses (in the energy equivalent) the existing deposits of the traditional energy resources. The RES in question are hydropower, wind power, photo electricity, bioenergy, solar power and heat, geothermal energy and marine power (power of tides and waves).

To sum it all up, Kazakhstan with its sizeable amounts of oil and gas, coal and uranium is an important energy player in the world. However, with these natural energy resources in abundance, the Government and the country's energy sector keep an attentive eye on the global energy trends. An optimal energy mix, its efficient use, the environmental dimension of the energy policy, research and development of renewable reserves – all these issues are on the country's energy policy agenda.

Kazakhstan aims at a diversification of its energy export routes and continues to adhere to its multi-vector policy. Kazakhstan is open for dialogue with its partners to develop new ways of ensuring global energy security.

Improvement of Infrastructure

In the age of globalisation, the improvement of infrastructure acquires a great significance. Over the last 10 years, we have witnessed the construction and renovation of four thousand kilometres of roads. In 2006, the Transport Strategy 2015 was adopted, which provides for 80 investment projects worth US$ 30 billion. Under the new programme, 1,600 km of new railroads will be constructed and 2,700 km of railways will be electrified. 50 thousand km of highways will be constructed. The National Maritime Commercial Fleet, Sea Ports and internal shipping ways will be developed. So, with the time passing, Kazakhstan is turning into transport and transit hub of Eurasia.

The people of Kazakhstan will be provided with the modern telecommunication services. Today, the number of internet users in Kazakhstan is about 1.8 million. By 2010, 3.5 million people would be using the internet. The Centres of IT excellence are being opened in Kazakhstan adding to the existing courses for IT education. 65% of schools in Kazakhstan have access to internet. Next year, 2,000 schools will have broadband connection (85%).

The aim is to achieve a 100% of coverage of schools with the internet connection in the nearest future.

Professional Government

Kazakhstan's ambitious tasks cannot be implemented without a professional government. We have adopted all necessary laws ensuring a better performance of authorities, including the Laws on Public Service, Fight Against Corruption, the Code of Honor of Public Servants, etc. E-governance has been introduced in the country to raise the efficiency of public service and make it more available to the general population.

Our goal here is to form a highly professional state service and efficient government structures. The main idea is that government officials should be as effective and highly paid as businessmen in the corporate sector, cutting down on red tape and delivering the government service in a time-bound manner.

Kazakhstan Energy Indicators

Current Oil Reserves: 32.5 billion barrels (twice as much as the North Sea)

Projected Oil Reserves: 100-110 billion barrels by 2015 (will be among top 5 world oil exporters)

Oil Production: (III quarter 2007) 41.2 million tonnes Current Gas Reserves: 3 trillion cubic metres Projected Gas Reserves: 5 trillion cubic metres by 2015

Natural Gas Production: (III quarter 2007) 21.9 billion cubic metres Coal Reserves (2006): 35 billion short tonnes (Mmst) Coal Production: (III quarter 2007) 62.7 million tonnes

Electricity Generation: (III quarter 2007) 54.6 billion kilowatt-hours (kWh)

Uranium Reserves: 1.5 mn tonnes (or 19% of the world reserves)

Uranium Production: (2006) 5279 tonnes

Main companies: KazMunayGas (vertically-integrated state oil and natural gas company); Kazakhstanugol Corporation (state coal company); Kazakhstan Electricity Grid Operating Company (KEGOC); Kazatomprom (National Atomic Company)

Major Oil and Gas Fields: Tengiz (oil), Karachaganak (natural gas and gas condensate), Kashagan (off-shore, oil), Uzen, Kumkol, Korolev, Tenge, Uritau Zhanazhol (natural gas),

Major Oil Ports: Atyrau, Aqtau, Bautino and Kuryk on the Caspian Sea

Oil Export Pipelines: Caspian Pipeline Consortium (CPC) – Tengiz–Novorossiisk (Russia); Uzen-Atyrau-Samara (Russia); Kenkyak–Orsk (Russia) line which transports oil from the Aktyubinsk fields to the Orsk refinery, Kenkyak–Atyrau, Atasu–Alashankou (China – under further expansion).

Major Oil Refineries (crude oil refining capacity): Pavlodar (162,666 bbl/d); Atyrau (104,427 bbl/d); Shymkent (160,000 bbl/d)

Major Power Plants (capacity): Ekibastuz No.1 (4,000 megawatts, MW), Yermak (2,400 MW), Zhambyl (1,230 MW)

Conclusion

Looking back to 1997, and comparing it with 2008, we can conclude that a lot has been achieved since the adoption of Kazakhstan 2030. As we move forward on the Strategy, its aim remains the same, which is to enter the ranks of the most developed countries by 2030.

Whatever achievements that we have reached were possible because of the constant support and help of our friends and partners. India continues to support Kazakhstan's overall development and economic progress, for which we are grateful.

Our bilateral cooperation is on a dynamic rise. At present, the trade turnover between the two countries increases by 74%, reaching the US$ 210 million mark. An excellent political dialogue between our countries creates favourable conditions for fruitful engagements in many other areas.

It has been recognised that Kazakhstan is emerging as a regional hub of economic activities and regional integration. Based on the above successes in nation-building, Astana is poised to achieve new landmarks in ensuring prosperity and development of the country.

13

Socio-Economic Development of Uzbekistan and Indo-Uzbek Relations

Saidkamal Saydaminov

Uzbekistan has celebrated 25 years of its existence as an independent state . The Independence Day is an important date in the country's history. For it is the perfect opportune and right time to assess the past, to draw some conclusions about the traversed path, and design plans for the future.

To appreciate *what has been done* by the leadership and people of Uzbekistan during the sixteen years of independence one needs to know in a better manner about the geographic, climatic, demographic and socio-economic peculiarities of Uzbekistan.

Country Profile

The Republic of Uzbekistan is located at the heart of the ancient Silk Road – at the centre of Central Asia, between two big rivers – Amu-Darya and Syr-Darya, and has historically been the linking bridge between the East and the West. It shares borders with the Republics of Kazakhstan, Kyrgyzstan, Tajikistan, Turkmenistan and Afghanistan. The territory of Uzbekistan is 4,48, 900 sq. km. It is a landlocked country and stretches 930 km from north to south and 1,425 km from the west to the east. Almost 80% of its territorial areas are constituted of deserts or semi-deserts. This makes the country's climate very hot, dry and sharply continental. The western and central parts of the country have the most severe climatic conditions – in winter, cold waves come from the north, and summer is hot and dusty because of its surrounding desert areas and the saline bed of the dried-out Aral sea. The eastern part of the country – Ferghana valley, Tashkent and Surkhandarya regions – provide the most favourable climatic conditions.

Consequently, while the average population density in the country increased from 35.6 people per sq. km in 1980 to 59.26 people per sq. km in 2006, in some regions the population density is much higher: in the Andijan region – 551.2; Fergana region – 419.6; Tashkent region – 294.8 and in the Namangan region – 275.3 people per sq. km. Today, the total population of Uzbekistan is about 26.6 million. It is estimated that by 2010 the total population of Uzbekistan will increase up to 28.5 – 28.7 million. Nearly 64 % of the total population lives in rural areas.

Under the arid zone conditions, an increasing population leads to a greater anthropogenic pressure on the environment and creates additional ecological, economical and social burdens on the densely populated regions of the country.

From the previous Soviet regime Uzbekistan has inherited the one-sided economy, based mainly on supplying raw materials, including cotton, agricultural products, as well as strategic mineral resources to the centre. After the disintegration of the Soviet Union all economic links with the former Soviet Republics have almost been cut. Uzbekistan has become a doubly landlocked country; that is, to reach any open sea or ocean, it is necessary to cross at least two foreign countries. In some regions, inter-state railroads partly passed through the neighbouring countries – Turkmenistan and Tajikistan – which has caused additional transportation problems both in connecting the regions of Uzbekistan and in delivering cargo to and from any open sea.

The Uzbek Model of Socio-Economic Development

After the country gained independence, it chose its own way of economic development and transition to market relations, more known as the *"Uzbek model"*.

The cornerstone of such a model has become the economic policy, aimed at a radical restructuring of industry, establishing and mastering the new and progressive methods of production, equipped with the latest technologies, as well as raising the share of the ready-made products in the exports. The task of ensuring peace and stability and carrying out the stable and strong socio-oriented policy has turned into a landmark task of economic development during the early stages of reforms in the country.

The five basic principles, elaborated by Islam Karimov, the first President of the Republic of Uzbekistan, served as a basis for political, social, and economic reforms in the country: the state is a main reformer; the supremacy of economy over politics; the superiority of law; the gradual reforming and the strong social protection of the population.

In its path towards the *democratic reforms*, the Government of Uzbekistan is altering the structure and role of the executive and judicial branches of the government. The powers of the executive, previously lodged with the President, have been altered to accommodate a new Prime Minister.

The parliamentary elections that have taken place in Uzbekistan, became important landmarks in its history with its focus on a further democratisation of the state. For the first time in the history of its parliament, the bicameral parliament was established, consisting of the Legislative Chamber and the Senate.

The establishment of the bicameral parliament allowed for an enhancement in the role of the Legislative Chamber, and stepped up the control of execution of adopted laws.

From 2004 parliamentary elections were peculiar due to the fact that they were held on a multi-party basis. This allowed for the promotion of the active role and participation of the five registered parties in Uzbekistan.

On the liberalisation of the judicial system: Since 2001, the new system of laws has been developed and adopted which meets all international standards. Particularly, on August 1, 2005, President Karimov signed a decree to abolish death penalty. According to the decree, starting from January 1, 2008, the death penalty is changed to long-term or life-term imprisonment. Currently, only two clauses of the Uzbek Criminal Code envisage death penalty, and they are terrorism and premeditated murder in aggravating circumstances.

Another decree has been signed in August, 2005, on *"Transferring to Courts the Right to Issue Sanctions for Arrest"*, which secures the provision for the efficient protection of human and constitutional rights and freedoms.

In conformity with the Article 83 of the Constitution of the Republic of Uzbekistan, the President put forward for the consideration of the Legislative Chamber of Oliy Majlis (Parliament) the draft of the Constitutional Law "On strengthening the role of political parties in renewal and further democratization of state administration and modernization of the country", and a draft law "On introducing the amendments to particular articles (Art. 89; Clause 15 of the Art. 93; P. 2 of the Art. 102) of the Constitution of the Republic of Uzbekistan". The aim of the first new law is to strengthen the role of the political parties in the process of democratisation of the state administration and the modernisation of the country. It provides the definition of a political fraction, and states that a fraction of a political party that receives the majority of seats in the Legislative Chamber makes up the parliamentary majority. It also outlines the rights of the parliamentary opposition, the order for the election of the speaker and his deputies, the appointment and removal of the Prime Minister of the country, as well as the *khokims* (mayors) of the regions and the city of Tashkent. The

Constitutional Law and the amendments to the Constitution of the Republic of Uzbekistan will enter into force from January 1, 2008.

Religion and Society are Crucial Aspects of Any Country

There are over one hundred ethnicities and about twenty religions existing peacefully in Uzbekistan. Most of the population follows Sunni Islam. The Law *"On freedom of faith and religious organizations"* (1998) secures the right of public for practising religions freely, maintaining and developing ethnic customs and traditions as well as languages. It is all thanks to the Government's efforts that religious tolerance, mutual understanding, inter-ethnic accord and friendship reign harmoniously in the country.

Uzbekistan sets the policy of enlightened, tolerant and peaceful Islam against religious extremism. Speaking on this, President Islam Karimov stressed that "...we can set an idea against an idea, thought against thought, enlightenment against ignorance...". A number of important steps have been taken in the country to fill the void in ideology and to introduce the religious education of the 1990s to study and preserve the great legacies of such theologians as Imam Bukhari, Imam Termezi, Imam Maturidi, Burkhaniddin Marginani, Abdukhalik Gijduvani, Najmiddin Kubro, Bakhouddin Naqshband and other scholars from Movarannahr who had elevated Islam up to the level of science. A great deal of endeavours have been made to make the young generation feel proud of the great legacy of its ancestors, respect and learn scientific and religious heritage, and study religious and secular sciences. The young people should be brought up in the spirit of tolerance and respect for other nations and religions, being aware of their rights and responsibilities. The old good traditions of such world-famous Madrasahs as Mir Arab in Bukhara and Kokaldash in Tashkent have been resurrected. In total, there are two religious high schools, ten Madrasahs and the Tashkent Islamic University in Uzbekistan, which train theologians in the spirit of traditional, peaceful, tolerant and enlightened Islam. More than 2,000 mosques operate in the country.

Environment Protection Policy

In the period of transition from an administrative command system to the market economy, the task of primary importance became the optimisation of micro-economic planning with the environment protection policy and its integration into the policy in the social and other spheres. The environment protection policy of Uzbekistan aimed at changing the practice of protection of the specific elements of nature to the comprehensive protection of the overall ecosystem with the aim of securing optimal parameters of live environment for the human beings. The realisation of such policy is creates a sustainable development of the economy and society. The Government of Uzbekistan acted admirably to create a new national legislation to bring about a more sustainable order to development. Strategies were devised to strengthen its environment protection and management systems and the development of a comprehensive environmental policy. A number of strategic documents have been developed and adopted to address environmental challenges.

Economic Policy

Today, Uzbekistan's well-balanced economic policy has yielded considerable results in all spheres of society. In particular, the country has achieved self-sufficiency in grain and energy resources, the industrial production has been sustainable growth, and the machine-building, aviation, mining, as well as car-making industries has now been developing fast.

In particular, in 2006, the country strengthened the macroeconomic and financial stability, and extended the balance of economy and its specific branches. The GDP grew by 7.3%; annual inflation rate was 6.8 % (7.8% in 2005). Industrial production rose by 10.8% (7.3%), including a 20.6% (17.7%) growth in consumer goods manufacturing. Agricultural production grew by 6.2% (6.2%). The 2006 State Budget was executed with a surplus of 0.5% (0.1%) of the GDP. The steady rates of GDP growth, which have been more than 7% for the last three years, are noteworthy. Since 2000, the economy has grown by 30.1% while since 1991 it was growing by 28.2%. This tendency is a result of the systematic, consistent and persistent work on the gradual realisation of a well-elaborated model and a long-term programme of market reforms and the modernisation of the country.

Since 2000, the economic growth (at a factor of cost in real terms – at 2000–2006 prices) has accounted for 45%; the industrial production grew 1.6 times; agriculture – 1.5 times, foreign trade turnover – 1.7 times; exports – 1.9 times; gold and foreign currency reserves – 3.7 times; the real salaries of employees – 4 times; the volume of the direct foreign investments has increased by 9.3 times and have accounted for US$ 2.5 billion. The total bank capital exceeds UZS 1 trillion and it grew 7.4 times. The network of banks has been doubled. At the same time it is necessary to signify that the annual inflation rate has dropped fourfold. Considerable progress has been achieved in increasing the efficiency of production. As a result, the labour productivity in the industry has grown by 1.7 times.

The country's economic growth also impacted favourably on the trends in human development. The life expectancy index rose from 0.735 in 1995 to 0.792 in 2004; the education index – from 0.913 to 0.917; real GDP per capita – from 1973 to 2834.8 PPP (PPP – purchasing power parity of national currency), and the overall human development index – from 0.704 to 0.752.

Summing up the results of the social and economic development of our country last year, we may confidently state that the year 2006 has become a year of the implementation of profound market and democratic reforms, the year of high economy growth rates and the year of positive changes for enhancing the level and quality of life of the population.

The IMF approved the economic policy of Uzbekistan for the last two years and in its last annual report mentioned that the potentials of the country in economic development during the coming years are quite promising.

The Main Priorities and Goals in the Economy for the Year 2007

The then President Karimov in his address at the session of the Cabinet of Ministers in February 2007 comprehensively analyzed the overall results of the social and economic development of the country in 2006 and highlighted the most important priorities of deepening the reforms in 2007.

He underlined that the first and foremost objective is to ensure A sustainable and balanced development of the economy as well as the continuation of the structural changes and modernisation of the economy, technical and technological renovation of the equipment of its most important sectors and a further liberalisation of the tax policy.

The Oliy Majlis (Parliament) of our country has approved the following main indicators of the economic and social development for 2007: the increase in the GDP by 7.7%; industrial production by 7.8%; agricultural production by 5% and the volume of investments bound for the development of economic sectors by 25.5%. At the same time, it is envisaged to conduct a strict financial-credit and fiscal policy and on this basis to curb the inflation rate down to 5–7%.

The measures to further liberalise the tax policy and improve the activity of the tax bodies will be continued. The expenses of enterprises channelled to maintain the medical, educational and sports facilities will be exempted from their taxable base, and three types of tax payments practiced in the trade shall be replaced with a single tax payment. A profit tax rate is going to be reduced from 12 to 10%, the single tax rate for small businesses – from 13 to 10%, as well as the unified social payment rate will be down to 24%.

Such sectors of the industry as the energy, oil, gas and chemical complexes, gold mining and non-ferrous metallurgy, chemistry and construction material industries, the light industry (particularly textile), the sectors of the raw-material processing, and the spheres of information and communication technologies will constantly be in the focus of attention of the Government.

Our country is possessed with a large *agricultural base*, and we are extremely interested in the development of export-oriented processing and manufacture of food and agricultural products. So another important issue, which requires special attention, is the need to consistently continue the structural changes in the agriculture. On these issues, the Cabinet of Ministers worked out a comprehensive programme for the period of 2007–2011 that encompassed all regions of Uzbekistan. Necessary measures, and particularly, financial, tax stimulus and preferences for the implementation of the key directions of the countryside development, will be envisaged in this programme.

In accordance with the National Programme on social protection of people, the Government will provide livestock—first and foremost, the milky cow—free of charge to 60,000 needy families in the rural areas.

The Government is also going to pay special attention to the development of the *service sector* of our economy. This sphere of the economy generates 39.5% of the GDP; 58% of the able-bodied population is employed in it. It worth noticed that during 2006 the public services increased by 15%, educational and social services for children and disabled increased by 30%, and financial services increased by 2.5 fold. In 2007 the share of services in the GDP increased up to 42–43%.

A significant part of the structural transformations in the economy are the *communication systems* – the railroad and automobile transport infrastructure, electrical, gas and plumbing networks. The Government paid special attention to the implementation of the *"Concept of the development of highways for the period until 2010"*. Particularly in 2007, it was planned to extend the railroad lines to the south, along with the new railroad, Tashguzar-Baysun-Kumkurgan. A sum of US$ 450 million of foreign and local investments have been channelled for this enormous project.

In the sphere of implementation of economic reforms, the main priority direction will yet remain as the creation of all necessary favourable conditions for businesses, and particularly, the private business and consistent reduction of the state participation in the economy.

The attraction of the foreign investments, and the most important – direct foreign Investments – into the country's economy will remain as one of the most important priority concern. In 2006, it was all thanks to the creation of a favourable system of privileges and preferences that more than US$ 20 billion-worth of foreign investments were attracted to our economy. For over the years 2000–2006 alone, the volume of the foreign direct investments has increased by 9.3 times and accounted for US$ 2.5 billion. In accordance with the Investment Program for 2007, it is planned to utilise US$ 3.95 billion investments, including US$ 1 billion of foreign investments, in the major and most important sectors of our economy and in the implementation of the large investment projects in the social area.

Another priority task in 2007, which required a particular attention, was to *consistently increase the salary of employees and the people's living standards*. It is obvious that raising the salaries directly depends on many factors and reasons, and firstly, on the effectiveness of economic development, the growth of financial stability of the enterprises and the entire country, the balance of the money turnover and the stability of our national currency – the Som. According to the statistical and sociological research data, by the end of 2006 the average real salary in Uzbekistan accounted for UZS 185,000 or nearly US$ 150. Taking into consideration that the firm and stable foundation has been created for the economic development of our country as well as looking at the latest developing tendencies of the economy, it is planned to increase the real salaries by at least 1/3rd by the end of 2007, and by 2010, i.e. within the nearest three years

– by 2.5 times. Consequently, other payments such as pensions, stipends and other allowances of the people will grow accordingly.

The fifth important priority is to provide a comprehensive support for the accelerated development of small business and private entrepreneurship, and a resolution on this basis on the issues of the employment of people and a clear-cut agenda for raising the prosperity of the people. At the beginning of 2007, the number of the small and medium business and private enterprises had reached 350,000, or has grown 2.3 times in comparison to the year 2000. At the moment, the share of the small businesses in the GDP accounts for 42.1%. Our permanent objective in this is to ensure the consistent growth of the small and medium business (SMB), and to take its share in the GDP up to 45% in 2007 and up to 50–52% in 2010.

The sixth priority objective is to further deepen and expand the scope of the ongoing reforms in the banking and financial system. For over the last year, certain particular positive changes have taken place in the banking system. Nowadays the total bank capital exceeds UZS 1 trillion and it grew 7.4 times more in comparison with the year 2000. The network of banks has been doubled.

The seventh priority direction is related to the further deepening of the reforms in the field of communal services. In this context, there is a task to achieve the full realisation of the adopted Housing Code of the Republic of Uzbekistan, the Law "On the communities of private housing proprietors" and other normative and legal documents. With this aim the Government along with the involved entities, the Council of Ministers of the Republic of Karakalpakstan, municipalities of the provinces and the city of Tashkent will develop the program on further reforming the communal sphere, improving the management system and introducing the energy-saving technologies, modernising the networks of boiler plants as well as the system of heating and water supply, and reforming and modernising the drainage system.

Foreign Policy

Since its independence Uzbekistan has become an equal member of the international community, and has gained its proper place and voice in the international arena. Unlike the countries, those who have just started to participate in world affairs, from the early days, Uzbekistan has boldly stressed on the priority of national interests in its foreign policy. Its all thanks to a number of initiatives and proposals that have been put forward to provide for regional and global security that Uzbekistan has become an active participant in international affairs. The international community has highly appreciated the initiatives of the country's leadership such as to set up an international centre to combat terrorism under the UN Security Council, to bring peace and stability to Afghanistan, and to establish a nuclear-free zone in Central Asia. Uzbekistan has not limited itself to initiatives, but has also taken an active part in the implementation of those progressive ideas.

The participation at the Shanghai Cooperation Organization (SCO) came as one of the important directions of Uzbekistan's foreign policy. The country's government has been paying enormous attention in expanding relations with the member-states of this organisation in the field of security, trade and economy.

The engagement at the SCO has opened up new opportunities for the economic cooperation of Uzbekistan with the member-states of the organisation. In particular, the strengthening of cooperation with such countries as Russia and China renders a positive impact upon a further expansion of ties with Europe and the countries of South-East Asia. The exploitation of the economic potential of the member-states within the framework of the SCO activities, as well as their capacities in the sphere of transport communications and investments, shall favourably impact Uzbekistan.

India and Uzbekistan have centuries-old history of trade, economic and cultural links. Even during the *Soviet period*, in spite of the artificially closed borders, Uzbekistan, and in particularly Tashkent, has been one of the centres, contributing greatly to the development of the relations between India and other republics of the former USSR. In fact, the Consulate-General of India in Tashkent was formally inaugurated on April 7, 1987. H.E. Mr Jawaharlal Nehru, the then Prime Minister of India, accompanied by Indira Gandhi visited Uzbekistan in 1955 and in 1961. H.E. Mr Lal Bahadur Shastri, the former Prime Minister of India, visited Tashkent in January 1966. Unfortunately, he passed away in Tashkent. His name has been commemorated – a street and school have been named after him and a statue and a bust have been erected in his memory in Tashkent. H.E. Mr R. Venkataraman, the former President of the Republic of India visited Uzbekistan in 1988, and H.E. Mr V. P. Singh, the former Prime Minister of India, visited Uzbekistan in July 1990.

We appreciate greatly that India was among the first countries in the world to recognise *Independent Uzbekistan* on December 26, 1991 and the diplomatic relations were officially established shortly after this on March 18, 1992. On the same day, the Consulate-General of India in Tashkent was upgraded to the level of Embassy, and in September 1992 the Consulate of Uzbekistan was opened in Delhi, which was upgraded to the level of Embassy in 1994.

During these years, Indo-Uzbek relations have developed progressively in all spheres. The regular exchanges of high level visits and exchanges of other delegations have been maintained. As the ambassador of Uzbekistan to India I am very much happy that our bilateral relations have gained a fresh momentum during the last two years. The visit of President Karimov to India in April 2005 heralded a new dimension in bilateral ties. Along with cooperation in political spheres, the leaders of both the countries recognised the need to enhance trade, economic and investment cooperation and linkage in the banking and finance sector, which have been indicated in the Joint Statement and 12 important agreements signed between these countries. The Official Visit of the Prime Minister of the Republic of India, H.E. Dr Manmohan Singh to the Republic of Uzbekistan on April 25–26, 2006, has demonstrated the special friendly relations and the continuation of the dialogue on comprehensive cooperation between these two countries and creation of the effective mechanisms for the accelerated development of the multifaceted interaction between Uzbekistan and India. Besides the official negotiations and signing of several bilateral agreements, H.E. Dr Manmohan Singh officially commenced the operation of the Indo-Uzbek Centre for Information Technology in Tashkent, which has been named after prominent Indian leader Jawaharlal Nehru.

The close friendly relationship between India and Uzbekistan, which is characterised by a mutually beneficial all-round cooperation, is based not on our shared historical and cultural ties only. In more recent times, our countries have come to share common values such as secularism, tolerance and strong opposition to the forces of fundamentalism and terrorism. We have a common vision of stability in our region, and peace and prosperity of our people, and we are determined to work together to achieve these aims. Our cooperation is underpinned by over 60 agreements in different areas.

Today, we can say that the trade and economic relations between Uzbekistan and India over the years have largely been very successful. For the past decade, our mutual trade turnover has grown by more than 12 times and in 2004 reached almost US$ 150 million. Unfortunately, in the last two years our mutual trade turnover has dropped significantly and from both the sides, there is an intention to improve the situation.

Thus, the third India Trade Exhibition was organised by the India–CIS Chamber of Commerce and Industry in last October in Tashkent with the participation of 60 major Indian companies. The exhibition attracted a large number of Uzbek entrepreneurs who held negotiations with their Indian counterparts for bilateral trade and investment in Uzbekistan. The Indian textile company Spentex bought two Uzbek textile mills for US$ 81 million last year. Other Indian companies are interested in investing in textiles, pharmaceutical and oil and gas sectors in Uzbekistan. Two major commercial delegations and several Indian businessmen have visited Uzbekistan last year, and more are expected during this year.

The Uzbek-India Inter-governmental Commission for Trade-Economic and Scientific Technological Cooperation held its seventh meeting in April , 2007 in Tashkent. The meeting was conducted as a part of the visit of a delegation of Indian businessmen headed by the country's Minister of State for Commerce, Mr Jairam Ramesh. In his greeting speech, the Uzbek Co-chairman of the Commission, Deputy Prime Minister of Uzbekistan, Mr Abdulla Aripov emphasised that the Uzbek–India cooperation is of strategic importance to both parties and is being built on the foundation of mutual respect. He also said that the two countries have attributed a high importance to the intensification of collaborative efforts in all spheres of cooperation.

Our export to India primarily consists of aircrafts, products of metallurgy, services, agriculture, silk and cotton and chemical industry products while the imports from India are services, pharmaceuticals and medicines, machinery and equipment, organic and chemical products, optical equipment and devices, textiles and many more.

There are currently forty-five large enterprises in Uzbekistan, which have been established with the direct participation of the Indian companies and investment: twenty-six of them are joint ventures and nineteen – enterprises with 100% Indian capital. To name a few and the most distinguished ones: Diamond Uzbekistan International (tourism), Emsam Trading (construction and tourism), Multi Channel Impex Ltd. (cotton processing and commerce), Spentex (textiles), etc. These enterprises are making a valuable contribution to the development of Uzbekistan's pharmaceutical, tourism, construction and many other industries.

At the same time, however, we believe that the current level of economic cooperation between our two countries does not meet its significant potential. We surely have enormous opportunities to expand this cooperation in many areas, including the following:

- To study India's experience and expertise in privatisation and the investment in large enterprises and banks with a direct participation from Indian experts in this process.
- Deeply interested in introducing new data-processing techniques into electronic management, banking and financial sectors.

We are keen to advance cooperation with a partnership from India to develop its own export-oriented pharmaceutical industry. India's investment in this sector would undoubtedly bring considerable benefits to both our countries.

All of the aforesaid is the evidence of wide-scale reforms undertaken in Uzbekistan to preserve the environment and to provide a sustainable development to the economy and society, which vividly demonstrate their consistency and efficiency. The figures and facts show an evolutionary nature of the ongoing transformations. At the moment, there are still the most important objectives of modernising the country, extending and raising the efficiency of the ongoing reforms and environment protection measures. Life introduces its corrections, and in dealing with some urgent tasks we have to make adjustments, but at the same time, our strategic goals should remain immutable.

The most important aspect is that political and economic reforms are going on without interruption like one continuous process, and they have now become irreversible.

14

Economic Policy of the State Concerning Small Business: Experience of St. Petersburg

Vyachislav Shavshukov

With the origin and evolution of family, liabilities and private property, the state has been assigned with full concerns to craft and devise policies to enhance the manufacturing and small business. On their own basis, the basic institutions of a society – family, property and the state – have become stronger and developed.

They are one of the major parameters of development in terms of both the market, and mixed, socially guided economy.

Generating about 25 million jobs and contributing about 12% to the country's gross national product, the small business in the Russian Federation for 15 years of the self-development has acquired a pivotal position in the national economy. The statistics of 2003 show that in St. Petersburg, about 12.5 % of all small enterprises of the country, making goods and services for the sum of more than 80 billion rubles, operate. Their contribution to cumulative tax revenues to budgets of all levels makes up 30%, and their share in the spheres of wholesale–retail trade is 50%, industrial production and construction – 9%, transport – 4%, and research and development – 3 %. The aggregate number of subjects of small business in St. Petersburg exceeds 236 thousand enterprises and businessmen. It has generated more and more job opportunities than its recorded formal employments.

The small sector of the Russian economy already carries out a social and economic role. With its help, key problems of the economy are solved: the market of the food and industrial goods is quantitatively sated, and the free competition has become an element in the sphere of trade, services, transport and industrial production.

The development of small business greatly depends upon the kind of a state policy. Its core task is the creation of favourable legal and administrative conditions for the development of national capital for the major sectors of the national economy.

In 2001, the Government of St. Petersburg accepted the Target Program, that is, the State support for the small business of St. Petersburg, for 2002–2004. For its realisation, three innovative – technological centres, seven subcontractive centres and the centres of business development in five areas of the city have been created, and two exhibitions are carried out to Lenexpo. The small business with its four social sectors has guided the tender under the regional order: the technology of success and an information-analytical infrastructure (newspapers, magazines, radio and TV for the small business).

The first forum of the small and average business of St. Petersburg was passed in April 2003, on which the cooperation agreement on the development and their support for both legislative and executive authority and public associations of businessmen has been signed. The Code of Honour of the Businessman of St. Petersburg has also been accepted.

From 2000 to 2002, the actual volume of the city fund of support for small business has grown 2 to 3 times (from 27.5 to 62.4 million rubles), that correspondents with the growth in 2 to 1 times of the total sum of tax payments from the subjects of small business for the same period (from 14.3 up to 30.1 billion rubles).

At the same time, certain negative tendencies are marked in the economy of small business and the state policy revolving round it. The rates of growth in case of a number of small enterprises are reduced; their potential in the industrial production, construction, research and development, and high technologies are poorly used. A poor quality of goods, works, services, and a low level of culture and ethics of business have caused for claims and objects on the part of the consumers and society.

The Budgetary-Financial committee of the Legislative Assembly of the city, in search of the clauses (articles) of indemnification of deficiency of the budget of St. Petersburg, has made the decision on the termination (discontinuance) of financing for 2004 (already reduced in 2003 in 2 times from 62.4 to 30 million rubles) of the Target Programme (the state support of small business in St. Petersburg, 2002–2004).

So, for 15 years, there was an economy of small business in St. Petersburg. The nucleus of a class of proprietors working in the market for more than 5–10 years was generated. The level of development of the given sector testifies to the performance of a significant social and economic role by it. Small enterprises operate in all branches, introducing the competition, mobility and elasticity to dynamics (changes) of demand. The incomes of 35% of the population of St. Petersburg are directly connected to the activity of small enterprises. 12 % of the Gross Local Product and 30% of tax revenues are generated in the given sector.

The strategic priorities for the development of St. Petersburg as a multipurpose megacity, the sphere of services, construction, transport, housing and communal services, and tourism demand fuller use of the capital of all patterns of ownership in industrial production, innovations and cultures. The potential of the small businesses in their development is immense. However, the potentialities have not been harnessed. Above the listed circumstances, the state should dictate for a fuller use of the capital, and should develop smooth ways for the competitive advantages of small business in the development of the priority branches and directions of St. Petersburg.

Sometimes, it is easier to reveal problems than to devise ways to carry out their decisions in an effective way. In a prospective series of clauses (articles), the decisions, frameworks, programmes of development and support of small business in St. Petersburg for the period 2005–2010 is offered.

The Branch Analysis of Statistics of Activity of Small Enterprises in St. Petersburg

Payment

From 1998 to 2003, the monthly average wages of the workers of small enterprises in the current prices have grown by 420% (from 874 to 3,666 rubles). The greatest growth has taken place in trade – 735% (from 629 to 4,622 rubles), information services – 681% (from

496 to 2,404 rubles), transport – 508% (from 937 up to 4,758 rubles), industries – 469% (from 1,282 to 6,010 rubles), finance – 390% (from 666 to 3,810 rubles) and construction – 240% (from 1,472 to 3,539 rubles). Leaders on an absolute parameter are industrial and transport agencies (6,010 and 4,758 rubles accordingly).

However, the analysis in real terms (base of 1998) testifies to a considerably more modest dynamics (changes) and other branch leaders on the size of wages. The greatest gain has taken place in trade (146%), finance (114%) and transport (102%). In the other set for the above branches, the growth of wages for five years has on the average made 79% and was in a range of 48–97%. Thus, the statistics register only the so-called "white" wages making it dependent on the branch from 40 up to 60% of a real payment. Law is traced – leaders on a payment (trade, transport and the finance) had a mid-annual growth of wages of 24%, and in the industry, construction, and information technologies – 16%. The break is covered by the big size of the 'grey' salary.

Quantity of Small Enterprises, Total Proceeds and Tax Revenues

For the five years, 1998–2002, the quantity of small business in St. Petersburg grew by 159 %. The mid-annual rate of growth touched 32%. The greatest growth has taken place in public catering (187 %; mid-annual rates of growth have made 37 %), trade (176% and 35% accordingly) and research and development (130% and 26 % accordingly). There was a reduction of 1% in the quantity of small business in industrial production. Marked dynamics (changes) reflect the higher rates of development in trade and public catering, i.e. in spheres of higher speed of the rotation of the capital and the size of profitability.

The volume of manufacture (total proceeds) of small business for the five years grew in the current prices to about 751% (from 111 to 834 billion rubles). The greatest growth is marked in trade

(1,013 %) and industrial production (707 %). In real terms, the growth of volumes of manufacture has taken place in trade (two times) and the industry (1.4 times); a fall in total proceeds is marked in science (44%) and in public catering (440%). High mid-annual rates of growth in real terms in trade (40%) and the industry (28 %) testify to positive dynamics (changes) of economic development of the small business in the city and the growth of the solvent demand of the population. The falling of volumes of proceeds in public catering testifies to the opposite—about an insufficient quantity of small business in this sector, and the low intra-branch competition, allowing the rendering of services with no effective costs and under the prices from a high inflationary component.

The positive changes of tax revenues from the subjects of small business in the budgets of all levels for the period 1998–2002 (growth has made 25%) occurred as a result of a tax policy of decrease (reduction) in rates and application of the simplified system of the taxation. In 2002, the expert system of taxation was passed on 23,150 quantities of small business (or 17% of all-quantity small enterprises of the city); from them in trade 13,025, and the industries 2,125 of the total small business.

At the same time, a stated by expert estimations, in a shadow revolution, there are great volumes of manufacture. The branch picture of this revolution is not identical – tourism, up to 95%, trade about 50–60%, public catering around 45–55%, transport (passenger transportation – 60%, cargo – 20–30%), construction (private or individual repair of habitation, offices, construction of summer residences, houses) – 60–80%; contract – 30%), and industrial production about 20–30%.

Low rates of growth of small business in the industries and research and development (for five years there was even a reduction of their number in the industry around 1%) gives rise to, in particular, the branch distribution of tax privileges. In 1998, the share of privileges for the people working in the industry, made 23%, research and development – 2% and trade – 37%. In 2002, the branch distribution of privileges essentially did not change: the industry – 9.4%, science – 4.7%, and trade – 35%. If for five years there was a relative reduction of tax privileges for small business in industrial production in a total sum of privileges it is not necessary to speak about a stimulating tax policy in this sphere.

Employment in Small Enterprises

For five years (1999–2003), employment in SMALL BUSINESS has grown by 0.8% and has made 623 thousand persons employed. Moreover, in comparison with its peak growth in 2000–2001, it was reduced to 0.8 %. Low rates of growth of employment confirm the following basic thesis. The internal areas of the city that stand as opportunities and resource hubs for the development of small business, giving rise to employment potentials, are exhausted (settled).

The dynamics (changes) of branch concentration of labour for five years has not changed. In trade, 48 % are occupied in small business, in the industry; 17% are concentrated, and in the construction sector 16% are placed.

At the same time, the rates of growth of employment in these branches testify to having a growth of output in these sectors of the economy. For five years, the number of workers grew in small business – in transport 70%, industry – 37%, construction – 33%, information service – 12%, and research and development – 10%. In trade, employment was simultaneously reduced to 21% and in the sphere of the finance – 60%. The decrease (reduction) in number of workers in trade speaks of the occurrence and expansion of networks of department stores and reduction in the number of trading booths. In this sphere, of the economy there come modern forms of trade and processes of concentration and centralisation of capital.

A Comparative Analysis of Development of Small Business in St. Petersburg and the USA

Branch structure in Russia and St. Petersburg reflects an initial stage of accumulation of the private (individual) capital. In trade, 46% and 50% of all small business is concentrated, while in the USA about 30% are concentrated accordingly. The concentration of small business in the USA is higher than the parameters of St. Petersburg—in the industry (12% against 9%), construction (16% against 9%), and consumer services (25% against 5%). If a break in the industry and construction is insignificant, in the sphere of services it is huge. The comparative analysis of branch distribution of small business shows directions of stimulation of its development – consumer services, industry and construction.

Comparability is one of the characteristics of the lines of parameters for the activity of small business in the USA and St. Petersburg. In particular, the size of the starting capital makes for US$ 20,000–25000; the concentration of people occupied in the enterprises number about 1–4 persons (50–60%).

At the same time, the majority of parameters are qualitatively multifarious that reflect a different stage and levels of small business in different countries. So, the revenue of the American small business which is included in the National Federation of Independent Business, makes for US$ 3,50,000 (though mid-annual profitableness of small business in the USA is US$ 40,000), and in St. Petersburg small business makes for US$ 1,10,000, a share of small business in manufacturing of gross local product – accordingly 51% and 12%, charges on financial and legal services – US$ 25,000 and US$ 200, the number of small businesses on 1,000 persons – 74.2% and 20.1%, mid-annual rates of growth of small business in 1991–2001 – 8% and 12.3%, and a share of small business in the manufacture of innovations – 55% and 5%.

The analysis of interrogation of heads of municipal and territorial formations (educations) and directors of the small and large enterprises:

Results of the questioning of heads of small enterprises

376 heads of the small enterprises working in the sphere of services (36.8%), industry (28.9%), trade (23.6%), research and development (9.2%) and construction and finance (6.6%), participated in the interrogation and these stimulating samples of the respondents reflect and confirm the tendencies of the development of branches and interests of small business.

Among the respondents and the enterprises existing in the market for more than 10 years, (34.2%) dominates the number of the occupied 5–20 persons that testifies to the experience of management in conditions of initial accumulation of the capital, the financial crisis of 1998–1999 and the gravity of plans for the further development of business.

Interrogation has revealed and justified the reasons of preservation of business within 5–10 years among which competent marketing and financial strategy (57.9%) and uniqueness of business (35.5%) are marked.

The principal causes for the delay of the further development (progress, growth and diversification) of small business in St. Petersburg, according to the interrogation, are the instability of the tax laws (48.7%) and a low level of development of an infrastructure for the support of small business (28.9%).

At the same time, the policymakers have not arrived at a common platform in their points of view to devise policies to develop infrastructure for the support and development of small business and on the other, certain ideas, points of views and approaches have dominated over others. In the stated points of view, it is possible to allocate the following: the participation of small business in industrial exhibitions, the creation of informative–analytical systems (about the markets, and the normative–legal base) and the simplification of procedures of crediting. In the state policy, the centrality is concerned with the place, role and development of small business and in measures of support to it.

As prime measures of support for small business, respondents have the specified necessity of perfection in a tax policy (24.9%); in particular, the reduction of the tax burden (11.8%) and the granting of tax privileges (5.2%).

The second group of offered (suggested) measures is dominated by offers "to not prevent" (11.8%), information support (6.6 %) and reduction in the price of a rent (3.9%).

Results of questioning of the heads of the large enterprises

92 heads of the large enterprises representing the industry participated in the interrogation. The purpose of questioning was to garner views for the enhancement of the conditions of expansion of cooperation and communications (connections) between both large and small enterprises.

During the time of interrogation, it appeared that the directors of the large enterprises are not ready to systematise a condition of expansion of cooperation and communications (connections) with the small enterprises.

Obviously, the large enterprises yet do not consider (examine) small enterprises as worthy business partners. Over time, among the possible (probable) forms of cooperation can be dominated with leasing the equipment (80%).

Results of questioning of heads of territorial managements and municipal formations (educations) of administrative areas of St. Petersburg

Interrogation has shown the absence of a dominance of respondents in ordering problems for the development of small business in various areas of the city.

During that time too, the absence of the information in MCP, a subject of conduct and, hence, in the analysis of the segments of the consumer market, has not prevented the respondents to specify those sectors of economy which should be developed with the help of small business. This list is dominated with household and social service, construction and housing and communal services.

The question on the transfer of a part of functions of the city to the local self-government institutions for the effective development of small business in the area has revealed the following offers:

- The organisation of trade, consumer services and public catering;
- Granting of independence to MO in questions of privileges;
- Registration of businessmen without the organisation of the legal person;

Foreign experience of the state development and regulation of small business

Role and place of small business in the economy of the countries of the OEDC

The 1990s have been characterised by two essentially new phenomena in the economic sphere, e.g. globalisation and the intensive formation of a post-industrial technological development. Despite the known fears of the World Association of the Small and Average Enterprises, the International Congresses on Small Business, National Federations of Independent (Small) Business, and small enterprises of the EU, Japan, the USA, and the Great Britain, they have accepted new calls to what positive dynamics (changes) of their development testifies.

The small business has confirmed that it is one of the viable and dynamically developing spheres of economy of the countries of the Organization of Economic Cooperation and Development (OEDC unites the 29 most advanced countries of the world). Small enterprises make up 50–60% of the gross national product, and their share in an aggregate number of employment makes up 50–80%, and in export, proceeds of 25% with dynamics (changes) of growth of 1% in one year).

The statistical data presented in Table 1 testify to a fundamental role of small business in the social and economic life of the countries that is determined by objective laws. Small forms of business give to economy flexibility and mobility, and focus on demand. Their high elasticity is caused by its ability to structure and cause technological shifts. These qualities help the mass development of the sector and certain financial supports enable it to save up not only for overcoming the deficiency of the market but also for diversifying its other segments and for improving technological and innovative skills. The given thesis proves to be a true experience of Germany, Japan, South Korea, Spain and the USA.

Particularly in the USA, small enterprises make innovations in two times more than large enterprises, and the cost of production on one borrowed (occupied) on the enterprises from one up to four persons makes for US$ 31,748 per one thousand, and in firms, its number is more than five hundred persons – US$ 16,241. High economic efficiency is caused not only by smaller costs regarding an overhead charge, but also by relative increase in a share of complex (difficult) works (40.2 % of exports in the field of high technologies are concentrated in small businesses of the USA).

The sector of small business in conditions of its transition to a post-industrial stage of development and globalisation of economy (the open economy aggravates a competition) has shown a high survival rate and dynamism of self-development in the 1990s. So, for the period 1991–2001, the annual gain of small enterprises made in England for 1.1%, France – 1.5%, Germany – 3%, and the USA – 8%, i.e. on the average 3.4% of these four countries. In this background, the mid-annual rate of growth of small business in St. Petersburg in the industry, transport and construction sectors is about 1.7% and they are the indirect certificate of presence of barrier to expansion in the given branches of this sector of the economy.

Despite the distinctions in different countries in reference to the classification of the enterprises of small business, their number on 1,000 persons changes within the limits of 50–70 (in the countries of the EU – 45, Japan – 49, and the USA – 74.2). the parameters of Russia (6 small businesses on 1,000 persons) and St. Petersburg (20.1) testify, on the one hand, about the non-uniformity of the development of small business in the country, and on the other, testify to a serious backlog of this sector in comparison to the countries of the OEDC.

For subjects of small business of the EU and the USA, typically, an equal distribution of the enterprises (10–15%) on a scale of the revenue proceeds is – the income of US$ 51,000 up to US$ 1,00,000 (12.5 %) of the enterprises, from US$ 1,00,001 up to US$ 2,00,000 – 17%, from US$ 2,00,001 up to US$ 3,50,000 – 15%, from US$ 5,00,001 up to US$ 1,00,000 – 14.5%, and from US 10,00,001 up to US$ 30,00,000 – 13 %.

In spite of this fact, the size of the starting capital in small business, for example, in the USA (70% of the enterprises begin the business with US$ 20,000) and St. Petersburg is approximately identical (in trade and construction – US$ 25,000, and services – US$ 20,000 – US$ 15,000). However, the proceeds from the activity of the small enterprises are not comparable to the manufactured products of high technologies. 80% of small enterprises of St.

Petersburg have annual proceeds from 1,00,000 to 2,00,000 USD that testify to the small added cost and low purchasing capacity of the population.

It is a characteristic phenomenon that for a branch accessory (belonging) of the small business of the countries of OEDC, there is a concentration of small business in the four sectors of the economy: consumer services (25%), retail trade (24%), construction (16%) and industrial production (12%). In the second echelon, there are the enterprises working in three sectors of the economy – finance, insurance and operations, with the real estate being 8%, wholesale trade (5%) and municipal services (3%).

A comparative analysis of a branch accessory (belonging) of small enterprises of St. Petersburg confirms that the small business in Russia still is at the initial stages of the development. 51% of the enterprises are concentrated in trade. In the sphere of consumer services, a share of small enterprises is very less corresponding to the parameters of the countries of the OEDC which is more by five times – in the industry – 44%, construction – 25% and finances – 50%.

Infrastructure for support of small business in the countries of the OEDC

As an economic system, small business possesses its own infrastructure. The given term has appeared in the beginning of the twentieth century. As an infrastructure in a broad sense, it has begun to refer to the set of the branches promoting the production of goods.

The infrastructure for the development and support of small business represents the systems of the state, public, commercial and non-commercial organisations providing the development of small business and rendering to it on a preferential or paid basis the services in financial, educational, consulting, information and technological spheres.

This system includes the specialised institutes: state – (administration of small business funds), private (individual) (associations of independent businessmen, funds, module guarantee, mortgaging, credit; the insurance organisations, the leasing companies, technoparks, business incubators, industrial zones, ranges, educational, consulting, information structures, etc.) and mixed institutes. The basic elements of an infrastructure are presented in Table 1.

Table1. Basic Elements of an Infrastructure of Small Business

Institutes	*The Maintenance (Contents) of Programmes of Support*
Funds of support of SMALL BUSINESS and other financial institutions (National banks, cooperative banks, special banks, Society of Medical Credit)	Soft loans, warranting, selective indemnification of interest rates
The leasing companies	Leasing of the equipment
Business – incubators, technoparks, industrial ranges	Granting of premises (rooms) and the ground areas, the equipment, services
Agencies and the centres of development of SMALL BUSINESS	The information, consultation, training, exhibitions, business contacts
The mass-media focused on business	Propagation of SMALL BUSINESS, creation of favourable public opinion, the information, advertising

The purpose of formation of an infrastructure for small business is the creation of favourable conditions for its development by the maintenance of complex and address support of CPM. Through an infrastructure, the state support for small business is provided, and the feedback allows focusing all systems on real needs (requirements) and interests of small business.

Structural state support in the countries of OEDC is submitted in Table 2.

Table 2. Structure of System of the State Support of Small Business in the Countries of the OEDC

System of the state support of small business		
Conceptual programme block	The organisational–resource block	The functional block
The concept of support	State bodies	Regulation of factors of an environment of SMALL BUSINESS
Programmes and subroutines of development and support of small business	Objects of an infrastructure of small business	Address and target support of SMALL BUSINESS
The purposes of support	Bodies of public support of small business	Monitoring of programmes of support of SMALL BUSINESS and their updating
Methods, forms, mechanisms, tools of regulation, stimulation and support		

The conceptual programme block is focused on the realisation of a principle of a programme-target orientation. The organisational resource block creates an infrastructure for the support of small business. The functional block focuses on the creation of a viable environment, which is vital for the functioning of small business (for example, the system of cooperation communications (connections) between large and small business). The functional block is always connected to address and target the movement of resources and services in a concrete direction of the CMP. More often, it is carried out through specially created institutes of an infrastructure of support. At last, for the purposes of monitoring the constant activity for the perfection of the system of support of small business controls, the state structures (*US SBA*), and associations of small business (*US NFIB*) are created.

Between state bodies, there is a division of powers on the regulation and support of activity of small business.

Support at a national level is reduced to the performance of four basic functions:

- Development of uniform principles of the organisation of small business;
- Definition of priorities of state help for small business;
- Formation of state budgetary fund and its distribution in regions;
- Coordination in activity of various institutes of the government, interested in the development of small business.

The state support on regional, city and municipal levels carries out ten functions:

- Direct subsidisation of small business (especially in agriculture, research and development);
- Preferential crediting and selective warranting of credits;
- Preferences under the taxation;
- Transfer of a part of the state property;
- Granting of favourable state orders;
- The simplified procedures of registration and licensing of activity;
- Legal and economic preferential consulting;
- Assistance on professional training and expansion of the networks of the educational centres for small business;
- Maintenance of legal privileges of enterprising activity in free economic zones;
- Assistance and coordination of activity of the unions and associations of independent businessmen.

The experience of the countries of the OEDC shows that four directions of the state support of business are the most effective: economic, social, legal and ideological.

Within the framework of these directions, and the practice of state regulation and stimulation of business, the small business has developed its basic forms of support for stimulating its economic growth (See Table 3).

Table 3. Forms of State Support of Small Business in the Countries of the OEDC

Forms of Support	Tools
Financial	The state target programmes, warranting of loans, granting of preferential and gratuitous grants and participation in formation of funds of credit and financial and investment organisations.
Management	Consultation preparation, retaining of personnel information services, financing and participation in the work of the organisations, rendering direct support for SMALL BUSINESS, creation of favourable conditions and the help in development and transfer of new technologies.
Tax policy	Preferential system of taxation (the profit tax, tax to employment), the accelerated amortisation and exception of depreciation charges of object of the taxation
Antimonopoly policy	Maintenance of fair and equal rights of conditions of contract attitudes (relations) and transactions under the state orders, and also maintainance of good relations between large and small enterprises, creating measures for the prevention (warning) of delays of payments on the part of the large enterprises to small contract organisations for the prevention of bankruptcy of small business enterprises.

The special system for the support of small business is allocated (removed) to the financial mechanism including methods, levers, legal, normative and supply with the information of the CMP.

Bank crediting of small business in the countries of the OEDC: Problems of adaptation of experience

The ideas of cooperation of S. Furje and R. Ouena of the nineteenth century have been to the full extent putting forth the importance of crediting farmers and handicraftsmen. In the nineteenth and twentieth centuries the handicraftsmen, farmers, fishermen, woodcutters and wood workers in the absence of guarantees under commercial credits, began to unite the liquid means and savings with the purpose of mutual crediting on the basis of mutual trust. This way of crediting was caused by two reasons. Firstly, mutual credit is the simplest way of taking decisions in case of a problem of the starting capital and shortage of turnaround means. Secondly, being professionals, they felt that they knew it better than others about the conjuncture and tendencies of the market.

Within hundred years of its development, mutual and cooperative crediting has kept the status of the basic creditors of small business. The reason for that is covered in adherence to a principle of wide decentralisation and democratisation. In the chapter (head) of everyone of "local cash department" there is an administrative advice (council) from professionals of a concrete segment of the market. Subsequently, in all countries, the majority of boards of these local cash departments began to feel the necessity in federal, and then the national bodies, for the centralisation of accommodation of liquid means.

It is not casual that networks of mutual and cooperative crediting became national and were beyond the initial sector of the market and offered an entire spectrum of bank service without any dependence on the size of the capital of the client–borrower. At the same time these networks at operation with small enterprises use privileges of federal and regional authorities.

The mutual crediting of a network has shown aspiration in its association with the framework of Europe. So, the French Cooperative Bank for agriculture, the Dutch Rabo bank, the German DG Bank, the Belgian Spaar bank, the Austrian bank RTSB and the Finnish Obo Bank have signed the frame agreement on partnership.

Let's consider Some Country-Specific Networks:

France: In this country, there exist four kinds of mutual and cooperative crediting: a huge Agricultural bank of mutual credit, a network of National banks for crediting handicraftsmen, the small and average enterprises (the network of National banks totals 31 regional banks), the Bank of the Mutual credit in Alsace (about 3,000 mutual cash departments and about 5 million members), and at last, the Cooperative Credit and the Sea-Cooperative Credit. All these banks had a monopoly for residual loans for the clients of the market (so, the National banks had monopoly for easy loans to city handicraftsmen, and the Bank of the Mutual Credit possessed monopoly for free percentage incomes). All these banks for a long time have been released (exempted) from profit taxes. Now, these monopolies are cancelled. Banks have left the limits of the initial markets and have a set of clients from among the small and average enterprises and private persons.

Germany: In the middle of the nineteenth century, Fridrickh Raiffaizen, the burgomaster of district Vajerbush, in order to fight against famine, created the first grain association, which built a cooperative bakery on the loan, and provided grains to the community through wood mortgage. So, the main principles of the mutual credit such as Rajffajzen's, based on an idea of religious solidarity and the unlimited responsibility of members of the company, have been incorporated.

Since then in Germany, there have been two competing networks of the mutual and cooperative credit: a rural network of "Cash Department of Rajfajzen" and a city network, "National Banks". But now in Germany, one finds 10 thousand establishments and 11 million members. The principles of work of these networks were pulled together. The clearing of calculations between cash departments is made by five central banks (*Raiffaizen-Bayerische Zentralbank, SZG Bank, Norddeutsche Genossenschaftbank, Westdeutsche Genossenschafts Zentralbank, and Deutsche Genossenschaftbank – DG Bank*). The cumulative activities of the banks, which are included in networks, make about 1 billion euro.

Italy: Cooperative banks are more poorly advanced in Italy than in France and Germany. Nevertheless, 129 national banks serve handicraftsmen and small enterprises (more than 1 million people).

England: Three kinds of credit institutions are engaged in providing credits to small and average business: the commercial banks, the specialised credit establishments (Industrial-Trading Financial Corporation, created in 1945, the Bank of England and clearing banks), and cooperative banks (for example, the Cooperative Bank has more than 100 branches and 1.5 million clients).

In Commission Banks, the specialised branches under the brave capital for the small and average enterprises, for example, the National Westminster Grow Options Ltd., have been created. Cooperative banks have received a smaller development in comparison to continental Europe as the national network of the mutual and cooperative credit has not historically been created.

The specialised credit institute, "The Finance for the Industry", which swallowed up the "Industrial Trading Financial Corporation", gives small business credits from 8 to 15 years for a total sum up to £1 one million. However, the volume of preferential crediting in the given financial institute is insignificant.

Within the framework of rendering assistance to the development of regions, three regional financial establishments work: Kosira in England, the Scottish agency on development, and the Welsh agency of development. They give mid-term and long-term credits to the small and average enterprises in the regions.

The USA: The cooperative movement in banking, created in 1909, has not reached (achieved) big successes. But in the 1990s, on a background of lack of relative interest of Commission Banks in fine accounts and credits, the credit unions have started to compete with banks seriously. Since 1974, the movement has authorised them to open check accounts under per cent (interests). In total, it has 20 thousand credit unions. They have no vocational counselling and orientation on crediting private persons, and also on small business.

In 1953, the Administration of Small Business, having 15 regional agencies, was created. The administration is the federal organisation giving credits to the small and average enterprises, and rendering to them services in the field of innovations. Credits are provided on 25–30% to the borrowers.

There are specialised banks (the Bank of Development of Industrial Competitiveness and the Bank for Industrial Hypothecary Association), that guarantee bank loans to the companies, give plans to increase productivity, suggests innovations and plans for carrying out research and development.

Japan: In the fiftieth year (by analogy to the American Administration of Small Business), the Corporation of Small Business – a public institution, oriented to small and average business has been created. There has also been created a "National Financial Corporation", focusing on family businesses, and the

Central Cooperative Bank for financing cooperative societies in industry and trade. Thus, small business in the countries of OEDC has historically been financed through cooperative banks and mutual unions.

At the same time, large commercial banks also work with small accounts and microcredits, or within the framework of the state target programmes, or create special branches for the brave capital and innovations (the branch of National Westminster Bank in Manchester provides strategy for the development of the city, innovation of new ideas and high technologies).

For the financial support of small business banks along with the capital of the state, they have essential value for crediting the industry and trade and for encouraging investments. So, the French banks offer national credit, the credit on the equipment for the fine and average enterprises, finance the fine and average enterprises in the sphere of industrial production, and also finance business in the sphere of hotels, cafe and restaurants. These banks give soft loans, and also guarantee the credits which are given out by other banks. In a number of the countries (the USA, Japan)the specialised state institutions are created for the support of small business.

To a question on the adaptation of the experience of the countries of the OEDC in conditions of Russia and St. Petersburg:

A mechanical carry-out of experience of foreign countries to Russia is capable of deforming the social and economic nature of the institutions and tools of support of small business, and can be negatively reflected in small business.

In Russia, traditions of cooperative movement and societies of mutual credit are broken. the associations of small enterprises are not yet ready to proceed for the creation of a regional and national network of the cooperative banks, i.e., the specialised banks for small business.

Therefore, the most simple way for the maintenance of financial needs (requirements) of small business is the mechanism of guaranteeing fund support to the small business through commercial banks, and also a selective indemnification of interest rates (up to 25%) on crediting those small enterprises which specialise in the field of industrial production, innovations, high technologies, construction, tourism, services, culture and sports.

The second clause (article) is devoted to the analysis of the efficiency of the state policy in the field of tax regulation, ownership, an investment climate, the real estate, the administrative barriers, the financial- credit infrastructure, the productivity of budgetary measures of support of small business, and the third – to the concept and the programme of development and support of small business in St. Petersburg till 2010.

Table 4. **Distribution of Small Business on the Branches of eEonomy in the USA and the Russian Federation, St. Petersburg (%), 2001**

№	Branch	THE USA	Russia	St. Petersburg
1	Mining industry	2-7	4	
2	Agriculture	6	1.6	
3	Construction	12-16	14.4	9
4	Industrial production	12	15.3	9
5	Transport	2	2.2	4
6	Communication	2	0.4	2
7	Trade, including Wholesale Retail	7-520-24	46.3	50
8	Finance, Insurance, Operations with the Real estate	8	1.5	4
9	Consumer Services	41-25	10	12
10	RESEARCH AND DEVELOPMENT	2	4	
11	Public Health Services	2	4	
12	Other kinds of commercial activity	8	0.3	2

* Source: The Russian statistical year-book: The Statistical Collection /Goskomstat of Russia. – M, 2002. – With 320; NFIB 107th Congress, 2002. – W., 2002. – P.5.

** The first figure for a range of the data on the USA – the Bureau of Statistics of the State Department, USA; the second – sample of members of the National Federation of Independent Business, USA.

Table 5. A Branch Accessory (Belonging) of the Enterprises of Small Business in the National Federation of Independent Business, USA (NFIB)*

Branch	NFIB	St. Petersburg **
Agriculture	6	
Construction	15	9
Finance	6	4
Manufacturing Industry	11	9
Retail Trade	21	38
Services	24	5
Transport, Communications	3	4
Mining Industry	8	
Other	6	2

* Source: NFIB 107th Congress, 2002.-W., 2002. – P.5. ** Given (Data) КЭРППиТа

Table 5.1. Employment at the Enterprises of Small Business of Members of the NFIB and Subjects of Small Business of Saint Petersburg (in %)*

Employment, People	NFIB	St. Petersburg **
1	12	
2	14	
3-5	28	5.2
6-9	16	
10-14	10.5	
15-19	5	48.7
20-30	7	
31-50	4	22.4
51-100	2	14.5
More than 100	1.5	

* Source: NFIB 107th Congress, 2002. – W., 2002. – P.5.

** Source: the Data of interrogation of Open Company "INSEI"

Table 5.2. The Revenue (Total Proceeds) of the Members of the NFIB and the Enterprises of the Small Business of St. Petersburg (%)*

The revenue, ($)	NFIB	The Enterprises of Small Business of St.Petersburg **
Less than 50000	6.5	5
51000-100000	12.5	7

101000-200000	17	25
201000-350000	15	45
351000-500000	9	18
501000-1000000	14.5	
1000100-3000000	13	
3000100-10000000	7	
More than 10000001	3	
NA	2.5	

* Source: NFIB 107th Congress, 2002. – W., 2002. – p.5. ** A source: the Data of Open Company "INSEI"

Table 5.3. Parameters of Development of Small Business in the USA, the Russian Federation, Saint Petersburg (%)*

No	Parameters	THE USA	Russia	St. Petersburg
1	The starting capital, $ 5000150002000025000	10% of 70 %	60%	Hi-Tech Services, Trade, Construction
2	The revenue, $	40000	25000	110000
3	Workplaces, people 1-45-910-19 from above 20	60% of 18% of 11%	5% of 25% of 30% of 40	5% of 20% of 30% of 45%
4	Share of small business in manufacture of innovations, %	55 (in 2 times it is more than at the large companies)	3 %	5 %
5	Concentration of experts in area hi-tech in small business, %	40.2	11%	15%
6	Share of SMALL BUSINESS in production by a private sector, %	50		
7	Share of small business in employment in non-agricultural private sector, %	52		
8	Share of small business in gross national product	51	12%	12%
9	Share of small business in opening new workplaces, %	60.2%	20%	35%

10	Mid-annual charges of small business on the lawyer, financial advisers, the insurer, $	25000	200	300
11	Tax payments on the person in one year, $	7000		
	Cost of production on 1 borrowed (occupied): small business with number 1-4 persons, $ software more than 500 persons., $	3174816241	250	440
13	Charges of small business on the maintenance (contents)1 borrowed(occupied), % from proceeds	19		
14	Number of small business on 1000 person of the population: the USA of EU Japan	74,24549,6	6	23
15	Annual gain of small business in 1991-2001, (in %) in the USA, England, Germany and France	81,131,5	The industry, transport, construction – 1.7, trade – 6	12.3 Industry – 5.9
16	Quantity of small business, one million	10	0.9	0.235 (including businessmen without formation (education)

* Source: NFIB 107th Congress, 2002. – Washington, 2002. – P. 3-7; Small Business Economic Trends/NFIB. – 2002, Jan. – P.12-16.

** Source: the Data of interrogation of Open Company "INSEI", given(data) www.cedipt.ru/

Appendix 1

Classification of small enterprises in different countries:
According to the internal structure and environment of small business, four groups can be formulated by the character of productions (the branch approach), by specificity of management, by a condition of the limited resources (personnel, material, financial), and by the influence of external factors (legal regulation, a tax and customs policy.

In the countries of the EU and the USA, quantitative criteria are usually used for determining the character of the sizes of small enterprises. This set of parameters is applied: number borrowed (occupied), volume of an annual turnover, the size of the authorised capital, a share of participation in the authorised capital, the enterprises belonging to bodies of the state (municipal) authority and management, to other enterprises, the organisations and physical persons.

Approaches to the definition of parameters of small business depend on a level of economic development of the country, market conditions and a phase of a cycle, traditions, ideology and a macroeconomic policy (politics) concerning the given sector of economy.

Table 5.4. The Use of Quantitative Parameters of Reference of the Enterprises to a Class of Small in Different Countries*

Parameters	THE	Japan	GERMANY	England	France	Italy
USA						
Number borrowed (occupied)	+	+	+	+	+	+
Sales volume	+	+	+	+	+	–
Volume of the	+					
revenue						
Degree of participation in the capital of other firms	–	–	+	–	–	–

* Source: A.O. Small's "Pancakes Business: Organizational and Legal Bases of Activity" – M.: the Axis – 89, 1997.

In the European countries, the USA and Japan, there is a wide scattering of quantitative criteria of small business, but on an average, the small business carries the enterprises with numbers up to 500 persons (among them, 1–20 persons – craft; 20–99 – small; 100–500 – average).

Table 5.5. Classification of Small and Average Enterpreses in Foreign Countries and Russia*

The country	Criteria of the enterprise
Belgium	Annual turnover – less than 0.47 million euro, the revenue – less than 3.4 million euro, active – less than 1.6 million euro, number – no more than 50 persons in the industry and 40 persons in trade.
England	Annual turnover – not more than 2.3 million euro, the revenue – not more than 1.5 million euro, number – not more than 50 persons in the industry and 40 persons in trade.
GERMANY	Annual turnover – not more than 50 million euro, number – not more than 500 borrowed (occupied).
France	Parameters for the craft enterprises: number – not more than 10 Borrowed (occupied) and not more than 5 members of family participating in business
Sweden	Number – not more than 200 borrowed (occupied). For classification are used a number (line) of other parameters: *stages of growth (initial, survival, expansion) *Geographical segment (local, regional, national scales) *Branch *Specified proprietors (women – businessmen) *Typologies of problems (financing)
EU	*The average enterprises:* an annual turnover – less than 16 million euro currency of balance – less than 8 million euro number – from 50 up to 250 person *Small enterprises:* an annual turnover – less than 4 million euro currency of balance – less than 2 million euro, number – up to 50 persons
USA	Small enterprises: *Management with independent proprietors* do not borrow (occupy) a leading position in the market. Quantitative criteria, the Administration of small business in the USA for each branch establishes: *Agricultural facilities (an economy) – an annual turnover $3.5 million *Construction – from 7 up to $17 one million * extraction of minerals – number borrowed (occupied) up to 500 person * the industry – 500 person (in separate branches from 750 up to 1000 person) * transport – up to 500 person or an annual turnover $3,5 one million* wholesale trade – up to 100 person or an annual turnover $3,5 one million* services – an annual turnover US$ 3.5 one million (in separate branches up to US$ 13.5 million)

Japan	*Manufacturing industry and transport:* number – up to 300 persons, the authorised capital – up to 100 million yens, *Wholesale trade:* number – up to 100 persons, the authorised capital – up to 30 million yens, *Retail trade and sphere of services:* number – up to 50 persons, the authorised capital – up to 100 million yens
Russia	*The industry, construction, transport:* number – up to 100 persons of research and development and an agriculture: number – up to 60 persons, Wholesale trade: number – up to 50 persons, Retail trade and consumer services: number – up to 30 persons.

Table 5.6. Employment at the Enterprises of the Various Sizes as a Whole on the Economy*

The countries	Less than 20 people	20-99 people	100-499 people	500 and more
THE USA	26.9	29.0	23.9	20.2
Japan	49.4	27.6	11.2	11.7
GERMANY	27.3	22.4	22.6	27.7
Italy	50.7	21.7	14.9	12.7
Switzerland	42.6	26.7	19.6	11.1

*Source: *Small Business in Russia/* Avilova, A.B., Alimova T.A. and other editors T.G. Dolgopjatova. – M.: Konseko, 2002. With 14.

Table 5.7. Small Business in the Developed Countries and Russia*

The countries	It is borrowed (occupied) SMALL BUSINESS in one million people	Share of SMALL BUSINESS in an aggregate number borrowed (occupied), %	Share of SMALL BUSINESS in gross in national product, %
England	13.6	49	50-53
GERMANY	18.5	46	50-54
Italy	16.8	73	57-60
France	15.2	54	55-62
EU	68.0	72	63-67
USA	70.2	54	50-52
Japan	39.5	78	50-55
Russia	9.2	11	10-11

15

External Energy Policy of Russia

V. N. Kharlamova and N. A.Philimonova

At the end of the twentieth century and the beginning of the twenty-first century, the role of interstate interaction and international regulation in the sphere of energy got strengthened and the international energy policy got activated. At the same time, a new sphere of diplomacy – energy diplomacy – took birth.

The demand for energy, the main sources of which are related to non-reusable ones, would rise during the next two decades more than 2% annually. In absolute figures, the international requirement would increase from 9 billion tonne oil equivalent in 2000 to more than 13 billion tonnes in 2020. About two-thirds of the demand then would be met by oil and gas.[1]

Export–import relations between energy producers and consumers go beyond an exclusive economic arena. Energy resources, first of all oil, turn into some kind of indicator of the level of political–economic integration between states and as a serious foreign policy instrument. There is a direct dependency between the price policy of the main energy resources and the current state of international relations and global stability.

In these conditions, an optimisation of the integration process of domestic energy into global energy space is linked to the transition of the country from the role of supplier of raw energy resources to the role of participant in the global transaction of energy with higher value added price, pursuing an independent policy in the international energy markets. It is necessary to strive for a qualitative change of the Russian position in energy cooperation.

Russia, the US and the European Union have crafted new versions of energy strategy that stipulate a new approach to the principles of international cooperation, including cooperation among the countries of G-8. The well-crafted external energy policy would not only help to protect national economic and geopolitical interests in the international energy sphere but also facilitate in ensuring the stability and predictability of the world gas and oil markets, and maintain a wise balance in interests of the major energy producers and consumers. This will also help in creating conditions for a more effective use of modern energy technologies, including the help of foreign investments and the transfer of the fuel and energy complex to an innovation type of development, and the solution of the ecological problems of world energy.

The place of the fuel and energy complex in the Russian economy is determined by, first of all, the huge resource potential of the country. Having 2.4% of the world population, 13% of the world territory, Russia possesses 12–13% predicted fuel and energy resources that include more than 12% proven oil reserves, more than 30% gas deposits and more than the proven coal deposits. Russia produces 23% produced gas, 10% oil, 6% coal and 6% hydroelectocity of the world.[2]

The energy strategy of Russia till the year 2020 says that the energy sector ensures the functioning of all branches of the national economy, facilitates the consolidation of subjects of the Russian Federation, and largely determines the formation of major financial and economic indicators of the country.[3] In 2003, the share of the fuel and energy complex in the total tax collection of the national budget and hard currency reserves constituted 50%.[4]

The significance of the fuel and energy complex as stable source of foreign currency earnings is largely determined by the export of gas, oil and oil products. The export of a large part of energy produced in the country leads to a shortage in the domestic market. Table No.1 shows the export quota in the oil and gas sector.

Table No.1: Export Orientation of Oil and Gas Sector of Russia (% of the production)

	1992	1995	1997	2000	2001	2002	2003	2004
Crude oil	35	41	41.5	42.9	44.2	47.8	50.6	55.2
Natural gas	30	32.2	33	32.5	30.4	30	29.1	30.3

Source: Vneshne ekonomicheski Bulletin, No. 9, 2000, P-23

Considering this role of the fuel and energy complex in the Russian economy, some major conceptual documents on the main principles and orientation to the external political activities of the country in the sphere of energy diplomacy were drafted. These include the Doctrine of Energy Security and the Energy Strategy of Russia upto 2020.

The Doctrine of Energy Security (August 23, 2003) is one of the first conceptual documents on energy stability and security of Russia, related to the domestic and foreign policy of the country.

The external threats to the energy security of the country include an unstable conjecture of global energy prices, discriminatory measures towards the Russian energy resources in the market by certain countries, undesirable steps by certain countries through which the Russian energy is supplied, an illegal collection of Russian energy by transit countries and an active and passive resistance to Russian capital in the energy sphere of the consumer countries.[5]

In order to ensure the energy security in all directions, the Doctrine declares the countries of the CIS, Europe, South and South-East Asia and the Far East as zones of strategic political interests of Russia in the sphere of energy. Stable political and economic relations with countries of these regions are viewed as a factor of energy security. The diversification of supplies and their geographical expansion is considered as an important principle of energy security.[6]

The Energy Doctrine up to 2020 has been drafted by the Government of the Russian Federation and it contains indications of the development of the fuel and energy complex of the country from the point of domestic and foreign policy. This is a conceptual and practical document "concretizing objectives, tasks and major directions of long-term energy policy of the state".[7]

The energy strategy pays special attention to foreign policy in the sphere of development of the Russian fuel and energy complex. The document points out that the external energy policy aims at ensuring a non-discriminatory regime of foreign trade activities in the energy sector in consideration with Russia's admission to the WTO along with the access of the domestic energy companies to the foreign energy markets, financial markets and advanced energy technologies, and also the preservation and strengthening of the Russian position in international energy markets. Providing a comprehensive diplomatic protection to the Russian interests and Russian companies abroad, a active energy dialogue with the European Union, the US, other countries and international organisations, the document has paved new directions and orientations for the foreign policy of the country .

It is necessary to note that out of all the partners of Russia in the negotiations regarding its admission into the WTO, it is the European Union that expressed maximum concern in the gas sphere. The European side advanced the so-called "gas ultimatum of Paskal Lami", without whose implementation the European Union did not give the consent for Russia's admission into the WTO. According to experts, the energy demand was artificially used by the EU as a tactic in the negotiations with the objective of getting serious concessions from Moscow in other areas, particularly in the market of financial services and insurance, by giving concession to Russia on the energy issue. The EU leadership openly linked the issue of Russia's admission into the WTO to the issue of the ratification of the Kyoto Protocol by Russia.

In course of complicated negotiations with the EU delegation, the Russian delegation could remove most of the demands of the "Gas ultimatum". On May 21, 2004, Russia and the EU finally signed the protocol on the completion of bilateral talks regarding Russia's admission into the WTO. During the talks, the Kyoto Protocol, the expansion of the EC and the issue of the European companies' access into the Russian financial, insurance, automobile and aviation markets were bargained. In exchange, the EU withdrew most of its demands on the reform of GAZPROM and the liberalisation of the gas market.

In course of the negotiations with the EU, Russia could remove number of sensitive issues (including the condition for the transit of natural gas through Russian territory) ranging from the sphere of multilateral obligations of Russia in the framework of joining the WTO to the sphere of a bilateral agreement with the EU.

The issue of liberalisation of gas prices in the domestic market emerged as the most acute problem. The Europeans were quite satisfied with the fact that Russia would bring the domestic gas prices more or less in correspondence with the market prices under its Energy Strategy up to 2010. The gas price for the industrial consumers would gradually be increased from the current US$ 27–28 for 1000 cubic metres to US$ 37–42 in 2006 and US$ 49–57 in 2010. Apart from this, the ways for resolving the issues linked to the ensuring of accesses of all the producers, including the foreigners to the major networks, were designed.

It is important to note that Russia has planned a gradual liberalisation of the gas market and created conditions for a market-based price formation in this sphere. As Russia is one of the largest gas producers in the world, its domestic gas prices cannot be expected to be compared with the average European price. It should be noted that the Russian domestic gas prices in 2010 would all the same be two times lower than the prices paid by Germany for gas supplied by the GAZPROM.[8]

The development of a fuel and energy complex largely depends on dominating the direction of the foreign economic policy of the country either towards export orientation or import substitution. In our view, it is good for Russia to have a policy of a rational combination of both the directions as factors for increasing the competitiveness of the national economy. The development of the export potential of fuel and energy sector of the economy as well as its other spheres should be based on the use of a comparative national advantage in the natural resource sphere as well as the competitive advantages based on scientific–technical achievements and innovations.

For the development of an effective energy export, the reduction of cost of production and for ensuring the diversification of its commodity structure and increment of the volume of export with a more value-added price, it is necessary to have several times more investment. The international energy agency has assessed that the investment requirement of the Russian energy sector in the coming 20 years would be to the tune of US$ 160–200 billion.[9] Here along with the steps for improving the investment climate and direct state support to most prospective investment projects, an important role should be played by the development of new forms of international cooperation in energy; first of all, production and scientific–technical cooperation between economic subjects and also the activisation of the creation of joint enterprises and integrated transnational corporations. It is also expedient to activate a sound use of agreements on the production share and concession agreements for the realisation of expensive projects.

Let us look at the major issues and directions of the external energy policy of the Russian Federation through the example of energy dialogue between Russia and the EU. The European direction traditionally occupies a leading place in the sphere of the foreign trade of fuel and energy resources.

The energy cooperation between Russia and the European Union has a strategic significance for both the sides. This is the main source of hard currency for Russia. In the second half of the 1990s, hard currency earnings from the export of oil and gas to Europe constituted 40–60% of the total export earnings of Russia.[10] The main buyers of Russian energy are the member-states of the European Union – 20% of gas consumption and 16% of oil and oil product consumptions of these countries are met by Russian supplies. 53% of the Russian oil exports and 62% of the Russian gas exports go to the EU.[11] 50% of the energy consumption of the new members of the EU is met by Russian supplies.[12]

In the year 2000, the EU became the initiator of drafting a massive cooperation programme with Russia for 20 years in the sphere of energy. The Chairman of the EU, Romano Prodi, proposed for partnership in a significant way. The essence of the proposal was to increase the Russian exports to the EU by one and half times in exchange for investment and technology.

Russian Deputy Prime Minister and Industry and Energy Minister Victor Khristenko from the Russian side and Matias Ruet, General Director of the European Commission, responsible for transport and energy from the EU side, participated in the talks.

In the primary research stage of the dialogue, the EU and Russia created four groups of experts for the study of key sectors representing mutual interest: energy strategy and energy balance; investment; transfer of technology and energy infrastructure; energy efficiency and ecology.[13]

Special attention was given to five major topics in course of the energy dialogue. They were:

- an objective assessment of the possibilities of balanced increment of supplies of all kinds of energy from Russia to the EU in consideration with the necessity to find a concrete solution of issues of ensuring a reliable transit, an equal access to transport systems and markets and the preservation of a system of long-term contracts as the foundation for financing energy projects;
- a complex analysis of significant trade, administrative and investment barriers in the particular area and practical methods of reduction, and also the possibility of reconciling the processes of liberalisation of the energy markets in Russia and the EU;

- the formation of a joint portfolio of concrete inter-regional projects in the sphere of production, distribution and transportation of oil, gas and electricity, which can stimulate European investment in Russia and Russian investment in the EC;
- the expansion of cooperation in the sphere of energy machine-building, and also the creation of a joint centre of energy technology with the objective of application of the modern energy technology in Russia, the harmonisation of technical standards and procedures, and planning of joint investment in electric energy;
- cooperation in the sphere of raising energy efficiency and prevention of changes in world climate on the basis of the Kyoto Protocol, defining an optimal mechanism of regulating these processes and financing corresponding programmes, and drafting a catalogue of joint projects in Russia, financed through a mechanism of joint realisation of the Kyoto Protocol.[14]

The energy strategies of Russia and the EU as a whole present mutually compatible programmes, whose maintenance largely forms the ground for building a systemic energy dialogue, whose importance has been noted in the Energy Strategy of Russia up to the Year 2020[15] as well as in the "Green Book".[16]

The major goals of the EU in the energy dialogue are ensuring the security of energy supplies, the reliability of energy supply in conditions of hard demands of ecology and raising the competitiveness of the European industry. A systemic solution, ensuring the strengthening of the integration of Russia and the EU in mutually beneficial conditions of minimised risks of export and import of energy resources, would correspond to the goals and tasks of the energy policies of Russia and the EU.

The security of supplies has been kept in the first place in the priorities of the European energy policy. The EU priorities include geographical and resource diversification of supplies. The EU develops bilateral relations with major oil-producing countries from different regions, including Lybia, Iran, the Black Sea and the Caspian Sea region. Priority has been given to the relations with Russia, and other countries of the CIS, first of all with Kazakhstan, Azerbaijan and Turkmenistan. In this context, cooperation with exporter countries as well as transit countries within the framework of the Agreement on Energy Charter, designed to create a system of collective energy security in one single geographic region, is important.

The EU demand for Russia to ratify the Energy Charter is the major issue in the Russia–EU energy dialogue. The European Energy Charter was signed at The Hague on December 17, 1991. It was designed as the mechanism of cooperation between Western and Eastern Europe on energy-related issues. The Agreement to the Energy Charter and the related protocol on issues of energy efficiency and corresponding ecological aspects were signed on December 17, 1994 and came into effect in April 1998. 51 countries of Europe and Asia joined the Agreement by 2006. 17 countries and 10 international organisations have an observer status under the agreement. Russia that has signed the agreement but not ratified it, participates in it on a temporary basis. The essence of the agreement has been concentrated in five major directions: protection and encouragement of foreign investments in energy; free trade of energy; freedom of energy transit through pipelines and networks; reduction of unfavourable impact of energy cycle on surrounding areas and mechanism for solution of disputes between states or between investor and the state.

As a whole, the Russian Federation views the Energy Charter as an important instrument of international energy cooperation and confirms its intention to continue to participate in the discussion of a wide range of problems related to the energy transit, trade, investment and energy efficiency within the Charter-based process.

The ratification of the agreement can create favourable conditions for the export of energy from Russia. However, the Charter has a weak mechanism for resolving disputes. There are questions related to customs duty. But the main thing is that the difference on gas transit has not been removed. Negotiations on the issue have been going on for many years, but no compromise has been found so far. The Charter stipulates to provide the foreigners the same kind of conditions that have been given to its own producers, partly an indiscriminatory access to own pipelines. Russia has taken the decision to permit foreign investors to have a share in developing the oil and gas fields. However, the EU wants that Russia should give access to its pipelines. In exchange, the EU is ready to provide access to its domestic distribution markets to GAZPROM. Russia so far refuses the liberalisation of pipelines, which is stipulated in the Agreement on Energy Charter. Khristenko, explaining the position of Russian government on the agreement to the charter, declared that since the EU and Russia are situated in different states of liberalisation of the energy market, the delay in the forward movement of negotiations on the protocol is called for by forces of natural economic reasons.[17] And, Moscow is against the liberalisation of export pipelines.

The ratification of Agreement on Energy Charter can weaken the Russian position, particularly the position of GAZPROM in the European markets and it demands to give access to Russian pipelines to the Central Asian states on subsidised domestic tariffs.

In our view, in the near future, the ratification of the transit protocol and subsequently the Agreement on Energy Charter without any modification can hardly take place. Notwithstanding Russia's firm position on the issue, the EU has s serious interest in preserving and raising the role of Russia as a reliable supplier of oil and gas. Ensuring a steady energy import from Russia would permit a significant reduction of the EU's dependence on energy supplies from the Middle East. In the long term perspective, the EU considers Russia as the most reliable alternative partner. The EU too takes into account Russia's interest in further strengthening this cooperation. Given that the radical restructuring and modernisation of the industry, agriculture and economic infrastructure in Russia will take 20 to 30 years, during this period, the energy export would be the most important source of hard currency earnings, necessary for covering the expenses connected with the import of the Western technology. The Russian strategy for the development of the energy sector envisages the increment of oil and gas production and their export to Europe, the laying of new pipelines not only on its own territory, but also in European countries including those of Scandinavia, the Balkans and the Pireneiski peninsula, the building of sea terminals, etc. According to the forecast, the export of Russian gas to Europe can increase from 167 billion cubic metres in 2001 to 270 billion in 2010, which is 62% higher. The export of the energy resources as a whole would increase from 510 million tonnes of conditional fuel in the year 2000 to 630 million in 2010, which is 23.5% more. The increase in production and export is also expected in the subsequent decade.[18]

Attracting investment is the key question in the energy dialogue. The EU took a necessary political decision on the question. Everything depends on institutional transformation, in every sector including in the oil sector of Russia. The decisions in this sphere are lagging behind. It is necessary that the state should pay more attention to the Fuel and Energy Complex and its institutional reform, and also to changes in the mining and licensing laws.

In the framework of the energy dialogue, both sides pay special attention to the implementation of projects that present mutual interest. This includes projects like the North European gas pipeline, the development of the Shtockman fields, the creation of an additional capacity of the Yamal–Europe gas pipeline, the integration of the oil pipelines of Druzhba and Adriya and the unification of the energy systems of Russia and Europe.[19]

The Shtockman gas field located in the central part of the Barents Sea towards the north-east of the Kola peninsula, is expected to be developed on the basis of production share arrangements. On the basis of production share arrangements, it would be necessary to part with almost 30% of the produced gas for covering the cost. The rest of the gas would be for generating revenue. The Shtockman field is planned to go on production by the year 2010. The cost of the project is estimated at around US$ 19–21 billion.

The specific nature of the project lies in the fact that a significant part of the gas would be sold in the form of CNG, for which a factory has to be built. The annual gas production at the field is expected to be 70 billion cubic metres.[20]

The North Europe gas pipeline was planned in 2002. This project provides for the construction of pipelines through the territory of the Leningrad district and under the Baltic Sea for supplying gas to Great Britain and Germany. The project also stipulates the construction of branch pipelines under the sea for supplying gas to Finland, Sweden and other states. The cost of the project is estimated at around US$ 6 billion.[21]

The realidation of the project would permit to increase Russian gas supplies to the EU and ensure an alternative supply root bypassing Belarus and Ukraine. There are no transit states on its way.

A programme has been drafted to implement different aspects of the project in 2005–2006. 55 billion M3 gas would be annually transported when the project will be complete. The construction of the first part of this pipeline with a length of 2,115 km is expected to be completed by June 2010. By 2012, 30 billion cubic metres of gas would be transported through this pipeline annually. By 2013, the capacity to transport full 55 billion cubic m gas through the pipeline would be built. In September 2005, the GAZPROM Chairman Aleksei Miller signed the order for the transfer of the project into the investment stage of realisation.[22]

The Yamal–Europe gas project, designed to raise the export efficiency of Russian gas to Europe, started its execution from 1994. The project stipulated the building of a gas pipeline from the northern parts of the Tyumen district to Germany through the territory of Belarus and Poland.

The construction of the German and Polish parts is complete and linked to the local gas distribution network. The part of the pipeline from the Nesvizhskaya compressing station has been given for exploitation in the territory of Belarus. The construction of the part from Torzhok, a key element of the unified gas supply system in distributing gas streams coming from West Siberia to the West, is complete.

Some experts doubt the economic effectiveness of the project. It is expected that transport charges would constitute 60% of the end gas price. Alternative routes for supplying gas from Yamal to Europe are under study.

The possibility for the use of the Druzhba pipeline for transporting Russian oil to the Adriatic Sea through the Adriya pipeline is under study. The Druzhba–Adriya pipeline passing through six states must send Russian oil through the shortest way to the Omishal port in the Adriatic Sea. An inter-governmental agreement on the project for uniting the pipelines was signed among Russia, Kharbatia, Ukraine, Belarus, Slovakia and Hungary in 2002 for a period of 10 years. The project includes the building of export routes for the transportation of oil from Russia and other countries of the CIS to the world market that would include North America, bypassing.

The Bofor channel. The total length of the pipeline would be more than three thousand kilometers. It is planned to transport 5 million tonnes of oil annually immediately after its completion, and 15 million tonnes of oil in the mid-term perspective.[23]

At the end of 2003, the Ukrainian parliament refused to ratify the agreement for the integration of the Druzhba and Adriya pipelines, after which it was clear that the start of the international project in the framework of the Energy Dialogue with which Russia has linked its growth of oil export, will be under doubt. Thus, Ukraine ratifying the Agreement on Energy Charter violates one of its most important chapters, which is an agreement on free transit. The unsanctioned collection of gas, its preservation in the gas stores for many years from the 1980s to 2000 along with other unfriendly acts, have all together often led the aggravation of the gas problem between the Russian Federation and Ukraine, and posed a threat to the energy security of West Europe.[24]

From the beginning of 2006, Ukraine that was paying 50 USD for 1,000 cubic metres of gas, after long negotiations, had to pay the international price. The EU–Russia Energy Dialogue envisages an integration of the electro energy markets, which is expected to bring significant benefits for the development of free competition, the strengthening of reliability of energy supply and the creation of new possibilities for cooperation in the sphere of the electro-energy of Russia and the EU.

The draft agreement on trade of nuclear materials has been prepared and is in the stage of discussion. There are not only political and economic barriers but also technical barriers that stand on the way of the integration of energy markets. It must correspond to the standards, and should not go beyond the permissible level of decline from the frequency. A high-quality electro-energy is necessary for unifying the energy systems with parallel work.

Steps taken for a further development of cooperation that would include the activities of the Russia–EU Technological Centre, inaugurated in 2002, the Russian participation in monitoring the energy market, created by the European Commission in 2004, and also the creation of a leading group on energy in the framework of a round-table of industrialists and entrepreneurs of Russia and the EU, are called for promoting a further improvement of the investment climate of Russia and EU and the solution of problematic issues. The Fifth General Report[xxv] of the joint working groups has incorporated directions of further development of the Energy Dialogue between Russia and the EU. It must facilitate a practical realisation of initiatives for creating a common European Space between the EU and Russia. In this connection, the issues creating mechanisms for investment support, energy efficiency, marine security, unification of electro-energy networks and trans-European pipeline systems would have priority significance.

However, at this stage there are several obstacles and unfinished tasks that complicate a significant progress in this direction. Coordinated decisions must be found for such concrete problems as a difference in the legislation and practice, the choice of best mechanisms for the development of the energy market and the ensuring of energy security, a difference in the assessment of long-term risks of the large energy projects and the most suitable methods for their financing.

Notes

1. Sovremeniye mezhdunarodniye otnosheniya and mirovaya politika/ edited by A.B. Torkunov Moscow, < Prosvesheniye > 2004, p-382.
2. Katasonov V.Y , Petrov M.V. , Investotsi v toplivno-energeticheskom komplekce Rossii:osnovniye pokazateli, istochniki I metodi finansirovaniye, Moscow 2003, p-78.
3. Energeticheskaya strategiya rossii ha period do 2020
4. Yusufov I, Russia v mirovou energotike. O strategii razvitiya otechestvenovo TEK / Moravaya Energetocheskaya Politika, 2003 No6 (16)
5. Saligin V.I Safaryan A.B. Energeticheskiye Problemi v mirovou politike./ sovremeniye

mezhdunarodniye otnosheniya I mirovaya politika, edi A.B. Torkunov . M. < Prosvesheniye> . 2004, p. 386 -387

6. www.rusenergy.ru
7. Energeticheskaya strategiya Rossii ha period do 2020
8. Zhiznin S. energeticheskaya Diplomatiya Rossii: ekonomika, politika, praktika. Moscow, 2005 ,p.189
9. Sovremenaya Evropa , 2006 No1, p.81
10. www.minfin.ru
11. energetika : www.delrus.cec.eu.int/ru/p_306.htm
12. Sergeyev P.A. Energetika Evrosoyuza v hachale stoletiya./ Sovremenaya Evropa. No3, 2004,p.86.
13. Press release of secretariate of Energy Charter, Brussels, 16th June,2004
14. The fourth round table of industrialists of Russia and EU// Voprosi Ekonomiki, 2002 No -6
15. "Energy strategy of of Russia up to 2020–Vneshnaya Energeticheskaya Politika" approved by Government of Russia on 28th August, 2003.
16. Final Report of the Green Paper "Towards A European strategy for the security of energy supply," Brussels, 26 July 2002
17. www.arnews.ru/news/606112.html
18. BIKI, 2005, No27,p.14
19. European Union Oniine, http:/europa.eu.int/
20. Ibid.
21. Gazprom, annual report, 2003, p. 61
22. "Conceptual aspects of the North-European Gas Pipeline Project and Stages of its Realization"., www.negp.ru
23. www.kommersant.ru/doc-y.html?docld=633921
24. Ibid.
25. "The EU-Russian Energy dialogue: Fifth Progress Report", presented by Russian Deputy Prime Minister Victor Khristenko and European Commission Director General Francis Lamoureux.

16

Energy Factor in Geopolitics

Valery Egozaryan

The intensive worldwide discussion on energy resources in the course of the last several years speaks about the aggravation of competitive positions between various states and the impacts on the deformation of the entire system of international relations. For a long time, it has been clear that this topic is directly linked to the political issues of security. However, it is increasingly difficult to determine what is primary and what is secondary – politics or economics in each case.

In the case of Iraq, it is possible to talk about primary economic interests, whose realisation was dictated by political goals. All the problems of this country began around 1891 when Sarkis Gulbekiyan, studying various geological data, made an expert assessment about oil reserves in Mesopotamia. All of Iraq's further history was entangled under the pressure of oil located in its earth, and so far has been blessed by continuation for the fourth year of the "Four-Day" war.

The history of Iraq clearly shows that one of the key factors for understanding the contemporary international processes is the realisation of the fact that the world's financial elite, possessing political interest, are capable of going to any extent in the struggle for money and power.

Events in some parts of the CIS, particularly on the territory of the Caucasus and Tans-Caucasus, serve as reverse examples when the political goals determine economic activities.

Few years ago, US Senator Sem Brownbek declared that the "US has huge interests in the Caspian basin, in the countries of Central Asia and South Caucasus, which surrounds it. This is the zone of vital political, economic and social importance for US."

Indeed, all economic competition in the region develops under an active participation of the US. The energy resources of the Caspian Sea have been declared as the main goal. The US as well as many European and Asian countries are keen to have access to Azeri oil and Turkmen gas. All this led to the building of the Baku–Zeikhan Transcaspian oil pipeline.

However, today we can say that the economic goals of US in this region serve as a cover to establish its dominance in international politics. The Baku-Georgia-Zeikhan project, considered as economically non-viable by many experts, bears evidence to the fact it is not economic interest but political interests which are important for the US. That is why the US is ready to fight in this region without bothering about funds.

The hydrocarbon reserves in the Caspian zone are much less than declared. Moreover, it is a difficult project from an extraction and transportation point of view. However, the energy resources of the region have no significance for the US. The region witnesses a fight for influence in the international arena. The increasing demand by Georgia and Western countries for pulling out Russian peacekeeping forces from the region and the Georgian–Ossetian conflict have to be seen in this context.

According to the data of the US government, the potential reserves of the Caspian Sea constitute approximately 186 billion barrels of oil with maximum proven reserves to the tune of 32 billion barrels, whereas proven oil reserves in the Persian Sea constitute 674 billion barrels. Only Saudi Arabia possesses 264.2 billion barrels of proven and 1 trillion barrels of potential oil reserves. If we talk about the Caspian Sea gas reserves, the littoral states like Kazakhstan, Russia, Azerbaijan, Iran, Turkmenistan and Uzbekistan together have proven and potential reserves of 15,848 trillion cubic metres while the proven reserves of the Persian Gulf stand at 54,420 trillion cubic metres.

These figures clearly show that the Caspian Sea cannot be alternative to the Arab oil and gas. That is why one should not think that the US in the future would aggravate its relations with Saudi Arabia, cool its relations with Kuwait and leave Iraq and Iran in peace.

The Caucasus, apart from natural resources, presents a unique transport corridor, connecting Europe with Asia. For Moscow, the moot question is whether this route would go through Russia or go in the southern direction through Turkey and the Trans-Caucasus bypassing Russia. What is important is who would control the transport corridor; whose economy would be benefited and who would be able to dominate the South Caucasus region. This corridor would be useful to transport not only energy resources, different commodities and raw materials but also to move troops quickly in case of requirement. For Russia, the Caucasus corridor is natural and the nearest to the centre of Russia, to the Volga region, and that is why it is an extremely dangerous route for a possible breakthrough of Islamic extremism.

The coordinated oil policies of the US and British corporations are an important part of the long-term general policy of the US in order to control the Near and Middle East, strengthen its influence in the Caucasus and Central Asia and isolate Russia from its ports in Black and Caspian Sea.

There is one more invisible player in this region, i.e. Saudi Arabia that has direct relation to the events in the Russian Northern Caucasus, being interested in promoting conservative Islam in the north and destabilisation of the situation in Southern Caucasus, again with the goal of reaping rich economic dividends.

Iran is not happy about such developments, because this would strengthen the economic blockade against it and complicate its economic links with the neighbouring countries. This would also create a real danger for depriving Iran of its regional power status.

Iran is leaving no stone unturned for preserving its economic presence in the region. In the backdrop of trade decline with Azerbaijan, it is developing all-round cooperation with Armenia, participating in various projects, first of all in the sphere of energy, transport and communication in which Armenia is interested, because the Baku–Zeikhan pipeline goes through Georgia bypassing the Armenian territory, though it is one-and-half times bigger in length and consequently more expensive.

However, Armenia has been all along a reliable strategic ally of Russia and moreover, Russia has its military bases in Armenian territory. This is the problem with Armenia. Its geographical situation and absence of border with Russia determine the possibility for blocking Armenia with the help of Azerbaijan and Georgia.

The oil policy of Azerbaijan is determined by the creation of possibilities with US help, to meet its own demand and the requirements of Georgia and Ukraine because it would help the strengthening of their independence from Russia. Besides, it is an opportunity for receiving additional, if not main, financial resources from exports.

Ukraine is no less an important element in the energy pipeline scheme. The massive pipelines like the Urugoi-Pomari-Uzhgorod, Soyuz and the southern branch of the Druzhba, built during Soviet rule, pass through Ukrainian territory. It is a known fact that Russia of late has been trying to diversify its hydrocarbon supply routes to the world market and strengthen its supply stability. This was partially buttressed by the inadequate policy of some neighbouring countries trying to blackmail Moscow in the political and economic spheres, using Russia's dependence on transport corridors and contracts with European countries.

Russia is being accused of using energy as an instrument of political pressure on other countries. I do not know the position of the Russian government on this issue. But I would like to ask what is wrong if Russia is doing so? What is the International Monetary Fund in the hands of the US, if not an instrument of political surgery?

After all, Russia is selling oil and gas which legally belongs to it, though of late some circles have started talking about the natural resources of Russia belonging to entire humankind. I would like to emphasise that it is Russian property. If any country has any overdeposits of resources in its earth, let it keep them at the disposal of humankind.

The same can be said of regarding whom and under which conditions Russia would sell its raw materials and products. This is its right.

Some people are trying to convince us that it is not good to sell gas under market prices to Ukraine and Georgia. We are accused that by doing this, we are strangling young democracies. But nobody has yet explained on which basis Russia would sell its gas at a loss to countries that have been pursuing anti-Russian policies.

The CIS countries have to determine their strategic relations with Russia. Many countries are ashamed of doing this under the so-called multidimensional policy. This terminology is heard in the capitals of the CIS countries along with the hue and cry that they are small countries without many resources and are struggling for survival. It is difficult for small countries to take a principled position because they have to resort to a multidimensional policy for their survival. The leaders of the post-Soviet countries while declaring this, try to get the understanding from Russia for getting the permission for pursuing this kind of political activities. This is a kind of license for engaging in prostitution because the wonder instrument for survival "*the multi-dimensional policy*" lies in a periodical to-and-fro movement between the world centres of power, accompanied by a shifting of principles and betraying yesterday's friends for money.

It is like drinking milk from two cows. However, this is only an outward similarity. Russia is not a a milking cow, and the US more so. It is ready to feed; the only issue is to whom and what for.

Moreover, Washington, which does not have a wide heart like the Russians, has an absurd habit of asking the result of the money spent. Manuel Noriega had to reply, Saddam Hussein had to reply, and Bin Laden is on the run.

Any country, however small it might be, has the right to have its own position and principles. Apart from that, strategic issues and tactical issues should be separated, and one should firmly defend one's political position in alliance with its strategic partner, and at the same time, one has to be a flexible effective economic partner for the others.

Nothing dangerous would happen if any of our neighbours firmly declares that it is with our strategic competitors. We will obviously know who does not need our oil, metal, money when there would be problems with terrorists or bad partners. It is necessary to recall that countries providing their territory for building foreign military bases cannot be strategic allies and friends of Russia.

Different CIS countries from time to time have been raising objections against Russia, sometimes justified. Sometimes they demand that Russia should sell them this or that commodity at very low prices. Some ask for electricity, some ask for helicopters, and some ask for clean water. On the question why should Russia give helicopters, electricity and water, you find naïve looks and protesting remarks that Russians are always indecisive, unable to define their interest, that Russians do not like us, etc. Let them explain why we should love them. Should we love them for their *multi-dimensional policy*?

Kiev, Tbilisi, Baku, and Ashkhabad have been holding talks on gas supply and transit for a long time. Kishinev is interested to take part in these talks. There is discussion about building a gas pipeline from Azerbaijan to Turkey through Georgia parallel to the Baku–Zeikhan oil pipeline. The role of Turkmenistan is enhanced in the context of these plans. The US is planning to build the "Caspian Defense Force" for which it is ready to spend 130 million dollars in the course of six years. Iran is located in the neighbouring territory. The Caspian Defense Force is being built keeping Iran in view. It is being planned to be built in participation with the military forces of Turkey, Azerbijan and Georgia. The command centres of this infrastructure and radio-electronic intelligence system would be located in Kazakhstan and Azerbaijan. Here, the state of democracy does not bother the US.

Regarding the issues of our common security and potential conflicts in the CIS, I would like to stress that Central Asia is an unpredictable and conflict-prone territory as a whole. Nobody can forecast how the situation would develop in that territory in the next 10 years.

Events in the neighbouring Afghanistan pose a real danger to the region. Tajikistan and Kyrgyzstan had the opportunity to experience this. The US controlling a large part of Afghanistan seems to be ready to close its eyes towards the growing drugs flow in the direction of Central Asia in order to establish its control over the oil and gas resources of Central Asia.

In such a situation when the competition in the energy market gets aggravated, taking the demands of the US economy and the growing economic systems of India and China into account, the need for a political and economic partnership between India and Russia is pre-determined. The strengthening of the geopolitical axis between Moscow and New Delhi will permit us to resolve the issues of energy, security, etc., more effectively. May be, the Shanghai Cooperation Organization, which is outwardly ignored by the West, can serve as a mutually beneficial, effective instrument of our interaction.

17

Chinese Interests in Central Asia: Policies and Challenges

Ramakrushna Pradhan

Any geopolitical and geo-economic debate of Central Asia will remain incomplete without taking note of the role of China in the region. China is the fourth largest in the world in terms of size and the biggest non-CIS neighbour of Central Asia. It shares a long border of about 3,500 kilometres with Kazakhstan, Tajikistan and Kyrgyzstan (Akiner 1994: 5). In addition to this, it has a certain commonness in ethnicity, culture and language with the northern part of Kazakhstan i.e., Xinjiang. Being the immediate neighbour and proximate player in the region, China is interested in several aspects like ensuring political stability and preventing Islamic extremism in the region as this is critically linked to the security of China. It is also interested in maintaining close cooperation and boosting up trade relations with the newly emerged Central Asian Republics. Therefore, the opening up of Central Asia and its emergence as a major source of energy resources beyond the western border of China stimulated it to engage in dialogue with the region and maintain close and cooperative relations with these countries for the achievement of its strategic interests and creating opportunities for trade, energy and security.

Chinese Interests and Policies in Central Asia

In brief, there are six core areas of China's expanding interests in the region such as ensuring peripheral security by expanding its relations with the neighbouring states of Central Asia, securing the energy resources of the region, preventing the rise of Uighur nationalism, militancy and separatism in the Chinese Central Asian province of Xinjiang, opening up the landlocked western China for cross-border trade, investment and communication links, ensuring geopolitical and geostrategic stability by creating a buffer zone and to maintain the status quo by reducing the Russian influence and preventing the US prominence in the region. An attempt has been made through this article to briefly analyse the expanding interests and active policies of China in Central Asia.

Geopolitical and Geostrategic Interests

The geopolitical interests of China in Central Asia are determined by the dynamic location of the area in the heart of Asia connecting Europe with Asia. As a beautiful mosaic at the crossroads of China, Russia and the Islamic world, Central Asia acts as a geostrategic lynchpin. In addition to this, the region sits on vast reserves of oil and natural gas along with a huge quantity of minerals, uranium and other valuable resources which are adequate to revitalise cross-border trade, create positive political interaction and to stimulate regional cooperation. Given the potential to recharge the economies of the neighbouring countries, these resources of the region have captured regional as well as global attention. And China is not an exception in this case.

Further, due to its proximity to Central Asia and the Caspian Sea region, China has become a serious competitor for profit and influence in the area. However, this has been supported by its contiguity, significant size, thriving economy and powerful military force along with closer cooperative relations with Russia and Iran.

Central Asia is not just a trade and investment hub for China but a strategic region as well. China's security policy that rests upon four pillars such as countering terrorism and Islamic militancy backing Uighur independence, military cooperation, countering the influence of major powers in the region inimical to China and strongly influencing Central Asia's multilateral security arrangements. China also seriously views Central Asia's opening itself as the route to the vast regions of Eurasia – the energy centres of Central Asia, Russia and the Middle East to Europe and the ports of Pakistan and the Gulf. Therefore, it is obvious on the part of China not to allow Central Asia to become Russia's backyard and America's chessboard. Hence, China has been cementing its position in Central Asia.

Central Asia: A Buffer Zone

Central Asia covering the total border with China in the western side of about 3,500 kilometers provides China with a safety and friendly buffer zone. Its location between Russian and radical Islamic countries like Iran and Afghanistan provides an important space to address China's security concerns. The Taliban that came to power in 1996 in Afghanistan stood as the greatest threat to the region's security, posing serious challenges to China in its Xinjiang region. Central Asia located centrally between China and Afghanistan has provided a safety zone to China in handling the crisis. The most important threat that China is encountering now is the eastward expansion of NATO beyond the Central Asian borders. Here again, Central Asia has stood as a strong support base for China. That is why China rates the region high in its security and strategic agenda.

Peripheral Security

The peripheral security of China in Central Asia has two dimensions. The first is the preservation of stability, economic well-being, political order and security of its western-most province Xinjiang-Uighur-Autonomous Region (XUAR) which shares a long and common border with Russia, Mongolia and three Central Asian states of Kazakhstan, Kyrgyzstan and Tajikistan. Intricately linked to this goal is the second aim to create a friendly and secure belt of states around the Xinjiang region. A crucial endeavour of its regional security policy is to ensure that Central Asia remains free from the hegemonic control of the powerful rival – the United States and the influence of Russia.

In this respect, China amicably solved the border issues with the Central Asian states, but the most contentious of the border problems was between Kazakhstan and China. In the recent years, however, the border problem has found a solution through the evolution of the SCO. Another problem that has raised its ugly head posing stern challenges to China as another Tibet in its external dealing with the community of the nations is Xinjiang – a region not just compounding border problems but also the issues of ethnicity and nationalism as well.

Xinjiang

The Xinjiang Autonomous Region is China's largest province in size occupying roughly one -sixth of the country's territory. It is an ethnically mixed region with 18 million population consisting of Uyghurs, Turks, Hans, Kazakhs and other smaller groups (Philip 2000: A12).

The Uyghurs and Turkic tribes constituting overwhelmingly the majority of Xinjiang, have made its integration into China problematic. They were keen to join in the Central Asian mainstream, because of their historical, cultural, linguistic and civilisational links and commonalities. The denial of this has therefore given rise to separatist movements in Xinjiang. Taking serious note of the events, China after 1991 waged a large campaign to crush the three evil forces of violent terrorists, religious extremists and separatists in Xinjiang. China says that the separatists are backed by the al-Qaida and other militants abroad such as the Hizb-ut-Tahrir (HUT), the Islamic Movement of Uzbekistan (IMU) in Central Asia and other militant groups operating in Afghanistan and Pakistan. However, the reality is more complex. A report filed in the *Washington Post* reads like this"

"Although recent reported scattered incidents of violence, the region seemed beset less by a coordinated terrorist campaign than by simmering ethnic tensions, made more acute by government policies. In dozens of heavy handed security tactics and uneven economic developments are aggravating relations between Xinjiang's 7 million Hans – the dominant Chinese ethnic group and its 8 million Uyghurs – Turkic speaking Muslims many of whom yearn for independence or at least greater autonomy from Chinese rule" (Dwivedi 2006: 142).

Xinjiang also produces one third of China's cotton and has the largest oil and gas reserves of the country.

That is why China is more concerned with Uighur separatism. China initiated the idea of the Shanghai Five (S-5) in collaboration with Russia, Kazakhstan, Kyrgyzstan and Tajikistan for an amicable solution of the problem. The main aim of this organisation was to settle the border problems of China with Russia and three states of Central Asia peacefully. Furthering this process, China also transformed the Xinjiang region into a free market zone in 1998, now better known as the Xinjiang-Uighur Autonomous Region (XUAR). China has done this in collaboration with Kazakhstan only to put an end the ethnic crisis and for establishing cooperative relations with its Central Asian neighbours. This may also be pointed out as one of the most important reasons of the Chinese support to the US in its global war on terror. However, the dust doesn't seem to have settled as the region is witnessing ethnic riots and unrest at regular intervals. The recent ethnic violence in Xinjiang that led to the killing of over 150 Uyghurs in July 2009 is definitely posing a serious concern for Beijing.

The Shanghai Cooperation Organization

The Shanghai Cooperation Organization – the successor to the Shanghai Five – was formed in 1996 for the purpose of solving the border problems among the member states peacefully. The founding members of the organisation are China, Russia, Kazakhstan, Kyrgyzstan and Tajikistan. Besides, the promotion of transborder trade was also one of the motives of the Shanghai Five. Uzbekistan which does not share a border with China was not a member of the organisation. However, it joined the organisation in its sixth summit from January, 14–15 2001. Since then the organisation came to be widely known as the Shanghai Cooperation Organization (Khojaev 2007: 35). Turkmenistan till today is not a party to the organisation as it has embraced the policy of positive neutrality since 1991.

China attaches great importance to the SCO podium and is actively involved in its institutional development. China has used the SCO mechanism to influence the region not just for defending its prominent interests but also to reduce the Russian influence and more importantly to prevent the US entry into the region. It has also used the SCO platform for garnering support of the member states for fighting against the separatist forces in the XUAR. It is also skillfully using this as a tool to control the region's Uighur population and in settling the long-standing border disputes with three Central Asian states.

Although the goals of the SCO are very broadly defined as a regional cooperation organisation, its foundation is based mainly on potential cooperation in three areas: (a) regional stability and opposition to the three evil forces of terrorism, extremism and separatism (b) economic cooperation and (c) potential strategic cooperation. Maintaining regional stability is the foremost objective of SCO where national interests converge and action is taken. That is the main ground through which China is trying to capitalise its hold over Central Asia and helps in posing some serious challenges to the US activities in the region. It also galvanises over certain aspects of the SCO through the help of which it set out to counter the eastward expansion of NATO.

Energy in the Chinese Strategy

China is the second largest energy consumer in the World and therefore has great interests in gaining access to the rich deposits of the hydrocarbon resources of Central Asia. As per the US Department of Energy estimates, the "Chinese consumption will increase to 10.5 million barrels a day and its import may touch 3 million barrels of crude oil per day by 2010" (Guacheng 1998: 43) and depending on the accuracy of the estimates, China might become the world's largest energy consumer in the coming years. A further net energy import of China grows persistently with the relentless increase of consumption while the production is sterile as it is clearly shown in Table1.

In order to meet this ever-increasing energy requirement, China needs a guaranteed supply of oil. Therefore, it is apparent on the part of China to depend profoundly on Central Asia, an energy hub accounting 1.7% and 5% of global proven recoverable resources of oil and gas, respectively (Dutta 2003: 155).

Central Asia as such is predominantly a gas-producing region along with significant amounts of oil reserves, uranium, coal mines and hydroelectricity resources. It has proven gas reserves amounting to 6.6 trillion cubic metres (tcm): 2.9 tcm in Turkmenistan, 1.9 tcm in Uzbekistan and 1.8 tcm in Kazakhstan. This represents about one-tenth of the known gas reserves of the CIS. Turkmenistan with 80 billion tcm per year and Uzbekistan with 50 billion tcm per year are the two leading gas producers although Kazakhstan produces a significant amount of gas in the region (International Crisis Group: 2007: 32).

As far as oil is concerned, Central Asia has an estimated 200 billion barrels of hydrocarbon reserves. Kazakhstan, the main producer of oil in the region, is projected to have between 30 to 40 billion barrels of crude oil reserves. Turkmenistan, the most important producer of gas also has about 600 million barrels of proven oil reserves. Uzbekistan also has a production capacity of around 600 million barrels (International Crisis Group 2007: 6-9). The Kyrgyz Republic and Tajikistan produce only small quantities of oil. According to some other estimates, Kazakhstan has the largest oil reserves in the region estimated at around 800 million barrels oil per day for which it is being said that the rich deposits of oil and gas of the nation could make it another Kuwait. Turkmenistan (32 bb) and Uzbekistan (1 bb) are the other countries to have the largest oil reserves (159 trillion cubic feet) in the region followed by Uzbekistan (110 tcf) and Kazakhstan (88 tcf) in the gas sector (Mattoo 2003: 56). Table 2 represents the energy resources of the Central Asian countries as the following:

Table. 2 Energy Resources of the Central Asian Countries, 2009

Country	Oil Reserves	Oil Production	Gas Reserves	Gas Production	Coal Reserves
Kazakhstan	30 billion Bbl	1.429 million bbl/d	2.407 tcm	33.38 bcm	120 billion metric tonnes
Uzbekistan	594 million Bbl	83,820 bbl/d	1.841 tcm	67.6 bcm	3000 metric tonnes
Turkmenistan	600 million bbl	189,400 bbl/d	2.662 tcm	70.5 bcm	No reserves
Kyrgyzstan	40 million	958.4 bbl/d	5.663 bcm	30 mcm	2500 metric tonnes
Tajikistan	12 million bbl	238 bbl/d bbl	5.663 bcm	15.3 mcm	Self sufficient

Source: CIA, World Fact Book, 2009

In addition to Central Asia, the Caspian Sea region has abundant energy resources of which

Kazakhstan and Turkmenistan are littoral states. Uzbekistan though not a littoral state, is generally considered to belong to the Caspian Sea region. According to the July 2001 report of the US Energy Information Administration, the Caspian Sea region possesses about 34 billion barrels of proven oil and 235 billion barrels of possible oil reserves (US Energy Administration Report). It is about one-fourth that of the oil reserves of the Middle East. The proven natural gas reserves of the Caspian region including that of Uzbekistan were quoted at 243–248 trillion cubic feet (tcf). As far as oil is concerned, 88 per cent of the Caspian reserves are located in the three states of Azerbaijan, Kazakhstan and Turkmenistan (Gidadhubli 2003: 149-157). Turkmenistan and Uzbekistan have the major parts of gas reserves in the region. Therefore, it becomes essential to study the Caspian Sea region while dealing with the energy sectors of the Central Asian states. Thus, in this context Central Asia not just provides the Chinese energy market with an opportunity to break the Russian stronghold but also allows a long-term access to the region where continues oil and gas demand is assured. Therefore, China is quite willing to consider as well as implement ambitious and clearly expensive pipeline schemes such as the gas pipeline from Turkmenistan and the oil pipelines from Kazakhstan.

China has emerged as a major player in Kazakhstan's oil exploration efforts. It has been actively participating in exploring the Aktyubinsk and Mangyshlak oil deposits and building an oil pipeline in the Kazakhstan–Xinjiang region. One of the most ambitious projects signed by China includes a 5,730 kilometres -long gas pipeline project estimated at a cost of US$ 11 billion between

Turkmenistan-Uzbekistan-Kazakhstan-China in which a consortium of companies from the US, Japan and China have already been conducting preliminary surveys for quite some time (Alaomolki 2001: 5-7).

China has been making constant and continuous efforts to outbid several big companies of the US, Russia and Japan in Central Asia. In June 1997, China's National Petroleum Corporation (CNPC) outbid its Russian and American counterparts to obtain exclusive rights to operate in the Uzen oilfields in western Kazakhstan for the next 20 years. In September 1997 Chinese premier Li Peng signed an estimated US$ 9.6 billion deal on oil shipments and the construction of two pipelines with Kazakhstan. Based on the agreement, the China National Oil Corporation (CNOC) projected to build a 3,000 kilometers pipeline from Kazakhstan to China's western border. The second 250 kilometre pipeline was likely to be built from Kazakhstan to the Turkmenistan border. The CNOC also continues with the development of the Uzen and Aktyubinsk oilfields in western Kazakhstan in the east of Caspian Sea with an estimated 1.5 billion barrels in oil reserves. UNOCAL and AMOCO, two major US oil companies, were also interested to get an entry in these two large oilfields. Despite lobbying from Washington, they could not come up with the terms guaranteed by China – which agreed to finance the pipeline (Ibid: 8-9).

In the process, China has signed "Treaties of Good Neighbourliness and Friendship" with Kazakhstan and Kyrgyzstan, and Beijing upgraded its political ties with Kazakhstan to the level of strategic partnerships in 2005 (Dwivedi 2006: 149). It has been pursuing vigorous politico-economic and diplomatic ties along with a regular exchange of ideas and leaders with the Central Asian states. In the last couple of months through the acquisition of oil companies by state-owned enterprises, the extension of a 3,000 km oil pipeline and a number of loans for oil deals, China has seemingly strengthened its grip over the energy resources of Kazakhstan (*The Hindu* 2009: 14). China is moving fast and systematically taking advantage of Kazakhstan's economic situation in the period of global recession. Kazakhstan, with a projected 4.5 million barrels of oil per day, is critical for energy security of China, Russia, US and India. However, in the race China seems to be emerging as the winner, as on August 20, 2009, China's top economic planning body, the National Development and Reform Commission approved a 49 per cent of stake worth US$ 40.5 million in a Kazakhstan oil company (Ibid).

Although, Turkmenistan and Kazakhstan are the main partners of China in providing access to Central Asian oil and gas resources, Beijing has also been very successful in securing its presence in Tajikistan and Uzbekistan's energy sectors. China has already invested in three projects in Kazakhstan and one in Turkmenistan. Nevertheless, China is keen to rapidly expand its economic ties with the Central Asian states. Its trade and investments in the region have grown significantly over the past few years. In a larger sense, China has met with considerable success in pursuing a strategy of advancing loans and making investments in the Central Asian countries. It has also helped substantially in developing their economies as a whole leading to enduring relationships with commensurate benefits in the energy sectors.

The following are some of the investments or proposed deals made by Chinese firms in Central Asia in the recent years:

- April 24, 2009: The CNPC agreed with Kazakhstan's state oil firm KazMunaiGas to jointly buy the oil producer MangistauMunaiGas for US$ 3.3 billion. As part of the deal, China agreed to lend Kazakhstan US$ 10 billion in a "loan-for-oil" deal.
- April 4, 2009: China's Guandong Nuclear Power Co. (CGNPC) and the Kazakh state nuclear firm Kazatomprom planned to boost uranium output in their joint venture.
- April 2008: Kazakhstan will support China in developing oil and gas resources on the continental shelf of the Caspian Sea, according to a joint communiqué by the two governments.
- June 2006: A subsidiary of China National Petroleum Corp. (CNPC) planned to spend US$ 210 million to look for oil and gas in Uzbekistan over the next five years.
- April 2006: China agreed to buy 30 billion cubic metres of gas from Turkmenistan through a new pipeline each year. Both sides later agreed to expand the sales to 40 billion cubic metres a year. Part of the pipeline is expected to be operational by the end of 2009.

- 2006: The state-owned investment group CITIC bought the Kazakh oil assets of Canada-based Nations Energy Co. Ltd. for US$ 1.9 billion. The cornerstone of those assets was the Karazhanbas oil and gas field, which has proven reserves of more than 340 million barrels and production of over 50,000 barrels per day.
- 2005: CNPC International paid US$ 3.96 billion to acquire a 33 per cent stake in PetroKazakhstan.
- 1997: Kazakhstan and China agreed to build a 3,000 km crude oil pipeline and would later double the capacity of the combined pipeline to 20 million tonnes a year (www.reuters.com, www.thehindu.com, Central Asian Times).

Economic and Trade

China's economic interests in Central Asia are related to a reliable supply–demand relationship based on the fair and reasonable prices of oil and gas. Central Asia has provided a huge and good market for the cheaper Chinese goods. Thus, China treats economic relations with Central Asia as a top priority. The increasing interests of China in the Central Asian economy can be seen in the light of the following facts:

- "The territory serves as a transit route for economic ties between China and Europe, South Asia and the Middle East.
- Central Asia is rich in natural resources. Oil, gas, gold, uranium, cotton, etc., attract international forces and boosts its economic importance.
- The newly independent states have turned the region into a vacant and easily accessible market for Chinese goods and a source of cheaper raw materials. Land transport communications have also offered more advantageous conditions for Chinese exports" (Khojaev 2007: 31).

After recognising their independence and establishing diplomatic relations with the Central Asian countries, China has signed a large number of treaties with these states. These treaties serve as a foundation for the development of economic ties and for opening airlines and simplifying the visa regime for Chinese nationals. Wholesale markets were opened in Beijing and several border towns. Customs duties for the exported Chinese commodities and imported raw materials were either lowered or annulled; transportation service for the export goods were established. Much has been done to repair and modernise the highways and delivery means. The VAT (Value-Added Tax) return system has been operating in the export of goods by ntermediaries. Many of the public and private producing companies have acquired the rights to export their products to Central Asia themselves. They got all or part of the paid taxes back depending on the share of exported products. The producers could import raw materials or equipments on easy terms or free of charge (Ibid: 32).

Military

Being the biggest non-CIS neighbour of Central Asia, China considers the stability of Central Asia as critical to its security. It concluded several multilateral and bilateral agreements in 1996 and 1997 on the demilitarisation of the common border with the Central Asian republics. It helped in strengthening measures of trust in the military field on the border areas. In an advance to this effort, China initiated the formation of the Shanghai Five in 1996 in collaboration with Russia, Kazakhstan, Kyrgyzstan and Tajikistan.

This has deepened military trust in the border areas and helped in reducing military forces on the front. At the end of 1996, twenty-two rounds of negotiations took place. The main goals of these negotiations were to reduce tensions on the border areas. According to these agreements, each country party to the negotiations would have to refrain from staging military exercises directed against the other. They also specified restrictions on military exercises in terms of scale, area and the number of such exercises that were permitted. In addition to this, all important military activities initiated by one party in the area between the borders and 100 kilometres from the border line needed to be announced to the other and an invitation to observe the exercises were also to be extended. It has also been assured the measures to prevent dangerous military activities and enhance friendly exchanges of armed forces in the border areas. All these meant specifically to maintain stability within the territory adjoining the boundary and to ensure the security and economic welfare of its people and to assure peace and stability on the border by promoting a belt of good neighbourliness and friendship by China.

However, the September 11 events led to a further US stranglehold in the region. The US involvement in Central Asia and its further military activities aggravated the Chinese position in the region vis-à-vis the world politics. China cautiously handled the otherwise tense situation and mobilised its resources and international reputation to bring back the things under control. Today, however, the Chinese position in Central Asia is more strong and positive in comparison to the US as there is no military base of the Americans in Central Asia for the time being. Recently, the US shut down its military bases in Uzbekistan and Kyrgyzstan in 2009.

Challenges to the Chinese Policy

In recent times, although China has upset the US in its desire for dominance in Central Asia and has succeeded to a greater extent in reducing the Russian influence in the region, it is not immune from challenges critical to its national security as a whole. Ethnic unrest in Xinjiang, border problems, an eastward expansion of the NATO, an active US involvement in the region, energy insecurity, regional instability and Islamic extremism and many other factors are shattering the bright hopes of China with regard to Central Asia.

The unrest in Central Asia holds much greater potential for affecting China's own internal stability than any other part of Asia. The dangers Beijing is visualising in Central Asia are basically due to the severely tarnished economic condition, poor infrastructure and the breeding corruption along with rising civil strife among the transnational ethnic or religious groups. The looming uncertainty of the region's future are all posing serious challenges for China to maintain its security from the domino effect. Along with this, the vulnerable southern border of Central Asia connecting (Talibanised) Afghanistan and other Islamic states pose a further pressure on the Chinese security set-up.

An eastward expansion of NATO following the Pentagon Report of 1998 which suggested the rising China and its growing threat to the US anywhere in the world, is certainly a serious issue of concern and challenge for the Chinese think tanks. Its growing expansion in the eastern direction started with the incorporation of Bulgaria, Poland, the Czech Republic and Hungary, the initiation of Programmes like the "Partnership for Peace" and "Operation Enduring Freedom that had eventually meant to embrace all the countries of the region, has seriously challenged the Chinese position in regional politics of Central Asia and Eurasia. Following the 9/11 attacks, the US utilised the opportunity more profoundly to promote its interests in the region. It entered into many bilateral, multilateral agreements and established military bases in the Central Asian region, wasting no time. However, the US has shut down its military base in Uzbekistan and transformed it into a mere air base in Kyrgyzstan just few months back; but, this has not removed the US fear from the Chinese cauldron.

However, the real worry for China comes from the Taliban, presently instable Afghanistan and other Islamic neighbours of the region. The growing American presence in the region also no less worries China in its dealings with energy-related matters. The Xinjiang syndrome has certainly some significant concern for the Chinese leaders because of the region's importance to China's continued economic development and to its national security.

Conclusion

From the above understanding, it can be said that China has enormous interests in Central Asia ranging from geopolitical and trade to energy and the question of the region's security and relations with Russia and its neighbours. These are also vital for the stability and economic prosperity in China's Xinjiang province as well. Central Asia is also an important source of oil and natural gas for the energy-hungry Chinese economy. To strike a balance in global and regional, geopolitical and economic interests, Beijing needs to pursue an active and balanced policy towards Central Asia.

Given the critical link of Central Asia to the Chinese security, it is on the Chinese onus to keep the region under its sphere of influence. Following the growing involvement of America and the subsequent eastward expansion of NATO, the Chinese threat perceptions from the western border and its deliberate encirclement have become very clear. Therefore, the Chinese attempt to capitalise on the SCO and to use it as a tool to strengthen its interests relating to security and geo-strategy is natural. However, only time will tell as to what extent China will succeed in preventing the American influence beyond its western border and a greater use of the SCO as a counter to NATO.

Notes

1. Akiner, Shirin (1994), "Post-Soviet Central Asia: Past is Prologue", in Ferdinand, Peter (eds.), *The New Central Asia and Its Neighbours,* London: The Royal Institute of International Affairs, p. 5.
2. Philip, P. Pan (2002), "In China's West, Ethnic Strife Becomes Terrorism", *Washington Post,* July 15, p. A12.
3. Khojaev, Ablat (2007), "China's Central Asian Policy", *Central Asia and the Caucasus,* 3 (45), p. 35.
4. Dwivedi, Ramakant (2006), "China's Central Asian Policy in Recent Times", *The China and the Eurasian Forum Quarterly,* 4 (4), p. 142.
5. Guacheng, Xing (1998), "China and Central Asia: Towards a New Relationship", in Zhang, Yongjian and Azizian, Roubeen (eds.), *Ethnic Challenges Beyond Borders: Chinese and Russian perspectives of the Central Asian Conundrum*, London: MacMillan Press Ltd, p. 43.
6. Dutta, Sujit (2003), "China's Emerging Ties with Central Asia", in Joshi, Nirmala (ed.), *Central Asia: The Great Game Replayed, An Indian Perspective*, New Delhi: New Century Publication, p. 155
7. "Energy and Cooperation in Central Asia: Challenges and Opportunity", International Crisis Group, 24 May 2007, p. 32.
8. "Central Asia Energy Risk", Asia Report no-133, 24 May, 2007, International Crisis Group, pp. 6-9.
9. Mattoo (2003), "United States of America and Central Asia: Beginning of the Great Game" in Nirmala Joshi (ed.), *Central Asia: The Great Game Replayed, An Indian Perspective*, New Delhi: New Century Publication, p. 56.
10. US Energy Administration Report 2001.
11. Gidadhubli. R (2003), "Politics of Energy Resources of Central Asia", in Nirmala Joshi (ed.) *Central Asia: The Great Game Replayed, An Indian Perspective*, New Delhi: New Century Publication, pp.149-157.
12. Alaomolki, Nazar (2001), *Life After the Soviet Union: The Newly Independent Republics of the Transcaucasus and Central Asia*, New York: State University of New York Press, 2001, pp. 5-7.
13. Ibid., pp. 8-9.
14. Dwivedi (2006), op. cit., p. 149.
15. *The Hindu*, August 22, 2009, p. 14.
16. Ibid.
17. Khojaev (2007), op. cit., p. 31.
18. Ibid, p. 32.

18

Diaspora: The Experience of Indian Diaspora for Russia

Felix Yurlov

The Russian diaspora abroad, including in the CIS and Western countries, runs into tens of millions of people. It constitutes an important reserve for developing Russia's relations with these countries. However, its economic, cultural and political resources and potential has not been studied adequately. In this connection, the experience of the large Indian diaspora in different countries including the US has a lot of significance.

The Indian diaspora consisting of more than 20 million people in different countries and continents of the world is India's large partner in its efforts for modernisation and globalisation. The Indians living abroad are energetic and effective middlemen in trade and economic, socio-political and cultural links between the countries they live in and their historical motherland.

The annual income of Indians living abroad is about 370 billion USD. For comparison, it may be mentioned that the Indian GDP in 2005 was equal to 857 billion USD.[1] The richest and most dynamic part of Indians abroad lives in the US, Britain, and Canada. A significant number of them live and work in the countries of the Persian Gulf, Malaysia and Singapore, in countries of the Caribbean basin, in Africa (South Africa, Kenya, Tanzania and Uganda), Fiji and Mauritius and others. The Indians living abroad transfer billions of dollars to their historical motherland every year, participate in joint ventures with India and finance many trade and economic projects in this country.

The Indian government pays a lot of attention to the Indians living abroad, and creates a favourable trade and investment climate for them in India. the Indian Prime Minister Dr Manmohan Singh speaking in a meeting of the members of the Indian community in Berlin in 2006 stressed that the Indians living abroad are important partners of India in the process of globalisation. He called them to participate in building a modern and prosperous India. The Prime Minister emphasised the significance of use of the advantages linked to the Indian diaspora.[2]

Indian Migration to Foreign Countries

The migration from India and formation of the ethnic minority of Indian origin in the countries of Central America, Asia and Africa goes back to the nineteenth and the beginning of the twentieth century. With all the differences in concrete reasons for migration to different countries, what was common was that the Indian migrants of the nineteenth century were formed out of contract workers, who were transported to these countries after the abolition of slavery in British colonies in 1833. This led to the running away of black workers from the plantations and shortage of labour. Under the pressure of the plantation owners, the colonial government of India in 1844 adopted a law for permitting the Indians to migrate. In 1921, in Trinidad alone, the number of Indian migrants rose to 120 thousand that constituted one-third of the country's population.

The Indian immigration to Fiji began in 1879, and at present there are about 335 thousand people of Indian origin, which makes 51% of the total population. A similar situation prevailed in Mauritius, where the Indian community constitutes 65% of the country's population.

The Indian mass immigration to South Africa began in 1860sBefore that, in the middle of the seventeenth century, the Dutch people had brought Indian slaves to the Kapski colony. Towards the beginning of the twentieth century there were 150 thousand Indians in South Africa, who with their hard work in the plantations created conditions for making Kapski and Natal one of the richest colonies of the British Empire. There were 800 thousand Indians living in South Africa towards 1980. However, the towards 1990s, their number reduced to 350 thousand. The majority of Indians, deserting South Africa under the pressure of apartheid, went to Europe.

The trade and cultural relations of India with East Africa (presently Kenya, Tanzania, and Uganda) led to the emergence of Indian colonies there long before the advent of the British. However, it was only after the imposition of the British colonial order that the migration of the Indians assumed a mass character. Towards the beginning of the twenty-first century there were 85 thousand people of Indian origin in both Kenya and Tanzania. And there were only 15 thousand Indians in Uganda, from where a majority of the Indians were thrown out under Idi Amin's regime. The Indians from East Africa migrated mainly to Great Britain, where their number reached 200 thousand. Similar situations arose in Malaysia and Singapore, where 1 million, 600 thousand and 200 thousand people lived respectively towards the end of the twentieth century.

After India attained independence in 1947, the emergence of new independent countries in the former colonies was accompanied by inter-ethnic conflicts and the ouster of Indians from there. Thus out of one million Indians in Burma (Myanmar) towards the end of the 1960s, there remained only 250 thousand. The rest of the Indians migrated mainly to India.

From the end of the 1950s, the nature of Indian migration changed from unqualified labour force to specialists, and here migration took place mainly to developed countries – like great Britain, Canada and the US. The Indian migration to the countries of the Persian Gulf reached three million towards the beginning of the twenty-first century.

Poverty, unemployment and the quest for a better life were the main factors of "forced" migration from India. The number of Indians in Great Britain grew by two-and-half times during the last decade of the twentieth century. They formed the third largest Asian group (about 2 million people in 2005), after the Chinese and Filipinos. If the present growth of population remains, the number of Indo-Americans in the first decade of the twenty-first century may rise two-fold.[3]

Indian Immigrants in the US : The First Success

The first big wave of Indian immigrants reached the US in the middle of the 1960s at the height of the Vietnam War. At that time there was an acute shortage of doctors as many of them had been called to serve the huge contingent of American troops in Vietnam.

The US authorities in their search for doctors paid their attention to India, which was widely known for its qualified doctors that had gained popularity in many countries, first of all in Great Britain. Moreover, this was not the last factor; they knew the English language which was the medium of instruction in medical institutes. The offer to come to the US was sent not only to experienced doctors; in 1964 in accordance with the agreement signed with the Indian government, many graduates from leading medical colleges received the invitation for working in the US.

A simplified procedure for formalising the documents for living in the US (Green Card) was offered, credit for travelling to the proposed destination was offered, and a permanent place of work was also offered. Of course – there was a reliability test which was introduced, where it was required to get a certificate from the local police certifying that the invited person was not linked to extremist, terrorist or similar organisations. After the doctors, people of other professions and specialisations, particularly people with higher education, many of whom had doctorate and other higher degrees, started going to the US.

The second large wave of Indian migration to the US was linked to the development of information technology—software programming for computers. This reached its peak in the 1990s. The Indians in the US achieved a lot of success. Their average income is 25% higher than the average American income. Almost all Indians have houses of their own. About 65% of Indians have higher education, whereas 23% of the population in the US has higher education. More than 60% Indo-Americans are employed as managers and highly qualified specialists. The Indo-Americans are usually programmers, doctors, advocates, experts, financial experts, journalists and scientists. They are college and university professors in technical disciplines, businessmen who are engaged in the sphere of high-tech, trade, hotel, motel, restaurant and medicine business.[4] 15% of the new companies in the Silicon Valley belong to Indo-Americans, 10–12% of doctors in the US are Indians and 40% of the hotel business in the US is controlled by Indians.[5] a significant number of Indo-Americans are elected and appointed to federal and local legislatures. The Indian entrepreneurs and professionals have formed an influential political lobby, including in the US Congress, which often stands to defend Indian interests. As a whole, the Indian community could confirm itself as a hard-working, law-abiding, affluent part of the American society, enjoying a remarkable popularity among the representatives of different ethnicities and cultures.

The Indo-Americans achieved a high success in information technology. The company formed by them in this sector is estimated to be worth 300 billion USD according to the NASDAQ index in the stock market. There are thousands of Indian millionaires living in the Silicon Valley of California. A majority of them are engaged in the sphere of information technology, including computer programming. One of them is Sabir Bhatia who invented Hotmail and sold it for 400 million USD to Bill Gates's Microsoft company.

It is not accidental that the following joke is popular in California: here it is shameful not to be a millionaire.

After receiving education in India, young specialists widely use their family and other connections to settle in the US. Arriving there with the help of working visa or getting married to Indian girls, having American citizenship or Green Card, they try to fit into the existing American system of business and social relations.

Relations with its community in India and the US, the knowledge of English help to evade the "cultural shock" that the immigrants from other countries often go through. The author of the book about Indians from Silicon Valley, Chidananda Rajghatta writes, "if you speak simply, 5 lakh Indians arrived in US in ten years, with 50,000 every year. They represent the best in India, the cream of Indian talent. Those who came to US in 1980s reached the peak in business and professional career. They could use the wave of technological explosion in US that began thanks to activities of such large companies as Hewitt Packard, Microsoft, Sisko and others".[6]

There are famous managers, bankers, brokers, heads of companies, etc., among the successful Indians. Thus Rono Datta heads the largest American aviation company- United Airlines; Rajat Gupta heads Mackenzie – one of the largest consulting firms; Indra Nooyi became Chief Manager of Pepsi in 2006; Gururaj Deshpande is owner of Sikamor Telecommunications Company, which has a capitalisation of 30 billion USD in the US stock market.

Laxmi Mittal who is quite famous in Russia, is among the largest steel barons in the world. Apart from metallurgical factories in the US, he has enterprises in Germany, Mexico, Indonesia, Kazakhstan and Ukraine. According to Indian media reports, he plans to invest 9 billion USD in India's metallurgical industry.[7]

The Roots of Success of the Indian Immigrants

The success of Indian immigrants in the US, particularly of the last wave, is directly linked to India's achievements in the sphere of higher education. Every year, about 150 thousand specialists graduate from Indian universities and colleges. Science-based information technology, programming and computer science develop actively in the country. The Indian immigrants use this Indian potential, recruiting engineers living in India for their companies. While living thousands of kilometres away from India, they prepare computer programming, which is then transferred to their partners and owners in US through electronic email. Thus, the work in the sphere of high technology is done both in the US and India, mutually enriching their knowledge and materially stimulating both the sides.

The explosion in the sphere of informatics and omputerisation in India itself led to the creation of computers, second only to American and Japanese computers. One of them is the Super Computer-10000. India did not have its computers in 1960s. India purchased this from the US, The former Soviet Union and other countries. When the US refused to sell its super computer Krei-X-Mp in 1990, on the pretext that the Indians could use this for military nuclear research, Prime Minister Rajiv Gandhi declared that India would build its own super computer. In less than a decade, India could build that kind of computer with trillion operations in a second. This achievement of India found its use in the Russian–Indian scientific cooperation. The Russian–Indian centre opened in Russia in the framework of a cooperation programme in the field of prospective research, using this and other computers of Indian production.

The development of high technology in India was accompanied by the creation of lot of companies, successfully working in this sphere. India's own Silicon Valley appeared in Bangalore. The success of India in this sphere found its credit in that 140 out of 500 largest companies of the world use Indian programs.[8]

The success of India in the sphere of science-based technology led to a significant growth in employment and the emergence of large entrepreneurs. Now India has thousands of Indian millionaires (in rupee terms), engaged in this business. Some of the more successful Indians from among them found their place in the ranks of techno-billionaires in the world. According to the famous financial journal *Forbes Global*, out of 39 such people living outside the US, six are Indians. This list is headed by Japan with 15 such people; India and Germany each have six such people; Taiwan and Britain each have 2 such persons; each of France, Hong-Kong, Canada, Ireland, Italy, Israel, Spain and Sweden have one such person. The second position in the list has gone to the Indian Azim Premjee (Wipro, with 21. 4 billion USD). Subhash Chandra is in the eighth place (ZEE Telefilms has 9 billion USD).[9]

India's achievement in computer science drew attention of such grand companies like Microsoft, which built its development centre in Hyderabad in Andhra Pradesh. In September 2000, Bill Gates and the head of the Indian company Infosys Technologies Narayan Murthy signed an agreement for cooperation in the sphere of information technology and the use of internet for sale of items of financial service and insurance. Both the companies are conducting joint work for expansion of the Indian computer market, particularly to create programming in Hindi and other Indian languages.[10]

Narayan Murthy himself considers that the US has been the main market for Indian computer programs (60 to 70% income was coming from the US). For ensuring a further development in this direction, Infosys Technologies created its centres in California and Massachusetts. However, this does not limit its activities only in theUS, but expands its market in Europe and Japan. Infosys Technologies has its branches in Canada, Germany, Switzerland, Sweden, Japan and Australia. The European headquarters of the company would be opened in Great Britain. The Indian companies producing computer programs have set a task to achieve the export of computer programs worth 85 billion USD in 2008 in a year.[11]

It is highly naïve to believe that all American-Indians are super-champions and millionaires in high and science-based technologies.

Most of them are engaged in common things, required for any country and any city. They are present in many spheres of the US business and social life. Besides, there are specific fields for the use of their labour and talent. To a great extent it is linked to the traditional occupation of their families in India itself. For example, the devotees of Mahavir brought production and trade of jewellery, for which they are famous for centuries, to their new motherland. High professionalism in this business coupled with their close contacts with India permit them successfully to compete with other entrepreneurs.

The inclination of Indians to work in the sphere of jurisprudence, which is based on British law, helps them to freely understand the American legal system and become part of the huge community of US legal experts. Even the Indians themselves, in the US, prefer the service of their countrymen, who are working as advocates, without whom it is difficult to survive in this country. The Indian advocates, specialising in migration law, enjoy a special reputation.

The advertisements about credits given by one of the banks managed by Indians provide some indication about the occupation of Indians in the US. The bank announces that credit worth of 1.5 million USD with payment installments for 25 years is extended for buying hotels, motels, petrol pumps, restaurants, drycleaning, shops and other similar places.[12]

One of the spheres where the Indo-Americans have been successful is the motel and small hotel service. The volume of this business can be gauged considering the huge number of roads running through the US and an increasing number of tourists travelling in all kinds of transport, particularly in automobiles. Many hotels belonging to Indians in some areas are managed on family principles. A big family with parents, their married sons with their wives and children, fully manage to provide service to the clients, maintenance of the hotel or motel. All of them work without considering time and holidays and the whole income goes to the family coffers and is actively used for business expansion.

In some American states this business became a sort of monopoly of Indians hailing from Gujarat, belonging to the Patel caste – traditional village heads. That is why Indians humorously name this business as "motel- patel". The owners of motels and hotels view this as an advertisement and continue to work hard, without taking rest. They increase the capital, buy old motels, repair them and sell them with significant amount of profits at the peak of the tourist season.

As the number of Indian restaurants and shops increased, the need for supplying goods like rice, spices, mangoes, etc., which the Indians love, arose. Companies busy in this sphere appeared in the US. One of such companies is Raj Foods that has its packaging industry and storing facilities in Ahmadabad and Mumbai, New York and Chicago. The company with an annual turnover of 30 million USD grew successfully. Like in other areas, the whole business is run on family links. Rakesh Patel is the President of the company and Svetal Patel is Vice-President. The President of the New York branch is Mahendra Patel while Paresh Patel is Vice President.[13]

The Indian immigration in America in reality is purely an economic phenomenon and that is why its main problems are related to this—particularly during the first stage when one has to adapt in the new place of work, accommodation, survival in the new socio-cultural environment, which are the main issues linked to integration with the American society.

The Indian Diaspora with its deep multi-confessional and polyethnic traditions found itself in a situation of multi-confessional and polyethnic American reality, complicated by racial relations. In the middle of the 1960s, when the first wave of Indians arrived in the US, this country was passing through a sick stage of freedom and cleaning from rigid racial discrimination. At this point of time was the wave of Afro-American movement for their rights, peak of which reached when their leader Martin Luther King was killed and laws were approved for the establishment of racial equality.

However, during the past years, the situation has undergone a lot of changes. First of all, now there is whole new generation of Indo-Americans born in the US. In conditions of heterogenic American society with its huge diversity, each part of which is proud of its historical past, it is completely normal to emphasise one's spiritual or family links with the historical motherland. This concerns all the British, Irish, Germans, Chinese, Russians and others.

The Indians are no exception. Moreover, they have a thousands of years-old huge, diversified culture and civilisation. Looking at historical roots by the Indian migrants is natural and logical and does not evoke any question in the conditions of today's American reality.

Bharati Mukherjee, an American writer of Indian origin, conducts a course on world literature and workshop on literary creativity in the University of Berkeley in California. According to her observation, during her talks with students – Indo-Americans – she hears the inner voice of the young people, born and brought up in the US and raised as Americans in many ways. Nevertheless, they try to find their roots in the past, which their parents left in India in the 1960s–70s as they left for the US in order to study and work. While the first generation immigrants in many ways stagnated in the cultural framework of India of the 1960s, their children on the one hand show a confidence typical of the Americans. On the other hand, if they do not share the feelings and mood of their parents; they nevertheless feel the requirement to get out of what is called "here and now".[14]

The striving to preserve tradition in the Indian Diaspora in the US finds its expression in building Indian temples, creating the Vedanta Society, the beginning of which was made by the great religious reformer Swami Vivekananda towards the end of the nineteenth century.

Apart from religious rituals and ceremonies, the Indian temples in the US are engaged in religious-enlightening activities, paying special attention to attracting the youth and explaining to them the essence of Hinduism. In many cities of the US, they have become the centre for communication among Hindus and the revival of the traditions of Hinduism. For this purpose, not only temples are used but also complex with cultural centres being built.

In the conditions of a multi-confessional American society, the bid to preserve the own Hindu identity does not contradict other religions. One of the specific features of the cultural–religious activities of the Hindu temples and the location of Indian cultural centers near them is the organisation of events with the participation of representatives of different faiths.

Vedanta centers and societies of the Ramakrishna Mission in San Francisco, New York, Washington, Chicago, Seattle, Boston, St. Louis and other cities are doing a lot for propaganda for Hinduism. Vedanta centers are engaged in religious–educational activities, and in this connection publish a lot of books and booklets. There are libraries in those temples for their members. Not only the Indo-Americans but also other Americans visit these centres. In some temples, Americans of non-Indian origin also work as heads.

One of the main ideas preached in these centres is that Vedanta is not an exclusive religion. The spiritual leaders of the Vedanta society stress that they came from India not as missionaries, but on the invitation of a group of people or group interested in Vedanta; they are not professionals, but spiritual leaders.

Indo-Americans get united not only on ethno-religious but also on aprofessional basis. For example, the Association of American Physicians from India and the Indian Medical Association are well-known professional organisations. The main objectives of these associations are extending a free medical help to the Indians in the US and India. For this purpose, they build clinics in both countries. Right now, the Association of American Physicians from India manages 13 clinics and is planning to expand its activities to all large cities.

The Global Organisation of People of Indian Origin functioning in the US was engaged in the issues of violation of rights of Indians in the world. At present, it concentrates its efforts in creating a favourable situation for the business growth of Indians coming from India, Mauritius, Trinidad and Tobago, Guiana, Fiji, Surinam and other countries.

Newspapers like the *India Tribune, India Post*, *India West*, *India Abroad* and others published in different US cities play a significant role in the life of the Indian Diaspora.

Indian businessmen, public and cultural figures and politicians display a keen interest in maintaining links between India and the Indian Diaspora. They use the contacts with the Indo-Americans for promoting their business and political relations with the US. The Indian Diaspora is a vital instrument for strengthening relations between the two countries. The Indian community in the US does an adequate lobbying for Indian interests at the local and national scale.

There is big group of lobbyists in the US Congress working in favour of India.

The Indo-Americans have gradually become involved in the active political life of the US. Some of them participate in elections at the city and state levels. The role of Indo-Americans at the national level is so far limited to the collection of funds in favour of political parties and their candidates. During the Presidential election of November 2000, the Indo-Americans did not keep themselves aloof from party and political struggle. Thus, the businessman Vinod Gupta and Sabir Bhatia contributed 1.6 million dollars to the election fund of the Democratic Party. Though a significant number of other Indo-Americans also supported this party and its candidate Al Gore, some extended financial support to the Republican candidate George Bush. The total amount contributed to the election funds of both parties contributed by the Indo-Americans reached about 3 million USD. This may be too small an amount compared to the total amount that was spent during this Presidential election, which was to the tune of 3 billion USD, according to some reports. What is important is that it took place for the first time. The time has come for an active participation of the Indo-Americans in US politics and social life, said Subhas Patel, founder of Sirrus Logic. "We were in isolation for too long", said Patel.[15]

All this together permit to conclude that the young Indian Diaspora in the US continues to preserve its original identity. It won't be an exaggeration to say that the process of assimilation has not touched it. This is quite evident among those Indians who are born, study and are raised in the US. Assimilation probably is one of the necessary conditions for success in the US. The significance of special features of American culture, business life, etc., gives the key for forward movement in conditions of serious competition. This concerns not only Indians but also all other immigrants. The market economy, consumer psychology, code of conduct, etc., as accepted in the US cannot but exert a significant influence on the lifestyle of the Indian Diaspora.

The ethno-social integration of the Indian immigrants in the US is simplified by the fact that different communities do not have a common language except English. That is why a bilingual practice of the majority of the Indian immigrants does not a create problem in this integration.

The native language remains as a means for communication in the family or in the ethnic community. But as the framework of such a Diaspora is not very sustainable and is subject to erosion in the process of communication with other Americans, including Indians, those who speak other languages, the ethno-linguistic isolation becomes impossible inside the Indian Diaspora as also in the American society as a whole. The second and third generations of the Indo-Americans are inclined towards acculturisation, in process of which the traditional culture of the ethos is subject to the cultural influence of American society. Sometimes, it so happens that inter-ethnic and international marriage becomes secondary to international marriage. What is common for many Indo-Americans is their affiliation to one religion – Hinduism. However, Indian Jains,

Muslims and Sikhs exist outside the framework of this important rallying factor. This weakens the consolidating role of religion.

Indians and the US Immigration Policy

The situation of the Indian Diaspora in the US should be viewed in the common context of the entire American social-economic, cultural and political life and should also take the state immigration policy into account.

The first large wave of Indian immigration practically began after the adoption of the most important immigration law in the history of the US in 1965, which was prepared in the course of 13 years from 1952, under the Presidentship of Harry Truman. The new law signed by President Lyndon Johnson did not have any discriminatory provisions in the immigration policy, which so far was giving lot of advantages to the immigrants from Britain,

Germany and Ireland. At the same time, the number of immigrants was doubled from 154 thousand to 290 thousand under the new law. This law removed the quotas for certain countries and gave importance to the reunion of families through a preserved immigration of highly qualified immigrants.

The Indians, like the representatives of many countries, widely used this opportunity. The Immigration Law of 1965 opened the door for people wishing to work and live in the US. The reunion of families was the mechanism that led to the unexpected growth of immigration. First of all this concerned the political refugees from South Vietnam in the 1970s followed by Cuban immigrants in the 1980s. This was followed by thousands of immigrants from Central America and Mexico. The Indians were a small number in this stream.

Reacting to the emerging situation, the US Congress adopted a law on Immigration Reform and Control in 1986 and the Immigration Law of 1990. Efforts were made to stop illegal immigration. The number of legal immigrants on the basis of the 1990 immigration law was raised to the record level of 825 thousand people.

The small Indian Diaspora used various loopholes for increasing its numbers. First of all, the Indians used the provision of family reunion and formation of new family. Single Indians, who were US citizens or Green-card holders began to bring their spouses from India, which was followed by their relatives.

The US has the requirement for highly qualified specialists, which are not satisfied by their universities and colleges. The majority of Americans are of the opinion that immigrants are the source for increasing the country's population and strengthening the might of the state. They say that American culture and US global interests are a product of ethnic diversity, which links the US with different regions of the world and transforms the immigration into a kind of foreign policy instrument. Besides, many teachers and parents of students think that by communicating with the children of immigrants, the schoolchildren are getting rid of their parochial mentality by widening their worldview.

Representatives of the business world insist on preserving big quotas for qualified immigrants. Several years back, during the annual debate in the US Congress on the temporary working visa (HI-B) for foreigners, the big businessmen from Silicon Valley tried to prove the necessity of the invitation to qualified specialists on computer programming under this category of visa. This concerned not only Indians and Chinese but also the Russians, who enjoy lot of reputation in the high-tech market.

The Indian government pays a lot of attention to the work with the Indian Diaspora in the entire world. A committee on dealing with the Indian Diaspora headed by L.M. Singhvi was formed in the year 2000. The objective of this committee was to analyse a wide range of issues concerning the present and future role of the Indian Diaspora in the economic, social and technological development of the country.

The members of this committee travelled to 20 countries where they discussed the questions of expansion of cooperation in many areas with the representatives of the Indian Diaspora. As a result of these visits, a comprehensive report containing proposals and recommendations was prepared for the Government of India.

The main conclusion of the committee was that the Indian Diaspora is an important factor in the development of relations of India with the countries of their living. The Diaspora has a huge potential for promoting cooperation with India, including in making it a superpower of knowledge. The Diaspora is an instrument for spreading genuine information about India among the people of the country where it lives.

The committee recommended creating an autonomous organisation for dealing with the issues of the Diaspora with the

Prime Minister as its Chairman, and to form a permanent committee in the parliament on these issues, which would maintain links with the parliamentarians of Indian origin in different countries. This work is going on.

It was proposed to strengthen the political interaction with countries that have a significant and influential Indian Diaspora. Special attention needs to be paid to the development of trade, economic and cultural relations with those countries. It was recommended to institute special awards for Indians living abroad and name streets, schools, libraries in recognition of their contribution, etc.

The constructive role of the Diaspora, its achievements and contribution in the development of relations with India are recognised in India through the celebration of the Indian Migrants Day in January, every year. Such important celebrations began in 2001. The International Conference of World Organization of People with Indian Origin was held at New Delhi which was addressed by the Prime Minister of India.

During the last several years a lot of work has been done for improving contacts with the Indian Diaspora, for its active participation in the trade–economic and cultural ties with India. Steps have been taken for simplifying their passport and customs procedure while travelling to India, extending legal assistance to the Indians travelling abroad and promoting the Indian culture and language abroad, particularly among the youth.

The Ministry of Overseas Indians Affairs pays a lot of attention to use its resources for increasing investment in India and the development of trade, economy and tourism. The possibility for creating special economic zones, meant for Indians living abroad and providing them with a single-window consultancy in this connection are under consideration.

A lot of attention is given to contacts with Indians working abroad in the sphere of education. Measures are contemplated for bringing scientists, teachers, etc., from among the Indian immigrants for working in the educational institutions and research centres of India. Plans are being chalked out for inviting the youth of Indian origin for getting education in India.

One of the directions for working with the foreigners of Indian origin is the use of media, controlled by the Indians migrant for acquainting the people of foreign countries with Indian culture, its achievements and problems. Work is going on for building a House of Indian Migrants in India with a library and an exhibition about the life of Indians living abroad, their successes and difficulties. The government is looking into the question of providing dual citizenship to the Indians living abroad.[16]

Conclusion

India would actively develop contacts with the Indian Diaspora in the countries of their habitation, using their resources for promoting its interests in trade, economy, science, high technology and foreign policy.

The contribution of the Indians living abroad to the fast growing economy of India would form a significant part of all investments, because the people of Indian origin have deep links with this country, know its culture and the specific nature of its economy and the financial system pretty well.

The Indian Diaspora will remain one of the instruments for strengthening the Indian influence abroad, particularly in the US, Britain, Canada and South Africa.

A large and powerful Indian Diaspora plays a significant role in the economic and social life of the US, Great Britain, Canada, and some other countries, and also in their relations with India. It is an important instrument for strengthening the contacts between the countries of its habitation and India.

The Indian community living abroad does adequate lobbying for the Indian interests in trade, economy and politics.

On its part, the Indian Diaspora is an important instrument for the countries of its living in their relations with India and for exerting influence on its economic and political elite.

Notes

1. *The Times of India*. 1 February 2005; *The Economist*, "The World in 2006", p. 95.
2. *The Hindu*. 25 April 2006.
3. *И.Ю.Котин*. Побеги баньяна: миграция населения Индии и формирование «узлов» Южно-Азиатской диаспоры. СПб: Петербургское Востоковедение, 2003; *Ф.Юрлов*. Индийская диаспора в Америке// Азия и Африка сегодня, 2001, № 5. С. 24-27; № 6. С. 9-12; Asia Annual 2003. Ed. Mahavir Singh. Maulana Abul Kalam Azad Institute of Asian Studies, New Delhi, 2003; *Ф.Н.Юрлов*. Рецензия на книгу Азия. Ежегодник 2003. Под ред. Махавира Сингха. Нью-Дели, 2003 // Восток, 2004, №4. С. 180-185; *Ф.Н.Юрлов*. Миграция индийцев за рубеж и формирование индийской диаспоры Рецензия на книгу И.Ю.Котина. Побеги баньяна: миграция населения Индии… // Азия и Африка сегодня, 2005, № 10. С. 72.
4. Wadhwa, Vivek, "Are Indians Model Immigrants?", *Business Week Online*, 14 September, 2006.
5. http:nytimes.com/renters/politics-india-usa-diaspora.html. February27, 2006.
6. "New Generation of Indian Americans creating Waves in US", NDTV-MSNBC Online, 10.08.2000.
7. *Times of India*. 26 December 1999; Итоги. 26 июня, 2006.
8. Подробнее см.: *Фирсова И.* Впечатляющие масштабы научно-технического прогресса. // Индия сегодня. Приложение к журналу Азия и Африка сегодня, август 2000. С. 25.
9. *Deccan Chronicle*. 26 March 2000.
10. *The Indian Express*. 15 November 2000.
11. *Deccan Chronicle*. 13 July 2000.
12. *The India Post*. California-Chicago-New York. 21 April 2000.
13. *The India Tribune*, Chicago, New York and Atlanta, 6 May 2000.
14. *The Sunday Times of India Review*, 31 December 1995.
15. *The Indian Express*. 03 November 2000.
16. http://indiandiaspora.nic.in/contents.htm/

19

Generation "Lost" and Generation "Next": The Two Generations of Russian Youth

Natalia Borozdina

The collapse of the USSR and the following socio-economic transformation in the territory of the post-Soviet countries were the matters of a great cultural shock for the grown-up, mature soviet people but also a larger scale for teenagers, whose identity was just forming. The collective mind was deeply injured; things which for decades had always been taken for granted, such as socialist ideals, dominant role of the communist party, secured workplaces for everybody, equal opportunities, condemnation of those who got personal profit out of sales and so on – all of that was thrown into the trash bin of history. New things such as entrepreneurial spirit and practicism started to emerge.

For the younger Russian population, it was especially difficult to survive this turn-over in moral values. The rapid transition from a soviet into allegedly democratic state hurt most of all those who were at the age of 12–16 at the beginning of the 1990s. It happened so because precisely at that age, the identity is being formed. The guidelines for that identity – stable moral values – are of vital importance. I myself belong to that generation. I never forget this disgusting feeling of being betrayed when the same teachers at school started to interpret history end even literature in completely the opposite way compared to what they had said several months before.

If before to be called an "egoist' was the worst curse, now the one who minds his own interest is the hero of the day; if before it was a disgrace to strive for a career and any work at any level was full of dignity, now only the successful and fast in their career came to be respected. Old values were defiled; the new looked vague and suspicious. We grew up with the feeling that everything is relative in this world and everything can be denigrated if it is needed. When you have a world perception like that, all forms of deviant behaviour seem most alluring.

Today we are 28–33 years old and Russian sociologists often call us the "generation lost" because now-a-days many people at this age do not have fixed moral values, are unable to build up a family or a long-lasting relationship, are politically passive, unstable as workers, unreliable as partners— not ready to take responsibility. Taking into account that in 10–15 years these people will be the backbone of the Russian ruling elite, the perspectives for the future is not so bright.

Fortunately, no turmoil lasts forever. Devastated and stressed by the overwhelming stream of Westernisation, Russia at the end of the 1990s started to regain its stability in a new form. Those born after or at the end of perestroika – at the beginning of the 1990s or at the end of the 1980s, went through the process of socialisation in more stable and defined conditions and that is why their identity nowadays is less dominated by the relativity syndrome, and reflects the changes in the Russian social climate. Though it is argued that in most post-communist societies there exists a huge gap between legitimised social norms and moral values and those standards that guide our everyday behaviour, the generation "next" in Russia is more consistent in formulating its moral values and life priorities and corresponding it with their behavioral patterns. It is especially important to study the identity and world perception of the Russian youth today due to the fact that in transition societies it is the values of youth that in 10–15 years become dominant among the whole population of a country, as it was argued by Ronald Inglehart in his article "Changing Values, Economic Development and Political Change."

So what is our Russian generation "next", people who never got any communist propaganda and who entered the middle school IN the era of Putin? To what extent can they be described as the representatives of "a modern personality" model, suggested by Alex Inkeles and David H. Smith in their book *Becoming Modern*?

According to these researchers, a "modern person is an active citizen with the deep sense of social responsibility, internally independent and intellectually mature, with the high level of tolerance and feeling for law and order". The high level of modernity is a very important prerequisite for the successful development of a modern society, especially the transitional one.

Our conclusions will be based on three researches. The first one named "The youth in the modern society" was conducted as an opinion poll in St. Petersburg, the second largest and, probably, the most politically influential Russian city. 1,000 young people from the ages of 14 to 25 years participated in the research, of which 11.1% were from 14 to 16 years old, 41.8% – 16–18 and 47% – 19–25 years old. In the selection of respondents the methods of quota and route sampling and target audience sampling were used. The respondents belonged to different strata, judged from the point of view of economic prosperity:

52.2% said that they have enough money for their daily needs and even can afford saving some part of it

29.1% – enough money only for daily needs

16.6% – some purchases cause financial problems

2.1% – have to deny themselves a lot of things

The data received show us the following picture: nowadays, the young Russian people are pragmatically oriented; they want to achieve material success in life and to improve their quality of life, being sure that an education is the best starting point for any career.

When asked "**What do you want to achieve in life?**", they answered:

Life goals	**General**	**Men**	**Women**
High salary, material prosperity	19.1%	17.6%	18.6%
Interesting work, the work I like	13.1%	14.4%	14.1%
Good relationship in family	11.6%	13.3%	12.3%
True friendship	11.3%	10.5%	12.1%
Happiness in love, intimate life	7.2%	8.8%	7.5%
Travelling around the world	6.1%	8.0%	6.4%
Entrepreneurial success (own business)	4.6%	4.4%	4.5%
Spiritual well-being	4.5%	4.4%	4.3%
Professionalism, high skills	4.2%	2.9%	4.1%
Independence, freedom	3.8%	3.0%	3.5%
Useful acquaintances, contacts	3.5%	2.4%	3.0%
Security	3.2%	2.3%	2.8%
Sense of security	3.3%	3.2%	2.8%
Full realisation of creative self-potential	2.1%	1.4%	1.4%
Fame, social recognition	1.9%	0.7%	1.2%
Power, chance to rule over others	1.9%	0.8%	1.2%
Easy job, relaxed life	1.9%	0.7%	1.1%

As for the future plans, 31.5% stated that they want to continue an education, with significant gender discrepancy on that point – only 26.4% for men and 36.6% for women. The second popular answer is to establish one's own business – 14.8% of all respondents (18.8% for men and only 10% for women).

The third option is to work according to received specialisation in commercial organisations – 12.3% (16.6% for men, 8% for women)

Fourthoption – to work in governmental organisations – 11.2% (7.8% for men, 4.6% for women)

What are our plans for the near future?

Answers	General	Men	Women
Continue education	31.5%	26.4%	
			36.6%
Start own business	14.8%	18.8%	
			10.8%
Work according to education in commercial firms	12.3%	16.6%	
			8%
	11.2%	7.8%	
Work according to education in govt organisations			14.6%
	7.5%	7%	
			8%
I have other plans	5.4%	7.2%	
			3.6%
I have no plans yet	5.2%	4.8%	
			5.6%
Go abroad for study or work	4.9%	5.4%	
			4.4%
Work NOT according to education in commercial firms	2.5%	2.8%	
	2%	1.2%	2.2%
Work NOT according to education in govt organisations	1.6%	1%	2.8%
	1%	0.8%	2.2%
Take care of the household and family			
			1.2%
Do scientific research			
Stay at the firm where I have a part-time job now			

The second research was conducted by the Center of Sociological Monitoring (Moscow). It compares the answers given by the graduates of the year 2000 (generation "lost") and 2006 (generation "next"). We can see that the perception of success is also quite different for these two generations, with self-assurance being the most valuable factor for the first one, and good education for the second:

What constitutes success?

The main component	Graduates, 2000	Graduates, 2006
	56%	45.6%
Self-assurance	33%	47%
Good education	46%	43.4%
Useful contacts	30%	37.9%
Business initiative	20.2%	32.5%
Money	37.8%	30.4%
Professional skills	10%	17%
Competitiveness	8%	12%

What are you prepared to do for your goal?

Type of action	Graduates, 2000	Graduates, 2006
Suffer from accommodation inconveniences	52.4%	30.7%
To be separated from parents	47.5%	33.3%
To work without weekends	46%	38.7%
To participate in fierce competition	41.3%	36%
To work for little pay	26%	21%
To marry by convenience	19%	21.3%
To work without social care package	16.5%	12%
To sacrifice moral values	14.5%	17%
To violate the law	11.5%	17.3%
To experience discomfort	11%	8%
To lie	9.7%	10.7%

The third research was a qualitative analysis of essays written by the young people in the Siberian city of Irkutsk, aged from 16 to 25, with the total number of participants amounting to 1220 persons. They wrote about the way they perceive modern life and their personal future. According to this research, the motto of our generation "next" is "To achieve success in life, have a high time and get all and at once".

Every second young person is striving for freedom and independence; they are ready to shape their future themselves and do not expect any support from the government. They are eager to make decisions themselves and hold all responsibility for that.

As for the brutal rules of market economy in Russia, 3\4th want to participate in it and start their own venture, every second person respects those who made a fortune regardless of their means, 1\3rd thinks that there are no honest and dishonest ways to make money, every fifth person would like to receive a lot money for nothing and only 15% considers business to be a fraud, with cruelty and exploitation.

Though the majority (49.3%) admits that our market economy has a criminal character, they are ready to accept it as an objective reality and tolerate it. They are prepared to adjust their behavioral patterns to the social reality of a modern Russia.

By way of conclusion we may say that in modern Russia there exists two generations of the young. The first one, which is often called generation "lost", is aged from 28 to 33. This generation suffers from the relativity syndrome, known as "dark age", and always foresees turmoil in any changes. Usually, these people hold a pessimistic worldview and are reluctant to trust in something or somebody.

Another generation of the young, aged from 14 to 25, is quite different in its nature. Born at the end of perestroika, when Russia opened itself to the foreign mass media, the generation "next" absorbed more than any other age group all the cultural standards the West had to offer. These young people are very susceptible to the influence of the consumer society; they want to get more entertainment, more informal networking, more pop-culture and more things to buy. They want to get more results for their invested efforts, and they want all their efforts be rewarded.

20

Can Eurasian Countries Catch up with the West?

Sergey Lounev[1]

Extremely complicated and diverse political–economic and socio-economic processes are taking place in the course of transformation of the world system at the crossroads of centuries. During the past twenty-five years, new socio-economic systems have appeared in the zone of developed powers, which have as yet, not received any name. Without giving details about all the changes, let us specifically note that a new interaction between production, science and informatics has taken place. Here, "Economics based on knowledge" is taking shape, and in countries like Japan, USA eighty per cent of the growth of the GDP is accounted for scientific–technical progress.

A process of emergence of industrialisation was observed in the non-West, at least in its large part. The model of "catching up development" was used in the entire world in the past. The developed countries were interested in some sort of modernisation of the countries of the East, and the centre of the world system systematically pushed capitalist impulses to the periphery. The main problem before this Eastern zone is the possibility of the postponement of this emerging system of the West. Considering the cardinal role played by science in the process of its formation, it is necessary to carry out an analysis of the formation of system of contemporary scientific knowledge in the developing societies of the East, in order to make real a assessment of perspectives for future development.

Europe's rapid development from the middle of the eighteenth century was largely linked with The application of new techniques and the European system of knowledge strongly influenced the Eastern societies. It is sufficient to note that this process led to stable changes in countries that had preserved their independence like Japan, China, Thailand, Turkey and Iran. Under the influence of growing economic, technical, and military advantage of the European powers, and the growth of their might, the Asian countries, in order to survive, were forced to borrow new techniques, and for their successful use to change laws and create corresponding organisational structures. First of all, they had to prepare capable cadres for using these techniques. However, the training of cadres in the European manner led to a division in the local elite, which was clearly reflected in the revolutions headed by Meidji Changcaisi, Young Turks and Gilyanski. In a known sense, these revolutions and their consequences could be considered as a "catching up" with the civilised characteristics.

During 15 years after the end of the World War, the colonial system saw its downfall; European education became widespread in most progressive colonies. The territory that was under British colonial rule needs a special mention in this regard. The system of European style education was introduced in India in 1835, and three universities were founded in 1857. Compulsory primary education was introduced in Ceylon from the beginning of the twentieth century. The French colonial authorities stared spreading European education later. The first university of Indo-China was founded in 1907. Holland and Portugal did not wish for the emergence of "foreigners" educated in a European manner.

The problems regarding the perception of achievements of new technology, the ability of the people to use it and the introduction of a European system of knowledge remain extremely complicated for the majority of states of the world. A major obstacle to the development of science could be called as an absence of the necessary infrastructure. Since fundamental science, particularly the expensive one, does not give quick direct returns, the Eastern society rejects such specialists. It is easier to use ready-made knowledge than to develop indigenous science. Young specialists receiving education abroad, in spite of their interest to work in their home country, are forced to go abroad where their knowledge could be properly used. It should be noted that many scientists from the countries of the East do not lag behind their European and US colleagues from the standpoint of their professional quality.

If we talk about modern science in the East, it was formed under the powerful influence of the West. This is related to, first of all, the use of Western apparatus and the perception of the problem. At the same time, the preservation of the powerful influence of traditional knowledge and values, which is manifested in the humanitarian sphere, is typical of Eastern countries.

The invasion of European techniques, science, education (in the form of American mass culture) evoked a sort of rejection in a number of the countries of the South. This is particularly so in the countries of the Middle East and tropical Africa. As a result, a serious development of science did not take place in these countries. Scientific research centres and universities live an absolutely isolated life, without any interaction with the society and the state. Their links with the international scientific centres are stronger. We can guess that these macro-regions do not have perspectives for building a system of science; there cannot be any interaction between science and production in the foreseeable future and development would continue to be based on the extraction of raw materials and industrial production not linked to high-tech spheres.

Another specific feature of the countries of Southern and Eastern Asia is the qualitatively higher stage of cultural dynamics and scientific–technical autonomy that dominates there. These characteristics ensure the ability of these countries to get out of the circle of backwardness, carry out enclave-type economic modernisation and not only skillfully use the imported high-tech but also independently develop scientific research, thus entering the new stage of a scientific–technical revolution, which gives additional opportunity for the expansion of influence on the processes taking place in the Afro-Asian region.

There is huge respect for science and scientists. Here, the state is represented by the ruling circles and their social institutions play an important role. The experiences of a number of states of the region bear testimony that the state's activity has had a fundamental significance in the course of formation of new structures, which have permitted such powers to master the scientific–technical achievements of the highly developed countries in historically short periods and end the process of industrialisation. The state possesses a key position in the Western countries too. A clear administrative system as seen in the Asian countries, is really less effective compared to the market-based system. However, this experience shows that any business in the absence of real control, would try to receive only maximum profit and would not protect the interests of the majority of the population and also does not promote the development of science and production based on high-tech.

The newly industrialised countries of East Asia are different from the developed countries in only quantitative terms, not in qualitative terms, and this gives the possibility to hope that they would enter the group of highly developed countries in the near future. Unfortunately, this is happening in relatively small countries.

The Asian giants face more complicated issues. In the former Dutch colony Indonesia, there was no development of science and no progress in the sphere of education during the colonial period. There is hardly any change in the contemporary period when the country with a population of one-fourths of a billion, has a very weakly developed science and technological production.

In the case of China and India (occupying the first place in the world in term of population and economic growth), the problems lie in a different sphere. These countries have highly qualified specialists, which positively impacts on cultural dynamics and the scientific–technical autonomy of the Asian giants. They are far ahead of the developed countries and the countries of southern Europe and Latin America in terms of rate of growth. The situation in China and India in the sphere of education is no ideal. But here, one has to consider their past.

If the civilisational paradigm of China can be called as state-egalitarian, in India, the main development path is elitist, which is directly linked to the caste legacy. It is in the sphere of education where the difference of the civilisational paradigm between China and India is clearly seen. While China is strong in basic mass education, India is strong in higher education.

In the technical sphere, China and India have showed the ability to handle imported high technology and create their own high technology. The share of high-tech branches in China's total industrial production has reached 25%, whereas India has remarkable achievements in information technology. It should be noted here that the Indian state creates the most favorable conditions for the development of this branch.

More than that, the Asian giants have displayed an ability to independently develop scientific research. The creation of nuclear weapons independently serves as an example in this respect. However, the Asian giants lag far behind the developed countries and Russia in the sphere of fundamental research.

The objective socio-economic situation of these countries, stand in their way of building a new society. The presence of a huge unqualified population does not permit them to adopt many models of developed countries. There is no sense for applying new resource-preserving technology because of the low cost of manual labour and the necessity to provide jobs to the huge population. It is not accidental that the majority of technological achievements are export-oriented. An annual exodus of tens of thousands of highly qualified specialists is also observed here, which may lead to a significant weakening of the positions of these states in the high-tech sphere, and a rapid deterioration of cultural dynamics in the future.

Russia, like a majority of the non-Western countries, builds on traditional capitalism (in new conditions with nationalist specifics). Russia, in principle, could have built a post-industrial society, particularly if it had chosen this path fifteen ago (the contemporary development of the West is the realisation of the idea found in the theory of convergence of capitalism and socialism).

Russia has an extremely weak state and influential bureaucracy. As a result, science-based production functions in an extremely distorted legal space, hardly facilitating the development of innovative activities. The state does not fulfil its functions in the sphere of unification of science and business, as it happens not only in the developed nations but also in the developing countries, whose experiences are very interesting.

If you assess the achievements of Russian science in the world market of science-based products, it looks rather modest. Only 0.3% of this market belongs to Russian know-how and technology. Our revenue from the sale of licenses is ten times less than that of the US. Such figures, coupled with a concentration of 10% of world scientists in Russia, serves as the basis for complains against market inefficiency. President Putin has drawn attention to this fact. Such position is not baseless however, there are a number of objections to it.

- If Russia's share in the world market of science-based products is determined not by number of our scientists, but by the budget allocation for science (which is less than the budget of a large US university), then the ratio is not so unfavourable for it.
- A significant part of Russian know-how and technology is not sold, but has gotten stolen because of the lack of protection of intellectual property.
- The sale of intellectual property presupposes its prior formatting as property, and Russia lags behind other countries in this field.
- The share of this or that country in the world market of science-based products speaks about

- its ability not only in production but also to sell it. In the developing countries, for each
- prospective scientific idea, there are on an average 10 managers, who push the product in the market while the number is several times less in Russia.
- It is necessary to build a system to provide special training to managers in this field.
- The poor state of production often obstructs converting scientific knowledge into new type of production.
- Russia has the problem of a permanent "idea drain". Tens of thousands of scientists are now working for foreign companies, and huge numbers of scientists have fled the country. Russia's real contribution to the world market of science-based products, know-how and technology is several times more than the registered statistics.

Thus, it is not Russian science that does not correspond to the requirements of the market economy. Rather, a Russian version of the market, based not on science-intensive but on trade and financial operations and raw-material extraction, does not correspond to the requirements of scientific–technical progress and is not capable of assimilating new scientific knowledge.

The Russian science itself has a fairly good market potential, which is manifested in those incidents when it comes in contact with the foreign market. That is why the Russian know-how and technology in a majority of cases is not finding application in our country and flows abroad.

Many branches of fundamental science in Russia, in spite of a lot of pessimistic assessment, maintain international levels. It is linked to the existing potential, preservation of scientific schools and brilliant scientists and also to the fact that fundamental science after all requires less financial resources as compared to the NIKOR. As a result of the last factor, a sharp reduction in the allocation of financial resources to science did not hit fundamental science so much.

Two weak points need special mention: inadequate materialisation of scientific achievements into technology and know-how, and their translation into ready-made items. It all existed during the Soviet times because of the rigid system. However, there was some sort of interlinking between the Academy of Sciences, the branch institutes and construction-bureaus. The last two elements simply disappeared during the post-Soviet period.

Russia can make a breakthrough to the post-industrial stage only through the strategy of development of human potential, technologically complicated and science-based branches and raising the role of science in production. It is clear that the strategy of reliance on raw materials and its practical status of the "villages of the West" leads to gradual degradation. There are lots of limitations for a traditional industrial path: low competitiveness of the basic work force; unfavourable climatic and geographical conditions, because of which cost of one unit of production rises by 10% to 15%. Among the European capitals, Moscow is located in the most severe climatic conditions. Even Helsinki is located in a warmer climatic condition than Moscow. The Urals and Siberia are simply incomprehensible from a market point of view in terms of the extraction of mineral resources.

Apart from this, Western countries would not facilitate the emergence of a new powerful competitor. More hopes can be pinned on the Asian countries. There was a time when the Moscow-Delhi-Beijing triangle was actively discussed in Russia. Unfortunately, the discussion took place in its military–political aspects. The perspective of economic cooperation did not receive proper attention, which has really a lot of potential. The combination of Russian scientific thoughts with Indian engineering thoughts and the low-cost qualitative work force of China has tremendous potential. The product produced through this combination can have a huge market. Two Asian giants are oriented towards the domestic market and will possess the highest rate of growth for a long time.

It is necessary to face these challenges of the century at the right time and comply with the national interests. The development of science should serve as the basis for strategic planning and in some respect serve the security needs of the country.

21

Institutional Developments And Political Practices in Kyrgyzstan

Sumant Kumar Swain

The nation-building process of a contemporary nation state requires strong institutional designing which would accommodate the wills and aspirations of all sections of the people. In a democratic society, well-designed institutions would facilitate active citizen participation in the state affairs. After the Cold War period, political development, especially in the communist bloc countries, provides a new imperative for political knowledge regarding the transitional political developments from the communist ideology to a democratic and liberal political system. The political culture, attitude, political behaviour and social acceptance of the general community as well as the political nomenclature of the communist society also changed according to the new political scenario. Efficiently designed political institutions are the key yardstick and instrument for a smooth functioning of the nation state in the contemporary political system. The design and formation of state institutions like the legislature, executive and judiciary, reflects country's political system and governability. In the present world order, institution-building is the most important aspect to accommodate and give importance to all sections of people, without discrimination. In the democratic form of government, institution-building plays a major role for creating a stable society. At the same time, institution-building is easier in a stable and mature society than in the newly independent states.

The Central Asian Republics got their independence after the disintegration of the Soviet Union in December 1991, though these republics were not willing to leave the Soviet Union. In the March 1991 referendum, 90 to 95 per cent of the electorate in the Central Asian Republics had supported the preservation of the USSR, as against only 53.5 per cent in the Russian Republic favouring its continued existence.[1] In spite of the Central Asian willingness to remain in the Union, the situation started changing following an abortive coup in Moscow in August 1991. As a result, on August 31, 1991, the Supreme Soviet of Uzbekistan and Kyrgyzstan declared the independence of their respective republics. After independence, Kyrgyzstan debated on whether the Parliament would operate on a full or part-time basis, as well as whether it would be unicameral or bicameral. In this debate, central leaders were divided on both the aspects. At last, they reached the conclusion and adopted their own constitutions. The Kyrgyz Republic directed itself on the way of building a strong democratic state governed by law. The Constitution of the Kyrgyz Republic was proclaimed on May 5, 1993 by the 12th Supreme Soviet of the Republic of Kyrgyzstan. This Constitution contained 97 Articles, divided into VIII chapters. This Constitution has also been amended so many times, like on October 22, 1994, on February 10, 1996, on October 17, 1998, on February 2, 2003, in November 2006 and October 2007 and June 2010, through referendums. The 1993 Constitution of Kyrgyzstan also declares the country to be a secular and unitary state and places the sovereignty with the people.

The Executive Branch

The President occupies the highest position in the Executive branch. The Constitution of the Kyrgyz Republic mentions the position of the President in the Chapter III and Article 42. This Constitution elaborates: The President of the Kyrgyz Republic is the head of the state and is the highest official of the Kyrgyz Republic. He is the symbol of the unity of the people and state power, and is the guarantor of the Constitution of Kyrgyz Republic and of human rights and freedoms. He also defines the fundamental directions of internal and external policy of the state, represents the Kyrgyz Republic within the country and in international relations. He takes measures to guard the sovereignty and territorial integrity of the Kyrgyz Republic, and ensures the unity and continuity of state power and the coordinated functioning and interaction of state organs and their responsibility to the people.[2]

Electoral Process

The Constitution of Kyrgyzstan clearly mentions the election process of the Executive branch in Articles 43, 44 and 45. The

President of the Kyrgyz Republic shall be elected for a term of five years and shall not hold office for two consecutive years. He may not be younger than 35 years of age and will not be older than 65 years. He has to have command over the official language and be a resident of the republic for not less than 15 years before the nomination of his candidature to the office of the President. The President of the Kyrgyz Republic shall be elected by citizens of the Kyrgyz Republic by a majority of the actual votes cast and elections shall be held on the basis of universal, equal and direct suffrage by secret ballot. The number of candidates for the office of President of the Kyrgyz Republic shall not be limited. Any person who has registered and has obtained not less than 50,000 voter signatures may be a candidate for the President of the Kyrgyz Republic. The election of the President shall be considered valid if more than fifty per cent of all voters in the republic have taken part in the election. In the first ballot, a candidate shall be considered elected to the office of President if he has obtained more than half of those votes cast in the election. If none of the candidates obtains more than half of the votes cast in the first ballot, only the two candidates who have obtained the largest number of votes shall appear on the second ballot. A candidate who obtains more than half of the votes cast in the second ballot shall be considered elected if not less than fifty per cent of all voters have taken part in the second ballot.[3]

After the adoption of these constitutional provisions for election, the Presidential election was held on December 24, 1995; Asker Akaev was the popular candidate and other two opposition candidates, Apsamat Masaliyev and Medetkan Sherimkulov, were not so popular. In this election, 81.1 per cent electorate participated and Akaev received 71.6 per cent votes.[4] He got elected for the second term. After the victory, Akaev expanded the presidential powers through a referendum. Thus Akaev, through a frequent use of the institution of referendum, gradually converted the Kyrgyz political system from parliamentary democracy which the 1993 constitution had conceived, to an executive Presidential system. Similarly, in the next presidential election, which was held on October 20, 2000, the incumbent President Akaev secured 74.4 per cent of the votes. His main challenger Omurbek Tekebayev secured 13.85 per cent of votes. The OSCE criticised the presidential elections and in a press release pointed out that "the Kyrgyz presidential elections fell short of the country's commitment to the OSCE".

In the parliamentary election in February and March 2005, there were also reports of huge irregularities in the election process that contributed to public protests. As a result, President Akaev fled the state and an opposition leader Kurmanbek Bakiev was appointed as an acting president until a fresh presidential election could be held. On July 10, 2005, a presidential election was conducted by the Election Commission according to the resolution of Parliament on July 10. The dynamic of the presidential race was shaped by an agreement on May 12 between acting President Kuemanbek Bakiev and Felix Kulov, a leading opposition leader released from prison following President Akaev's ouster. The agreement stipulated Felix Kulov's withdrawal from the electoral race and his immediate appointment as First Vice-Prime Minister. In this election, one woman candidate namely Toktayyam Umetalieva contested for the post of President. It was for the first time that a woman candidate contested for the post of President in Kyrgyzstan. Bakiev was declared the winner, with 88.71 per cent of the votes, on the basis of a reported turnout of 74.67 per cent.[5] For the first time a southerner was elected as the head of Kyrgyzstan, whereas since the Soviet period the northern clans had dominated the political scene that included the former President Akaev and his administrative staff. The south is more traditional and a large number of Uzbek minority populations live in that region and have been politically marginalised for a long period of time.[6] Over the period of time, President Bakiev got re-elected for a second term with 76 per cent of the vote in July 2009. Due to corruption and rising prices of the basic commodities, opposition activists and citizens protested against President Bakiev around the White House in Bishkek on April 7, 2010. As a result, this protest left 86 people dead and more than a thousand injured. Bakiev fled to his home in Jalalabad. Following these events, a provisional government was established, headed by Ms Roza Otunbaeva, a former foreign minister. By the referendum of 2010, Ms Roza Otunbaeva was nominated as the interim president until December 31, 2011.

Executive Powers

The Constitution of Kyrgyzstan also mentions the powers of President as the chief executive. These are the main functions: The President of the Kyrgyz Republic determines the structure of the Government of the Kyrgyz Republic. He appoints the Prime Minister of the Kyrgyz Republic with the assent of the Assembly of People's Representatives. He also appoints, in consultation with the Prime Minister of the Kyrgyz Republic, the members of the Government of the Kyrgyz Republic and also directors of the administrative departments, and relieves them of their offices. He accepts requests by the Prime Minister, the Government, or an individual member of the Government to resign, decides on his own initiative for the Prime Minister or Government to resign. He appoints, with the consent of the appropriate local Keneshes, the heads of state administration of districts and cities and relieves them of their offices. He appoints the State Secretary of the Kyrgyz Republic and determines his status and authorities, forms the Administration of the President of the Kyrgyz Republic and also forms and abolishes the executive organs not included in the make-up of the Government.

He presents to the Assembly of People's Representatives candidates for election to the offices of Chairman of the Constitutional Court of the Kyrgyz Republic, his deputy, and the judges of the Constitutional Court of the Kyrgyz Republic. He also presents to the Assembly of People's Representatives candidates for election to the offices of the Chairman of the Supreme Court of the Kyrgyz Republic and of the Supreme Economic Court of the Kyrgyz Republic, their deputies, and the judges of the Supreme Court of the Kyrgyz Republic and of the Supreme Economic Court of the Kyrgyz Republic.

The President of the Kyrgyz Republic presents draft laws to the *Jogorku Kenesh*, signs laws or returns them with his objections to the appropriate house of the *Jogorku Kenesh* for further consideration and publishes laws.

He speaks to the people in yearly messages on the state of affairs in the country, to be delivered at a joint sitting of both houses of the *Jogorku Kenesh*. He has the right to halt or annul the action of acts of the Government of the Kyrgyz Republic and acts of other organs of executive power. He has also the right to decide on the question of financing measures of an urgent nature at state expense, and to establish funds. He exercises full legislative authority in cases and by the procedure stipulated in Article 68 of the present Constitution.

The President of the Kyrgyz Republic has the right to call early sittings of the Legislative Assembly and early sessions of the Assembly of People's Representatives and to determine masters eligible for consideration. He calls a referendum on his own initiative, or takes decisions on calling referendum on the initiative of no less than 3,00,000 voters or a majority of the total number of deputies of both houses of the *Jogorku Kenesh*. He also calls for elections to the Legislative Assembly and the Assembly of People's Representatives, and carries out an early dissolution of the Legislative Assembly and the Assembly of People's Representatives in cases stipulated in the present Constitution. He calls for elections to the local *Keneshes* and carries out their early dissolution in cases stipulated in the present Constitution. He appoints the Chairman of the Central Committee on elections and the conduct of referendums and one-third of its members and Chairman of the Counting Board and one-third of its auditors.[7]

Legislature

The Kyrgyz parliament called as the *Jogorku Kenesh* comprises of two chambers – the Legislative Assembly (lower chamber) and the People's Assembly (upper chamber). The Legislative Assembly consists of 35 members and is a permanent chamber. The People's Assembly comprises of 70 members, sits twice yearly and represents regional interests. Members of both chambers are elected for a term of five years on the basis of universal, equal and direct suffrage by secret ballot. In 2003, a referendum passed by the Parliament with majority votes created the new unicameral Parliament consisting of 75 deputies elected in single-mandate constituencies for a five-year term.

Electoral Process

The Kyrgyz parliamentary election was held on February 20, 2000 according to the new system. The number of seats in the Legislative Assembly increased from 36 to 60; 15 of them being allocated to parties.[8] In this election the voter turnout was not high, with 57.8 per cent of the electorate casting vote in the first round and 61.86 per cent in the second round. Direct elections were held for 45 seats in the Legislative Assembly and for 45 seats in the People's Assembly and another 15 seats in the

Legislative Assembly were allocated on the basis of proportional representation. Most of the candidates running in single-seat electoral districts failed to win 50 per cent of the votes required to be elected. Only the former leader of the Kyrgyz Soviet Communists, Turdakum Usubaliyev and Akaev's brother got through the first round of the elections. Those who made it to the parliament represented the El (People) party, the Communist Party, the Ata-mekum (Fatherland Party), and the Kairan El party. Observes were highly critical of the elections. In 2000, the Communist Party won 5 out of 15 seats, the Union of Democratic Force election Block 4, the Democratic Party of Women 2, the Political Party of the Afghan War Veterans 2, the Ata-Meken Socialist Party 1, and My Country Party 1.[9]

As a result of the February 2003 referendum the new Constitution proposed by President Akaev was approved by 75 per cent of the votes polled. The referendum also approved the abolition of its bicameral parliament. The Constitution introduced the majority system of election to the parliament. Under Art. 54, the *Jogorku Kenesh* shall consist of 75 deputies who will be elected for a five-year term from single member constituencies. The voting in the referendum was

criticised by the Kyrgyz Committee for Human Rights which stated that "ballot boxes were carried from door to door to boost the turnout total". Elections for the new unicameral body or *Jorgorku Kenesh* were held on February 27, 2005, but the vast majority of positions remained undecided and were contested in a run-off election on March 13, 2005 and election irregularities caused widespread protests that resulted in the President being forced to flee the country. In this election, only 10 per cent of women participated and the OSCE reported that in the first round, 88 per cent Kyrgyz, 5 per cent Uzbeks and 4 per cent Russians have in this election.[10] The pro-presidential political party – Alga Kyrgyzstan – won a clear majority in that election.

The President tried to consolidate the executive power with his own associates and brought out a referendum on October 2007. According to this referendum, 75 deputies would be elected through a closed-list of Proportional Representation system. Political parties would have to clear a threshold of 5% of registered voters i.e., based on all eligible voters as opposed to the votes cast nationwide to enter the parliament. The parties also would need to clear a second threshold of 0.5% of all registered voters in each of the country's seven regions, plus the cities of Bishkek and Osh.[11] Following this referendum, the *Jogorku Kenesh* subsequently set the election date for July 23, 2009. In that election, three political parties were represented in the Parliament – the Ak Jol (71 seats), the Social Democratic Party of Kyrgyzstan (SDPK) (11) and the Party of Communists of Kyrgyzstan (8).[12]

In April 2010, President Kurmanbek Bakiev was ousted in a coup, which brought to power an interim government led by Roza Otunbayeva. She introduced the constitutional referendum on June 2010 for reforming the electoral system, the separation of powers, the judicial system, human rights, and local self-government. This referendum was approved by 90.55 per cent of the votes cast, with a turnout figure of 72.24 per cent. [13]

This referendum gave stronger powers to the parliament and resulted in a weakened presidency. It also extended the number of seats in parliament from 90 to 120, and set the cap for the maximum number of seats in parliament by any political party to 65. The new constitution also would allow the parliament to choose a prime minister and also to play a key role in forming the new government. In that direction, the new parliament election was held on October 10, 2010. According to the results declared by the Election Commission's office in Kyrgyzstan, five political parties passed the two thresholds. The CEC allocated 28 parliamentary seats to Ata Jurt, 26 to SDPK, 25 to Ar Namys, 23 to Respublika and 18 to Ata-Meken. The voter turnout was announced at 55.31 which represents 28 female members (23.33 per cent) and 14 members (11.66 per cent) belonging to a national minority. After that election process got over, no political parties got a clear-cut majority in the parliament. As a result, a coalition government came into force with five wining political parties in parliament.[14]

Political Practice

In Kyrgyzstan, on May 5, 1993, the Supreme Soviet session of the Kyrgyz Republic adopted a new Constitution based on democratic principles. The new Fundamental Law established a model close to the presidential–parliamentary form of government. The head of the state and the highest legislative body both had fairly wide powers.[15] The parliament played an important role in forming the government and its structure, and also identified the main trends in the country's domestic and foreign policies. The parliament and president had the right to submit the most important issue for a referendum. The constitution created legal conditions in which the legislative and executive branches could function relatively independently, thus making an agreement between them possible. The president could not rule independently of the *Jogorku Kenesh.*

However, in 1994, the president's power betrayed the first signs of strengthening at the expense of the parliament. In December 1993, the country was shaken by cabinet crises, and in September 1994, the legislature dissolved itself amid another crisis.[16] The president made a skilful use of his address to the nation to fortify his position more. The dissolution of the parliament was explained by the fact that the head of state and the legislative branch were at odds with each other. The national referendum of October 1994 set up a bicameral parliament elected in February 1995 in accordance with the majority system introduced to keep any potentially strong opposition party outside the parliament. This created a so-called 'pocket parliament'.[17] In December 1995, for the first time in its history, the nation went to the polls to elect a president from among several candidates. In that election process, the coalition supported the president for re-election and after the election process was over, the coalition demanded for another series of constitutional amendments in 1996. In this constitutional amendment, the republic acquired its final political image as an authoritarian state with elements of democracy.

The amended Constitution supplied the president with wide powers for forming the executive and judicial branches. In the absence of a checks and balances system, the hybrid regime could easily develop into a regime of personal power. In October 2000, about 10 parties united into an opposition People's Patriotic Movement bloc. The opposition was displeased with the president's wide powers, which it assessed as too wide and insisted that they should be redistributed in favour of the parliament.[18] They also insisted on the presidential–parliamentary form of government and wanted the Constitution to be amended accordingly. To normalise the situation, in September 2002, a Constitutional Conference was convened to discuss a new version of the republic's Constitution. On the strength of the referendum of February 2, 2003, the Law on the New Version of the Constitution of the Kyrgyz Republic was adopted on February 18, 2003. Maintaining the power balance, the *Jogoeku Kenesh* received the following powers – the approval structure of the government recommended by the president, giving its consent to the appointment of the prime minister and the member of the government, control over the government, giving a vote of no confidence in the government by a majority of no less than two-thirds of the votes of the deputy corps, giving its consent to the appointment of judges of the local courts, etc. (Art. 58).[19]

In spite of that, the head of the state has more power to control the cabinet. Due to the 2005 unfair elections, the opposition groups demanded the resignation of the president. Following a large demonstration and political crises, the President left the country. An interim government was set up under Kurmanbek Bakiev. The people at this time wanted to steer the country towards continued reforms rather than toward a new development model or a new socio-political system. In January 2006, the opposition moved towards greater unity within a newly established People's Coalition of Democratic Forces of 18 parties, movements and NGOs.[20] The new opposition insisted on more amendments to the Constitution regarding administrative and judicial reforms and more active anti-criminal measures. After the series of rallies in the capital city of Bishkek, finally, a new constitution was adopted on November 10, 2006.

This Constitution established a mixed form of government with wide powers to the parliament –the national security services earlier accountable to the president will be under the parliament, prominent heads were to be appointed by the parliament but the president retained the power to dismiss them, the number of deputies increased to 90 and the party that wins fifty per cent of the seats acquires the right to form the government and nominate a candidate for premier to be approved by the president. If none of the party wins half of the seats, the head of the state has the right to invite one of the parliamentary parties to select a premier. The *Jogorku Kenesh* has the right to pass a vote of non-confidence in the cabinet if dissatisfied with its annual report. All the power structures retain their power until their term expires in 2010.[21] In that respect, Akaev said that "the new constitution has a reasonable balance of President and Parliamentary Authority, which meets the expectation of society".[22]

After the November 2006 Constitution, the President also signed another Constitution in 2007. Many of the things remained the same and only few of the provisions of the constitution got changed. According to the 2007 Constitution, the president in the end decides whether to dismiss the cabinet or not. This constitution introduced new provisions that the president may set goals and tasks before the cabinet. In his own discretion, the president may interfere in the works of the cabinet, although the prime minister is responsible for the omission and commission of the cabinet. MPs elected from party list have the right to form a cabinet, which is better since voters elect the MPs. Besides, the president is placed above the parliament in the hierarchy of power due to a provision whereby the president commissions MPs from a political party to nominate the prime minister. Therefore, relations between the president and parliament are not of a relation of authority and subordination, but the relations of bodies that are independent of each other, having separate competencies and power in checking and influencing each other.[23] On April 13, 2010, President Bakiev offered his resignation due to huge protest by the opposition and common people. As the first steps, the provisional government led by Otunbayeva dissolved the parliament, the CEC as well as the Constitutional Court. It was announced as a so-called 'Return to Democracy' programme with the aim of a peaceful transition to democracy. In that direction, President Otunbayeva brought out the referendum in June 2010 aiming for parliamentary democracy. This referendum was historic among all the Central Asian Countries for minimising executive powers and giving more power to the parliament. This referendum brought major changes in the executive and legislature branches to promote democracy and proper representation.

This referendum has limited the president's power to serving a single six-year term. The president will invite names for the prime minister, but under the very restrictive conditions described under the powers of the parliament. Members of the government would be chosen by the prime minister, who is not required to even consult the president in the parliamentary form of government. The president signs a legislation but has no right of veto, just the right to send it back for reconsideration. That provision is certain to create a number of potential political choke points. On the other hand, in the event of the president's death or incapacity, the Speaker (*Toraga*) of the *Jogorku Kenesh*, becomes president, with new elections required within three months. The prime minister is second in line of succession.

The legislative power section lays out the structure of the parliament as well as its responsibilities, which include forming the government and electing its speaker. The parliament would consist of 120 deputies who serve a five-year term and are granted their seats on the basis of party lists. A prime minister and the prime minister's government are also subject to dismissal through a vote of no-confidence.[24] A request for a no-confidence vote would require only one-third of all parliamentary deputies, and the vote itself would require only a simple majority. In this instance, it would revert to the president to decide whether to dismiss the government. If there are two votes of no-confidence within a three-month period, the government must be dismissed. The prime minister may also call for a vote of confidence in the government, no more frequently than once a year; if it fails, the president must call for new parliamentary elections.

In a nutshell, Kyrgyzstan promotes the parliamentary form of government in the Central Asian region which minimises the power of the president. It needs a proper check and balance between all organs of the government for the smooth functioning of the political system. In the present political scenario, five political parties i.e. Ata-Jurt, the SDPK, Ar-Namys, Respublika and Ata-Meken socialistic party have succeeded in the parliament. They have formed the government as coalition partners but on the other hand, they did not have the experience to work as coalition partners. It needs the strong institutional design to accommodate all sections of ideology and political parties in the government and maintain a proper balance between executive, legislature and judiciary.

Notes

1. Kaushik, Devendra (2004), "Central Asia since Ozodi: An Appraisal", in K. Warikoo and Mahavir Singh (eds.), *Central Asia since Independence*, New Delhi: Shipra Publications, p. 1.
2. Article 42, *The Constitution of the Republic of Kyrgyzstan*, Bishkek, 1993.
3. Articles 43-45, *The Constitution of the Republic of Kyrgyzstan*, Bishkek, 1993.
4. Abazov, Rafis (2004), "Kyrgyzstan's Struggle for Democracy and Stability", in K. Warikoo and Mahavir Singh (eds.), op.cit. p. 45.
5. "Report on Republic of Kyrgyzstan Presidential Election" (2005), July 10, 2005, prepared by *OSCE/ODIHR Election Observer Mission*, Warsaw, 7, November, p.23.
6. Sjoberg, Fredrik M. (2005), "Post-Revolutionary Syndrome in Kyrgyzstan: The Struggle for Power Continues", *Central Asia-Caucasus Analyst*, Wednesday, July 13, p.1.
7. Article 46, *The Constitution of the Republic of Kyrgyzstan*, Bishkek, 1993.
8. Elebaeva, Aynura (2007), "Political Transformations in Kyrgyzstan (1991-2006)", *Central Asia and the Caucasus*, 44 (2), p.70.
9. Ibid.
10. '"Report on Republic of Kyrgyzstan Parliament Elections", 27 February and 13 March 2005, prepared by *OSCE/ODIHR Election Observer Mission*, Warsaw 20, May 2005, p.20
11. Weise, Gavin (2010), "Understanding the Proposed Kyrgyz Parliament", An IFES Briefing Paper, May 15.
12. Ibid.
13. According to information on the final results on the CEC website: http://www.shailoo.gov.kg/ru/news/svodnaya-tablica-cik-kyrgyzskoj-respubliki-po-itogamvsenarodnogo-golosovaniya-na-referendume-27-iyunya-2010-goda-svodnaya-tablica-cikkyrgyzskoj-r-espubliki-po-itogam-vsenarodnogo-golosovaniya-na-r/#more-3819
14. "Report on Republic of Kyrgyzstan Parliament Elections" (2010), 10 October, prepared by OSCE/ODIHR Election Observer Mission, Warsaw, 20 December, p. 23.
15. Elebaeva, op.cit., p. 69.
16. Ibid.
17. Ibid.
18. Ibid., p. 70.
19. Ibid.
20. Ibid., p. 72.
21. Ibid., p. 76.

22. *The Current Digest of Post Soviet Press*, 58 (45), 2006, p.7.
23. Iskakova, Gulnara, *Consitutional Reform and Power of the Highest Government Bodies in Kyrgyzstan: A New Balance*, available at http://www.ipp.kg/en/analysis/386/
24. http://kyrgyzstan.carnegieendowment.org/2010/06/kyrgystan%e2%80%99s-new-constitution/

22

The Basic Directions of International Activity of the Russian Orthodox Church

Olga Tserpitskaya

The Year 2009 was characterised with a lot of events which could be called as fatal in the life of the Russian Orthodox Church. With the death of His Holiness the Patriarch of Moscow and All Russia Alexy II, the whole "epoch of Church restoration" after the period of official Soviet godlessness has ended. And the first, "program" speech of the elected Patriarch Cyril was already the speech of "the Restored Church" leader.[1] In the official parts of both events – both burial and enthronement of the Patriarchs – the representatives of the Russian government participated as actively as it was possible and correct, showing how close and intimate the relations between the Church and the state became for the last 15 years. However, summing up His Holiness Alexy's stay on the patriarchal throne, it is possible to state with confidence, that he did the maximum not to allow the formation of such system of State–Church relations which had existed in the Russian Empire. It is not a secret now, that during both the Imperial and Soviet periods of the Russian history the central role in the life of the State was given to the Church, but the Soviet system focused the work of Church in the greater degree on international activity, not allowing it to deal with the internal life of the society.[2] But, both systems tried to hold the Church under rigid control, possibly not supposing independent actions.

His holiness the Patriarch Alexy in his speeches and works always emphasised that the Church and the State have various natures, purposes and tasks, but it does not exclude opportunities and prospects of their cooperation, considering the Byzantine tradition of the Church–State relations ("symphony", i.e. close connection of the Church and the State with a distinction of purposes and methods: the state takes care of the material side of the society life while the Church of the spiritual one which as a result leads to harmony), which the Russian Orthodox Church follows up to nowadays.[3] For state building, the Byzantine model is perhaps the ideal one – many times it has been stressed that spiritual values advocated and preached by the Russian Orthodox Church while taking into account its contribution to the Russian statehood and culture could become a basis for the Russian national idea. The principle of the symphony justifies itself even on the international scene (a vivid example is the State participation in the Russian Orthodox Church reunification and signing of the Act of Canonical Communion). Here, it is necessary to note that the Russian state (in any form of statehood) has always had the precise understanding of the degree of influence which the Russian Orthodox Church rendered on the image of Russia in moulding the opinion of the world community, and partly due to the Spiritual Missions (it will be described in more detail below). However, this fact imposes certain restrictions on those spheres of the international activity in which the State can and without consequences for its own image and harm for the image of the Church, use its help and support. So, the Church and the State can cooperate on the international scene in the following areas: peacemaking and peacekeeping, charity, development of joint social programmes, preservation of theglobal cultural heritage, science and creative activity, preservation of the environment and counteraction for the distribution of the pseudo-religious structures representing danger to the individual and society.[4]

It has already been mentioned that even the Byzantine model provides various methods for making the inter-relations of the Church and the State. The basic method of external relations of the Church (considering the long-term prospect in which the Church has recommended itself as a successful diplomat) is its "missionary activity". During the period of restoration, the Church has practically overcome personnel problems in the field of missionary work and even has changed the basic direction of the mission. "The Concept of Missionary Activity of the Russian Orthodox Church"[5] in its last edition of 2008 in the certain degree follows the needs of the Church and addresses mainly internal missions (missions inside the canonic territory which – and it is the essentially important point – goes beyond the borders of the Russian Federation). Thus, uniqueness of cooperation in the international affairs of the Church and the State is based in the fact that while Russia is already operating on the territory of a different State, the Russian Orthodox Church still remains in its own borders (for example, Belarus, Ukraine). Therefore, it frequently happens that what the Church names as an "internal mission", for the representatives of the government, turns out to be a foreign policy tool for the state. But here there is yet a tendency, a danger of the method of mission of the Church changing.

The most fruitful in the Russian Church history has always been and still remains the incarnation approach to the missionary activity[6] (the use of local language and ordination of the local citizens), which leaves place for the implementation of the certain State purposes like social work (especially in the "hot points") and the formation of the Russian image abroad as well. This method is effective in a long-term prospect as it can't be currently used in settling thorny questions on the new territories. And taking into account the extremely attentive attitude of the State towards the Church, there is a serious temptation to use another approach to the missionary activity – a political one[7] (with the whole support of the government). Its positive side is obvious: the problem can be solved within some days or even hours. But such an approach could be preferable only in case the incarnational approach had been already used in a disputed territory already for quite a long time (otherwise the Church can become dependent on the State policy; that will prevent the implementation of the Church interests on the international scene). The celebration of the 1020th anniversary of the Christening of Russia in Kiev can serve a good example: well planned by President Jushchenko, a public action on the transfer of the Moscow Patriarchate parishes to the Constantinople Patriarchate has been broken.[8] All representatives of the Russian side have worked effectively: the Church, diplomats and the common believers. But, probably the situation would have developed differently without a certain State resource and without the long-term internal mission, even such a bright victory would have been one-staged and having no continuation.

The method of mission in the external activity of the Church defines also such directions of the international activity, which the Department for External Church Relations of the Moscow Patriarchate (further – DECR) names the basic ones in 2008 (there is no comments on the 2009 priorities, but it can be supposed they will stay practically the same): foreign establishments and work with compatriots, inter-Orthodox communications and inter-Christian relations[9] (in the latter case, it is necessary to note that the dialogue with the non-Orthodox can also be included not on sense, but on fact).

The foreign establishments of the Russian Orthodox Church are an immense theme as many documents, capable of throwing light on their role in different events of the world history, remains closed till now. In spite of the strict instructions and the interdiction on participation in political events for missionaries, the Church establishments are frequently involved in the political life of the countries, and the changes of political vectors or foreign policy of the States point directly to Missions and parishes (the most vivid example here is the crash of the Russian Empire and disintegration of the Soviet Union). The principle of the work of foreign establishments of the Russian Orthodox Church plays an important role in all this. It is practically unified (ecclesiastical guidance of the believers, maintenance of good relations with the non-Orthodox, representation of the Moscow Patriarchy outside the canonic territory of the Russian Orthodox Church, the testimony about values of the Russian Orthodoxy and about the spiritual greatness of its Motherland to the whole world), but in the work of the establishments – the national and religious features of a host country are taken into account. Very often, such n approach results in the confidence of the host country's population in the representatives of the Russian Orthodox Church, and pilgrims from Russia consider Missions and parishes (two most widespread forms of foreign establishments) to be the basic instances providing quiet and safe travel (though this maintenance is not included as the duties of missionaries). But the interest of the State in foreign establishments of the Russian Orthodox Church (which has never been weak) is caused not only by its favourable image – many of the establishments possess a certain property which can be useful to the State. By the way, the Church has never objected to its lands being used by the State for the blessing of compatriots (or other people): one can even recollect the capture of hostages in the temple of Christmas in Bethlehem – then the operation on setting people free was carried out from the pilgrim house belonging to the Russian Orthodox Church.[10] In this view, especially strange seems the tendency of the recent one-and-a-half years when the State has been negotiating for returning the Church lands sold or lost during the period of the Soviet power, and returns them to itself though these lands have never belonged to the State. But even with such a development of events, the Church expands the presence outside of the Russian Federation, with the help of the State as well. As an example, the following data can be quoted:

> "During the period of 2004-2008, twenty-four objects of the real estate were built and registered as property. Construction of Orthodox temples in Rome, Havana, Tokyo, and Ulan Bator is being carried out. Building of the temple of "All Saints whose light shone forth in the Russian Land" in the Gorny female monastery in Jerusalem is fully completed. Overall reconstruction of the Hospital case in the St-Panteleimon monastery on the Sacred Mountain Athos is being carried out. The temple at the embassy of the Russian Federation in Bolivia has been built; the temples at the embassies of Russia in Beijing and Istanbul are under construction. Besides, during the given period

> the temple buildings in the city of Kiel (Germany), the city of Hobro (Denmark), the temple complexes with houses in the cities of Hamburg and Ulm (Germany), a large monastic complex in Amsterdam (Holland), two house temples on the Island of Sardinia have been registered as the property of the Russian Orthodox Church. The house in the center of Rome for the eparchial and pilgrim center has been bought. The transfer of a complex of buildings of the Farmstead of the Russian Orthodox Church by the city of Bari (Italy) to the Russian Federation became an important event".[11]

It is obvious that cooperation between the Church and the State in the aforementioned direction remains close enough and fruitful. Even the Act of Canonical Communion can be considered not only as a significant and symbolic event of Church life but also as the success of the Russian foreign policy in work with compatriots as the missionary activity of the Russian Orthodox Church outside Russia was not extremely successful on the world scale (and, probably, such purposes had not been set). And the term "compatriots" which appeared simultaneously both in the State and in the Church official languages in approximately identical meaning, shows the presence of the Church–State negotiations on a certain number of questions. Certainly, it would be the least strange if the State neglected such number of people focused on Russia, even if only by their Orthodox creed.

The total number of Russian-speaking Orthodox diaspora (the term "Orthodox diaspora" is already curious by itself and can be considered to be a new direction of activity as diasporas is the phenomenon which the State can work with in pursuit of its own purposes) in the world (including the Ukrainians and the Moldavians) is over 30 million. A significant part of them – the flock of the Russian Orthodox Church and many others – consider themselves as Russians or compatriots. Now the amount of the countries of the diasporas amount to 51 countries where there are 316 parishes and 16 monasteries of the Moscow Patriarchate. They are under ecclesiastical guidance by 8 bishops and 354 clerics (282 priests and 72 deacons). Also there are 89 Sunday schools currently working. This statistics does not include the Russian Orthodox Church Outside of Russia, but even without it the data looks quite impressive: some of the Local Churches have fewer believers.

Probably, the work with compatriots (or with the Orthodox diaspora?) is important for the Church also because it allows showing the position of the Church on a world scene openly. We can only recollect the speech of His Holiness the Patriarch Alexy II at the session of the PACE – would it be possible if the Orthodox diaspora were not so extensively widespread (including the European Union, after the disintegration of the USSR)? It is worth recollecting here a new form of foreign branches of the Church which though has already brought results – affiliations of the Russian Orthodox Church. They exist in such large political centres as Brussels, New York, Strasbourg and Geneva. And the geography of the Affiliations already causes a conflict of interest. Quoting the words of the then DECR's Chairman and Metropolitan, and nowadays His Holiness the Patriarch Cyril, Affiliations are created with the purpose "of informing the government and public of different countries about the attitude of the Church towards the modern lines of global development, testifying the necessity of the attentive and careful attitude to original spiritual and cultural bases of peoples' life, determining their shape and consciousness, to ennoble the voice of the Church against dissemination of sin and defect"[12]. It is also possible here to track one of the new and prospective purposes for the Church and the State: the interaction with the governments of the different states on the problematic circle of questions. During the long history of the Russian Orthodox Church it has become possible for the first time to set out such an idea as the purpose for the international activity of the Church. On the conference held in the beginning of 2009 in Sofia (Bulgaria), the reports of the representatives of the Russian Orthodox Church stressed the necessity of interaction with the international organisations as the Orthodox "traditions still remain badly-known and poorly represented in the international institutes",[13] but they create a special model of the Church–State relations out of from which modern Europe could borrow a lot of useful tendencies.

In the year 2006, as a result of five years' research, the author himself has allocated three basic directions of joint activity of the Russian Orthodox Church and the Russian Federation: "Yugoslavian" – rallying of the states which were afraid of the physical intrusion of peace-making forces (mainly the East Europe, the Balkans), "anti-American" – rallying of the countries against the "unipolarity" of the world according to the religious and/or national belonging (Greece, "east direction"), and the break-out of the Russian Orthodox Church from the "organizational isolation" – Its participation in activity of the European international organisations.[14] ("Neighbourly" direction, the CIS, at that moment has practically lost its urgency and, it is necessary to note, there is meanwhile no tendency to a new activity.)

It is interesting that the programme, conventionally named as "compatriots", works effectively in all three directions. But if the latter on participation in the international organisations is carried out with a sufficient degree of openness and soon it is going to pass into the "work with achievements" stage (certainly, this definition is conventional enough), the forecasts for the former two are more complicated even because two of these zones, both "Yugoslavian", and "anti-American," are rather closely bound with each other. Today, it is obviously impossible any more to divide the countries into such two directions even conventionally.

Therefore, the DECR's classification – Inter-Orthodox and Inter-Christian relations – seems to be rather convenient.

In the case with the inter-Orthodox interaction, quite a big amount of the countries happen to be in the "covered zone": there are all ancient Orthodox Churches and the Orthodox Churches of Europe. Unfortunately, those political forces which guide the Constantinople Patriarchate understand this too. And, if approximately till 2006, there had been a slight hope that Patriarch Bartholomew simply treated canonic rules differently and operated according to his treatment, today, after "overlapping" of the interstate and InterOrthodox problems, a number of not even coincidences but quite concrete regularities appear. According to these laws, the role of the Church seems to be valued greatly (and even greater is the role of the church schism). Unfortunately, all (or nearly all) Church problems on the territory of the former USSR represent the parts of one mosaic of this regularity.

Indeed, the existing problem of the 28th rule of the IVth Universal Council (concerning setting bishops "among members of different tribes" in Ponthian, Assian and Thracian areas[15]) has given confidence to the Constantinople Patriarchate that it (and only it) has the right of church jurisdiction over the whole world outside of its canonic territory. In the 1920s, when this treatment was declared, the Russian Orthodox Church, for clear reasons, was expelled from the participation in the theological dialogue and now, it does not accept this as an axiom. However, for today, it is favourable to certain political forces to maintain the given treatment and to support the most disputable of its derivatives, for example, the establishment of the second jurisdiction over one territory, as in the case of the Estonian one, or an automatic acceptance of the clergy under Constantinople jurisdiction (as it was in England). But the most tendentious is a claim for a superiority of the Constantinople clergy jurisdictions over the representation of all the Orthodox in the given territory. Thus, the current complicated situation in Ukraine is developing and not without the participation of Constantinople Patriarchate. It is difficult to imagine (as this information will remain covered for a long time), what personal efforts His Holiness the Patriarch Alexy II, DECR's representatives and the Russian Ministry of Foreign Affairs had to make to keep the Church in Ukraine from the next schism directly during the celebrations in 2008 when, it seemed that Constantinople Patriarch Bartholomew will not be able to reject president Jushchenko's gift of some of the Ukrainian parishes. Unfortunately, this act is one of the few uniting steps that happened because of the unwillingness of Patriarch Bartholomew to give independence to the Ukrainian parishes, which is against Jushchenko's wish as they may come into Constantinople's jurisdiction.[16]

The situations with the Moldavian parishes (foundation of the strange Bessarabian metropolia of the Romanian Orthodox Church[17]) and the schism in Bulgaria (more exactly, with that, the Constitutional court of the country, and then in the beginning of 2009 the Strasbourg court under human rights has taken the side of the dissenters[18]) are not so surprising already – on the territories, where the Russian Church pursued a policy of unity since 2001. Almost natural, unfortunately, seem also efforts of other political forces (for which instability in the regions is favourable) on separation. And, as in the politically shattered states and regions' belief and belonging to the united Church is that little, that can unite the population, attacks to the Church unity, obviously, will proceed with a new force.

Unfortunately, unsettled relations between the Orthodox Churches can also affect relations with the other Christian and non-Christian religions, and become a reason of numerous reproaches from more "liberally adjusted" religious currents.

Nevertheless, the Russian Orthodox Church has a very strong point which is difficult to challenge: the Russian Church at the given historical stage is the only major Church which has not admitted and allowed a dogmatic change or changes of traditional notion of divine service and the church life. Perhaps today, the Russian Orthodoxy remains one of the few that can freely carry on dialogue with the representatives of the other faiths or the secular organisations without compromises as no one can remember its earlier indulgences for the sake of other negotiating processes. But this positive moment becomes a starting point in the search of allies for the protection of moral values which are represented by the Russian Church. Among the Western Christian world, the important assistant is the Roman Catholic Church and a number of Protestant communities. Certainly, all sides understand the community of moral criteria, and also distinctions which do not allow to unite them more closely than necessary.

The situation with Catholic Church remains one of the most painful. On the one hand, the community of the purposes directed at the preservation of the European heritage and the experience of the friendly neighbourhood in Europe (when Catholic temples are given to the Orthodox parishes for divine services, frequently on friendly terms and free of charges). On the other hand, another obviously provocative action in Ravenna in 2007 (quoting only one of examples) when The representatives of the Russian Orthodox Church had to leave the Xth Plenary Session of the Mixed International Commission on Theological Dialogue between the Orthodox Church and Catholic Church because of the undesirable presence of the representatives of the "Estonian Apostolic Orthodox Church"[19] at the session. And, cases similar to this show that in Catholic circles there nevertheless exists the tendency to support the certain instability in the Orthodox world as a part of the initial territory of the Russian Church – Ukraine and

Belarus – that represents the big interest for the Catholic Church, and it obviously expects to receive even a part of these territories in case of a probable schism or a conflict. For the sake of these plans the "resource" of the Constantinople Patriarchate is involved which (the Patriarchate), unfortunately, by virtue of historical and modern position, does not possess independence in actions.

The further participation of the Russian Orthodox Church in the international religious organisations depends on the position of the Churches, but already in relation to the questions of ethics and morality. This question has lost the former urgency, and the unity of positions "on questions of economic globalisation, settlement of local conflicts, preservation of the environment and other socially significant themes" allows the Russian Church to participate in the sessions of the World Council of Churches and the Conference of the European Churches without damage to the reputation among the Russian Orthodox believers.[20]

Other rather complicated theme, to which has been given much more attention recently than it seems at first sight, is the question on the Orthodox Church in China. It received an autonomy more than 50 years ago (as a result of the long presence of the Orthodox Spiritual Mission in the region); this Church numbers up to 15 thousand believers, but remains without the Head and permanent clergy, with divine service held by visiting priests on the territory of the diplomatic missions of Russia in the Chinese People's Republic.[21] While negotiations with the Chinese authorities have not led to any appreciable result, this question is included into a number of the basic ones as the Constantinople Patriarchate is already trying to spread its jurisdiction over the Chinese Orthodox Church.[22]

In general, it is possible to predict the development of the interchurch and inter-religious dialogue with a certain care. First of all, it is connected with the personality of the new Patriarch

Cyril, who began his service under Nikodim, the Metropolitan of Leningrad and Novgorod. Metropolitan Nikodim is known (both in circles of the admirers of his memory, and among ill-wishers) as the person who managed to lead the ruined Russian Orthodox Church on the international scene, and saved it through these actions.[23] Metropolitan Nikodim realised that it was the international activity that would once become one of the major directions of Church life and his pupil being elected as the Patriarch has proved how right metropolitan Nikodim was.

However, as an echo of that time when the events wherein the Russian Church appeared to be involved in the opposition of the two states – Russia and Georgia – can be seen. Not so long ago in Moscow, there took place an event which coincided with the funeral ceremony to His Holiness the Patriarch of Moscow and All Russia Alexy II. On December 9, 2008, after the burial service and the burial of the Primate, His Holiness the Catholicos-Patriarch of all Georgia Ilia II was received by the President of Russia. This meeting ended with the brief information in press: "Dmitry Medvedev has met the Catholicos-Patriarch of all Georgia Ilia II".[24] Certainly, the subject of conversation will become known only when the Patriarch or the President will consider it possible to make it public, but the fact of the meeting is the original result of the certain steps of the State policy which the modern Russian politicians have started to carry out quite in spirit and traditions of the Russian empire and the USSR, and they do it quite successfully. Meanwhile, the position of the Russian Church during the conflict was, perhaps, more confident. It was quite clear that by supporting the actions of the Russian peacemakers, it supported those who protected the defenceless. However, in the heat of the conflict, the statements could be heard, that the conflict should not be transferred either in national or in religious or in any other way, that the essence of it lay only in the political sphere. The words of the Moscow clergy about the inadmissibility of association of the present Georgian authorities with the Georgian people was also seen as the original support to the Georgian Church.[25]

The most reverend Nikolay Balashov making comments on the meeting of Patriarch Ilia II and President Medvedev among other phrases made one very precisely describing the policy not so much of the States, but of the Churches: "The Orthodox belief which formed the culture and a history of our countries, is a primary factor which will promote an establishment of full mutual understanding between our peoples and the States".[26] Indeed, it is not the first time in Russian history when the representatives of the Churches have to solve diplomatic tasks, which diplomats are unable to solve because of the relations becoming aggravated. But today, rendering a certain help to the State, the Church does not carry out its own political line in parallel with the State' one – the Church declares its political life.

From everything described above, it is possible to draw a conclusion that the basic vector of the international activity of the Church has changed. If earlier the accent was made mainly on the interchurch and inter-religious dialogue, at the present moment, the emphasis has shifted to the strengthening of the Church and the achievement of its unity. And, as if summarising the international activity of the Russian Orthodox Church at the present stage, the words of His Holiness the Patriarch of Moscow and All Russia Alexy II, spoken at the Bishop Council of the Russian Orthodox Church on June, 24[t], 2008, become symbolic: "We should not compose ourselves thinking that we could quietly wait till the hardships passed, while the unity could be secured by itself just as a habit".[27] Probably, this position will help in determining the Church life further.

INDEX

9/11 attacks, 80, 124, 125, 249
Afghanistan, 19, 20, 23, 99, 110, 119, 124, 126, 129, 140, 141, 162, 173, 233, 237, 238, 249, 250
Akaev, Asker, 294, 295, 299, 303
Al-Qaida, 238
Algeria, 88
Amu Darya, 98, 99, 104, 112, 162
Argentina, 88
Arunachal Pradesh, 49
Australia, 39, 47, 50, 56, 260
Azerbaijan, 35, 36, 110, 155, 218, 228, 229, 230, 232, 233, 242

Bakiev, Kurmanbek, 295, 296, 300, 303, 304
Bangladesh, 43, 44
Basic Directions of International Activity of the Russian Orthodox Church, 308-322
Battle for Water in Central Asia and Regional Potential for Cooperation, 97-113
  differences in approaches of the sides to integration process, 103-106
  high-level group has been constituted and has had several sessions, 108-111
  obstacles in way of taking strategic decisions, 106-108
  possibility of achieving political consensus, 111-113
  specific character of water, energy balance in central asia, 98-103
Bay of Bengal, 49
Beijing, 21, 43, 48, 53, 118, 129, 239, 244, 247, 249, 250, 289, 313
Belgium, 207
Bhatia, Sabir, 257, 266
Bhilai, 2
Bhutan, 43
Bokaro, 2
Bombay, 2
Brazil, 39, 46, 79, 88
Bulgaria, 249, 316, 318
Bush, George, 63, 65, 66, 69, 70, 266

Cambodia, 42, 43
Can Eurasian Countries Catch up with the West?, 281-290
Canada, 246, 253, 255, 260, 271
Caspian Sea, 67, 97, 117, 118, 143, 152, 154, 155, 159, 218, 227, 228, 229, 236, 242, 243, 244, 245
Central Asia, 18-24, 41, 52, 53, 82, 89, 97-113, 114-131, 135, 136, 137, 138, 139, 140, 141, 147, 149, 155, 162, 173, 227, 229, 233, 234-250
Chagla, M.C, 12
Chandra, Subhash, 260
China, 4, 13, 16, 19, 21, 24, 39, 42, 43, 44, 47, 48, 49, 50, 51, 52, 53, 54, 128, 130, 135, 143, 153, 155, 159, 173, 233, 234, 235, 236, 237, 238, 239, 240, 241, 243, 244, 245, 246, 247, 248, 250, 282, 283, 285, 286, 290, 320
Chinese Interests in Central Asia: Policies and Challenges, 234-250
  central asia, buffer zone, 236-237
  challenges to chinese policy, 248-250
  conclusion, 250
  economic and trade, 246-247
  energy in chinese strategy, 240-246
  geopolitical and geostrategic interests 235-236
  interests and policies in central asia, 235
  military, 247-248
  peripheral security, 237-238
  shanghai cooperation organization, 239-240
  xinjiang, 238-239
CICA and the Contemporary World, 31-37
Contemporary Japan– Central Asia Relations, 114-131

conclusion, 128-131
introduction, 114-115
Japan's foreign policy after cold war, 115-117
Japan's foreign policy in central asia region, 117-128
Czech Republic, 249

Denmark, 77, 314
Diaspora: The Experience of Indian Diaspora for Russia, 252-272
conclusion, 271-272
Indian immigrants in US, first success, 255-258
Indian migration to foreign countries, 253-255
Indians and US immigration policy, 267-271
roots of success of Indian immigrants, 258-267
Dmitry Medvedev, Rossii, 62, 63, 69, 72, 76, 90, 93, 94, 321

Economic Policy of the State Concerning Small Business: Experience of St. Petersburg, 179-208
analysis of interrogation of heads of municipal and territorial formations (educations) and directors of small and large enterprises, 187-189
branch analysis of statistics of activity of small enterprises in St. Petersburg, 182-187
foreign experience of the state development and regulation of small business, 189-198
let's consider some country-specific networks, 198-205
Egypt, 39, 88
Energy Factor in Geopolitics, 226-233
England, 191, 199, 200, 205, 206, 207, 208, 317
Europe, 8, 19, 39, 40, 41, 42, 44, 51, 58, 67, 68, 70, 71, 72, 75, 77, 80, 82, 86, 88, 89, 94, 129, 140, 149, 154, 155, 173, 198, 199, 212, 215, 218, 220, 221, 222, 223, 228, 236, 246, 254, 260, 285, 316, 317, 319
External Energy Policy of Russia, 209-224

Fiji, 253, 254, 265
Finland, 221
France, 28, 77, 81, 86, 191, 198, 199, 205, 206, 207, 208, 260

Gandhi, Indira, 174
Gandhi, Rajiv, 259
Gates, Bill, 257, 260
Generation "Lost" and Generation "Next": The Two Generations of Russian Youth, 273-280
Geopolitics at Work: The Georgia–Russia Conflict, 60-72
conflict's purgative power, international dimension, 66-72
from frozen conflicts to military protectorates, 60-66
Georgia, 60-72, 81, 92, 155, 228, 229, 230, 231, 232, 233, 321
Germany, 39, 77, 78, 81, 190, 191, 198, 199, 205, 214, 221, 222, 258, 260, 314
Great Britain, 12, 14, 77, 86, 189, 221, 253, 255, 256, 260, 267, 271
Greater East Asia and Russia's Task, 38-59
energy problems and regional transformation, 51-53
global perspective for macro-region, 51
greater east asia and Russia, 55-59
new mega trend, winning or gaining old regions into macro-regional complexes, 38-41
perspectives for formation of greater east asia, 41-51
role of different powers in formation of macro- region, 53-54
transnational threats in east asia, 54-55
Gupta, Rajat, 258
Gupta, Vinod, 266

Haridwar, 2
Hashimoto, Ryutaro, 122, 123
Hewitt Packard, 258
Hitler, Adolph, 117
Holland, 283, 314
Hong-Kong, 260
Hotmail, 257
Hungary, 222, 249

Hussein, Saddam, 231

India, 1, 2, 3, 4, 5, 6-16, 20, 21, 23, 25-3035, 39, 42, 43, 44, 45, 48, 49, 50, 51, 52, 53, 54, 55, 56, 57, 58, 59, 79, 81, 82, 86, 119, 129, 135, 138, 140, 141, 142, 143, 144, 147, 148, 153, 155, 60, 174, 175, 176, 177, 233, 244, 253, 254, 255, 256, 257, 58, 259, 260, 261, 263, 264, 265, 268, 269, 270, 271, 283, 285, 286
Indo-Russian Strategic Partnership: The Bullwark of a Multipolar World, 1-5
Indonesia, 43, 47, 51, 142, 258, 285
Infosys Technologies, 260
Institutional Developments and Political Practices in Kyrgyzstan, 291-306
  electoral process, 293-296
  electoral process, 298-301
  executive branch, 293
  executive powers, 296-298
  legislature, 298
  political practice, 301-306
International System: Descending to Chaos or Looking up to New Opportunities, 75-96
  crisis in international security system, 82-90
  foreign policy concept of president Medvedev, 90-96
  positive and negative sides of unipolar world, 78-82
Iran, 20, 35, 36, 58, 81, 82, 86, 88, 89, 97, 98, 99, 113, 119, 129, 155, 218, 228, 229, 232, 236, 237, 282
Iraq, 64, 84, 86, 87, 91, 93, 227, 228
Ireland, 260, 268
Israel, 30, 36, 86, 89, 260
Italy, 77, 199, 206, 208, 260, 314

Japan, 41, 42, 43, 44, 47, 48, 50, 51, 52, 53, 54, 56, 88, 110, 114-131, 140, 142, 189, 190, 191, 200, 201, 205, 206, 207, 208, 243, 260, 282
Johnson, Lyndon, 267

Karimov, Islam, 22, 163, 164, 166, 168, 175
Kawaguchi, Yuriko, 125, 126
Kazakhstan, 18-24, 35, 36, 70, 98, 99, 100, 101, 104, 105, 110, 118, 120, 125, 133-144, 145-160, 162, 218, 228, 233, 234, 235, 237, 239, 241, 242, 243, 244, 245, 246, 247, 258
  land of peace and prosperity, 145-160
    conclusion, 160
    development of energy resources, 151-152
    domestic political stability and consolidation of society, 148-149
    gas, 155-156
    healthcare, education and well-being of people, 150-151
    improvement of infrastructure, 157-158
    national security, 146-147
    oil, 152-155
    professional government, 158-159
    renewable energy sources, 156-157
    sustainable economic growth, 149-150
    uranium, 156
  some aspects of regional security in central asia, perspective from, 18-24
Kenya, 253, 254, 255
King, Martin Luther, 263
Kirgizia, 100, 104, 110
Koizumi, Koichiro, 127
Kolkata, 2
Kremlin, 62, 63, 66, 67, 69
Kuwait, 228, 242
Kyrgyzstan, 21, 98, 100, 101, 104, 105, 108, 109, 110, 118, 140, 141, 162, 233, 235, 237, 239, 242, 244, 247, 248, 250, 291-306
  institutional developments and political practices in, 291-306

Laden, Bin, 231
Laos, 42, 43
Lebanon, 86, 89
Libya, 88
London, 6, 8, 9, 10

Mackenzie, 258
Malaysia, 43, 84, 142, 253, 255
Mauritius, 253, 254, 265
Menon, K.P.S, 8, 10, 11, 13
Menon, V.K. Krishna, 8, 9, 10, 11, 12

Mesopotamia, 117, 227
Mexico, 79, 258, 268
Microsoft, 257, 258, 260
Middle East, 13, 19, 20, 52, 63, 79, 81, 82, 86, 89, 118, 122, 23, 128, 220, 229, 236, 242, 246, 284
Mittal, Laxmi, 258
Mirziev, Shavkat, 101, 102
Molotov, Vyachislav, 9, 10, 12, 13
Mongolia, 110, 129, 135, 237
Moscow, 6, 7, 8, 9, 10, 11, 13, 15, 16, 21, 26, 30, 56, 62, 63, 64, 66, 67, 70, 71, 113, 118, 121, 129, 213, 219, 228, 230, 233, 278, 289, 292, 308, 311, 312, 315, 321, 322
Murthy, Narayan, 260
Myanmar, 42, 43, 44, 49, 255

Nazarbayev, Nursultan, 19, 22, 33, 135, 136, 146, 150, 152
Nehru, Jawaharlal, 7, 8, 9, 10, 15, 174, 175
Netherlands, 77
Nepal, 43
New Delhi, 8, 25, 26, 27, 29, 30, 233, 270
New York, 10, 262, 264, 315
Nixon, Richard, 70
North Korea, 86
Nooyi, Indra, 258

Pages from the History of the Establishment of Diplomatic Relations Between India and Russia, 6-16
  events paving way for establishment of diplomatic ties, 12-16
Pakistan, 20, 47, 49, 55, 86, 87, 110, 119, 129, 141, 142, 236, 238
Pandit, Vijayalakshmi, 12, 13, 15, 16
Paris, 8, 9, 13, 51, 72, 134
Peng, Li, 243
Pentagon, 84, 249
Pepsi, 258
Petrov, A.A, 13
Philippines, 54
Poland, 77, 81, 222, 249
Portugal, 81, 283
Premjee, Azim, 260
Putin, Vladimir, 3, 27, 63, 65, 68, 275, 287

Republic of Korea, 35, 36, 142
Ramesh, Jairam, 176
Russia, (*passim* throughout text)1, 3, 4, 5, 6-16, 19, 21, 25-30, 35, 36, 39, 41, 44, 48, 50, 52, 53, 54, 55, 56, 57, 58, 59, 60-72, 77, 78, 79, 81, 82, 85, 86, 87, 88, 89, 90, 92, 94, 95, 96, 99, 107, 112, 117, 118, 119, 121, 122, 128, 129, 130, 141, 153, 154, 155, 159, 173, 191, 192, 201, 202, 204, 207, 208, 209-224, 228, 229, 230, 231, 232, 233, 236, 237, 239, 243, 244, 247, 250, 252-272, 275, 279, 286, 287, 288, 289, 308, 310, 311, 313, 314, 315, 320, 321, 322
  maintaining long-range vision, and India: 25-30

Saakaschvili, Mikhail, 61, 64
Second World War, 7, 9, 32, 47
Shanghai Cooperation Organization (SCO), 19, 20, 62, 111, 129, 130, 140, 147, 173, 237, 240, 250
Sharma, Rakesh (Cosmonaut), 3
Shastri, Lal Bahadur, 174
Singapore, 41, 47, 142, 253, 255
Silk Route and Kazakhstan: A Historical Perspective, 133-144
Singh, Manmohan (Dr), 26, 175, 253
Singh, V. P, 174
Singhvi, L.M, 269
Sisko, 258
Socio-Economic Development of Uzbekistan and Indo-Uzbek Relations, 161-178
  country profile, 162-163
  economic policy, 167-168
  environment protection policy, 166-167
  foreign policy, 173-178
  main priorities and goals in economy for the year 2007, 168-173
  religion and society are crucial aspects of any country, 165-166
  Uzbek model of socio-economic development, 163-165
Some Aspects of Regional Security in Central Asia: A Perspective from Kazakhstan, 18-24
South Africa, 12, 39, 46, 79, 253, 254, 271
South Korea, 42, 43, 47, 51, 53, 54, 88, 190

Soviet Union, 3, 7, 8, 9, 10, 11, 12, 13, 14, 15, 16, 61, 97, 120, 163, 259, 292, 312
Spain, 77, 81, 190, 260
Sri Lanka, 43
St. Petersburg, 4, 179-208, 275
Sweden, 77, 207, 221, 260
Switzerland, 208, 260
Syr Darya, 98, 99, 105, 112, 162
Syria, 88

Taiwan, 41, 43, 47, 48, 88, 89, 260
Tajikistan, 35, 36, 98, 99, 100, 101, 104, 105, 107, 109, 110, 118, 141, 162, 163, 233, 234, 237, 239, 241, 242, 245, 247
Taliban, 237, 249, 250
Tanzania, 253, 254, 255
Taro, Aso, 126, 127
Tashkent, 125, 162, 165, 166, 172, 174, 175, 176
Tehran, 36
Thailand, 42, 43, 47, 142, 282
Tibet, 49, 137
Tokyo, 121, 123, 313
Truman, Harry, 267
Turkey, 35, 36, 88, 155, 229, 232, 233, 282
Turkmenistan, 98, 99, 101, 104, 118, 123, 141, 155, 162, 163, 218, 228, 232, 240, 241, 242, 243, 244, 245

Uganda, 253, 254, 255
Ukraine, 63, 66, 67, 70, 128, 221, 222, 223, 230, 231, 258, 311, 318, 319
United Arab Emirates (UAE), 37, 84
United Nations (UN), 4, 7, 10, 11, 12, 13, 33, 66, 80, 82, 89, 91, 92, 93, 129, 152, 173
USSR, 7, 8, 10, 11, 12, 14, 15, 18, 26, 78, 84, 115, 118, 137, 138, 141, 150, 174, 273, 292, 315, 317, 321
Uzbekistan, 21, 22, 98, 99, 100, 101, 104, 105, 109, 110, 118, 120, 124, 26, 140, 161-178, 228, 238, 239, 241, 242, 243, 245, 248, 249, 292
  and Indo-Uzbek relations, socio-economic development of, 161-178

Venkataraman, R, 174
Vietnam, 42, 43, 84, 87, 256, 268
Visakhapatnam, 2

Watanabe, Michio, 121
Washington, 30, 46, 63, 64, 65, 69, 70, 110, 118, 140, 205, 231, 238, 244, 264
Wipro, 260
World War I, 117
World War II, 78, 82, 117, 122, 128

Xinjiang, 99, 235, 237, 238, 239, 243, 249, 250

Yugoslavia, 81, 84, 91, 93